Evaluating Social Funds

**WORLD BANK
REGIONAL AND
SECTORAL STUDIES**

Evaluating Social Funds

A Cross-Country Analysis
of Community Investments

LAURA B. RAWLINGS

LYNNE SHERBURNE-BENZ

JULIE VAN DOMELEN

THE WORLD BANK
WASHINGTON, D.C.

9286072

©2004 The International Bank for Reconstruction
and Development / The World Bank
1818 H Street, NW
Washington, D.C. 20433
Telephone 202-473-1000
Internet www.worldbank.org
E-mail feedback@worldbank.org

Library of Congress Cataloging-in-Publication Data

Rawlings, Laura, 1964-
 Evaluating social funds : a cross-country analysis of community investments / Laura Rawlings,
Lynne Sherburne-Benz, Julie Van Domelen.
  p. cm. – (World Bank regional and sectoral study)
 Includes bibliographical references.
 ISBN 0-8213-5062-5
 1. Community development–Developing countries–Evaluation–Case studies. 2. Economic
assistance, Domestic–Developing countries–Evaluation–Case studies. I. Sherburne-Benz,
Lynne Darling. II. VanDomelen, Julie. III. Title. IV. World Bank regional and sectoral studies.

HN49.C6R39 2003
307.1'4'091724–dc21   2003052595

Contents

Tables

Figures

Abbreviations and Data Note

AAF	All-Armenia Foundation
ASIF	Armenia Social Investment Fund
BCG	Bacillus Calmette-Guérin
DPT	Diphtheria, pertussis, and tetanus
FHIS	Honduran Social Investment Fund (Fondo Hondureño de Inversión Social)
FIS	Social Investment Fund (Fondo de Inversión Social) (Bolivia)
FISE	Emergency Social Investment Fund (Fondo de Inversión Social de Emergencia) (Nicaragua)
FONCODES	Fund for Social Compensation and Social Development (Fondo Nacional de Compensación y Desarrollo Social) (Peru)
GDP	gross domestic product
IBRD	International Bank for Reconstruction and Development
IDA	International Development Association
INFES	National Social Infrastructure Program (Instituto Nacional de Infraestructura Educativa y de Salud) (Peru)
LSMS	Living Standards Measurement Study
NGO	nongovernmental organization
PIA	Plan International—Altiplano (Bolivia)
PRONAA	Targeted National Nutrition Program (Programa Nacional de Asistencia Alimentaria) (Peru)
PROGRESA	Program for Education, Health, and Nutrition (Programa de Educación, Salud y Alimentación) (Mexico)
SRP	Social Recovery Project (Zambia)
UNDP	United Nations Development Programme
UNICEF	United Nations Children's Fund

Data Note

Unless otherwise indicated, dollar amounts are current U.S. dollars.

Acknowledgments

This cross-country analysis was jointly coordinated by the World Bank's Social Protection Unit of the Human Development Network and the Poverty Analysis Unit of the Poverty Reduction and Economic Management Network. A study of this magnitude can only be the result of the efforts of many, from analysts and data collectors to program managers and financing agencies. The authors would like to express special thanks to Ana-Maria Arriagada, Robert Holzmann, Steen Jorgensen, Oey Meesook, and Michael Walton for their guidance and management support in terms of staff time and resources. The social funds in the six case study countries financed most of the costs of data collection and provided invaluable organizational and logistical support as well as keen program insights. Without their support and cooperation this study would not have been possible.

While it is impossible to recognize all of the people involved at the country level individually, the authors would like to acknowledge the essential contributions of the following country teams:

Armenia: Babken Babajanian, Robert Chase, Ghislaine Delaine, Julia Magluchiants, Caroline Mascarell, Kalpana Mehra, Hrachya Petrosyan, Malia Poghossian, Lynne Sherburne-Benz, and the staff of the National Statistics Office.

Bolivia: Ramiro Coa, John Newman, Menno Pradhan, Laura Rawlings, Geert Ridder, Miguel Urquiola.

Honduras: John Edwards, Gillette Hall, Laura Rawlings, Ian Walker and ESA Consultores, David Warren.

Nicaragua: Gustavo Bermudez, Florencia Castro-Leal, IDEAS Institute, Carlos Lacayo, Berk Özler, Menno Pradhan, Laura Rawlings, Julie Van Domelen, Andrea Vermehren.

Peru: Jorge Alfaro, Livia Benavides, Instituto APOYO, Norbert Schady, Francisco Soto, Christina Paxson, Roberto Wong.

Zambia: Clare Barkworth, Robert Chase, Lawrence Dowdall, Laura Frigenti, Kalpana Mehra, Lynne Sherburne-Benz, Julie Van Domelen.

The design and synthesis of the cross-country analysis and portions of the country case studies were supported with generous grant financing from the Government of Norway. The authors would like to thank the many other bilateral and multilateral agencies that also contributed to the field-work and analysis in the case study countries, as well the World Bank Editorial Committee and their selected reviewers.

Many colleagues in the World Bank and in the social fund community provided suggestions and insights invaluable in refining the analysis and policy implications. The report benefited from comments by Ana-Maria Arriagada, Robert Chase, Shanta Devarajan, Laura Frigenti, Robert Holzmann, Steen Jorgensen, Antony Levine, Caroline Mascarell, Berk Özler, Vijayandra Rao, and David Warren. Production and editing support were provided by Antony Levine and Kimberly Zellars. The opinions expressed in the report are those of the authors alone.

Photo Credits

Cover	Photo provided by the Nicaragua Emergency Social Investment Fund
Page 18	Photo provided by the Zambia Social Recovery Project
Page 84	Photo provided by the Zambia Social Recovery Project
Page 137	Photo provided by Steven Maber, World Bank
Page 148	Photo provided by the Fund for Social Compensation and Social Development
Page 164	(1) Photo provided by the Nicaragua Emergency Social Investment Fund; (2) Photo provided by Steven Maber, World Bank

Executive Summary

INTRODUCED IN BOLIVIA A LITTLE OVER A DECADE AGO, social funds have become one of the main tools of community-led poverty reduction. A departure from traditional approaches to development led by the central government, social funds encourage communities and local institutions to take the lead in identifying and carrying out small-scale investments, generally in social infrastructure such as schools and health clinics. The social fund model has proved to be a dynamic, replicable approach to community-led development, easily adapted and scaled up in diverse countries around the world. In Latin America, Africa, the Middle East, Eastern Europe, and Asia, social funds have now absorbed close to $10 billion in foreign and domestic financing.

Social funds have sparked many debates, particularly about their institutional role and their influence on the activities and effectiveness of central and local governments. Some observers have expressed concern that the funds' autonomy, combined with their proven ability to disburse funds rapidly to local development projects, may undermine governments' will to reform sectoral ministries. Research results from country cases have fueled a debate about whether social funds strengthen or weaken local governments and national decentralization efforts.

Despite the popularity of social funds and the active discussions of the political-economy issues they raise, their effectiveness as a mechanism for improving welfare has remained largely unmeasured. This study is the first attempt to conduct a systematic, cross-country impact evaluation of social funds using survey data and accepted evaluation methodologies. The research, carried out in Armenia, Bolivia, Honduras, Nicaragua, Peru, and Zambia, addresses four fundamental questions:

- Do social funds reach poor areas and poor households?
- Do social funds deliver high-quality, sustainable investments?
- Do social funds affect living standards?
- How cost-efficient are social funds and the investments they finance, compared with other delivery mechanisms?

Research Design

The technical challenges of robust evaluations are considerable, and assessing the impact of social funds is particularly complex. Their multisectoral investment menus and their demand-driven nature complicate pre-identification of the type or location of investments, as well as the selection issues that must be addressed in any impact evaluation. The study applied analytical approaches rarely used in evaluating development programs, including experimental and quasi-experimental designs incorporating control or comparison groups. Thus, it not only measured changes but also compared those changes with what would have happened without the social fund investment. Drawing on a range of methodologies, from randomized control designs to propensity score matching, the study examines the welfare impact of social fund investments in education, health, and water and sanitation in the six countries. The study also marks the first cross-country analysis of the poverty levels of social fund beneficiary households.

The study does not explicitly compare the outcomes of social fund investments with those of alternative interventions, except on cost-efficiency. Instead, through comparison with the counterfactual, it measures the net effect of social fund investments beyond the existing levels of service provision in the comparator communities, which often received investments from nongovernmental organizations (NGOs), public sector agencies other than social funds, or the private sector. The results establish a benchmark against which the welfare impact of alternative approaches can and should be evaluated.

The research is based on data from surveys of more than 21,000 households conducted for the purpose of the study, from national household surveys covering 42,000 households, and from facilities surveys of more than 1,200 schools, health centers, and water and sanitation projects. This use of both household and facility surveys allowed analysis of changes in the quality and use of services and in household welfare, as well as cross-checking of the data. Representative samples make it possible to detect impacts and generalize the evaluation results to the larger population of social fund beneficiaries in each of the case study countries.

Several approaches were used in constructing control or comparison groups. Some comparator communities were selected from those approved for projects that had not yet started ("pipeline communities"), while others were chosen using statistical matching procedures or random assignment. Statistical matching and random assignment are well-established practices in the evaluation field. The novel use of pipeline communities as comparators allowed the study to control for attributes that may make a community more likely to prepare a successful proposal and for the criteria used by the social fund in choosing eligible communities. This approach also establishes baseline information for subsequent impact evaluations.

In each country, designing the evaluations, collecting survey data, and analyzing the results required a high level of expertise, substantial commitments of time and money, and the combined efforts of national and international researchers. However, as the case studies show, robust impact evaluations require only a small share of program resources. The impact evaluations in the six case study countries cost less than 1 percent of program resources, on average.

Do Social Funds Reach Poor Areas and Poor Households?

Geographic Targeting

In each of the case study countries, social funds have achieved broad geographic coverage, generally reaching all districts and municipalities. The intensity of investment varies widely among communities; even within the poorest areas, some communities are more active than others in accessing social fund resources. The high levels of investment in some of the poorest areas refute the idea that such areas are systematically incapable of obtaining resources from demand-driven programs.

The geographic distribution of social fund spending was progressive in all six countries studied: poor districts received more per capita than wealthier districts. Moreover, the very poorest districts received shares exceeding their shares of the population. Among the six case study funds, the Peruvian social fund had the most progressive geographic distribution, in part because of its greater focus on rural areas, while those in Armenia and Zambia tended to have a more neutral geographic distribution. Overall, geographic distribution favored the poor more in the countries that use poverty maps to target resources to poor areas.

All six social funds reviewed have improved their geographic targeting over time. The better performance is attributable to a mix of factors, including active outreach by social funds, increased demand responsiveness, and, in Bolivia, the effects of fiscal decentralization.

Household Targeting

In all cases household data show that social fund benefits were concentrated among the poor, with poorer households more likely to benefit from a social fund investment than better-off households. In all cases the poor accounted for a greater share of beneficiaries than the nonpoor.

The percentage of beneficiaries beneath the national poverty line ranged from 71 percent in Zambia to 55 percent in Nicaragua. The poorest of the poor were well represented among social fund beneficiaries. Except in Armenia, the poorest 20 percent of the population accounted for 23 to 27 percent of social fund beneficiaries. (In Armenia the share was only 15 percent.)

Still, in most cases the distribution of beneficiaries at the household level mirrors national poverty levels, with little positive discrimination of greater representation of the poor among social fund beneficiaries, with the exception of Peru.

Household targeting results varied significantly by type of investment. Investments in latrines and health clinics did best in reaching the poor; sewerage projects did worst. Investments in education were pro-poor, and so were those in water systems, although slightly less so.

In addition to the type of investment, benefits also reach the nonpoor largely because of the nature of social fund investments, which are concentrated in community infrastructure and services, like schools and health centers, where everyone has access, poor and nonpoor alike.

Performance Compared with Other Programs

In countries where the geographic targeting of social funds could be compared with that of other social programs, social funds were more pro-poor. In Peru the social fund directed a larger share of resources to poor districts than did other targeted social programs. In Bolivia social fund resources were three times more likely to go to poorer municipalities than general fiscal transfers.

Household targeting by social funds, although neutral or only slightly pro-poor, nevertheless often compared favorably with that of other targeted social programs and with general social spending. In Peru the social fund was more pro-poor at the household level than other targeted social programs, while in Armenia the social fund was in about the middle of the range for social assistance programs. In Nicaragua social fund spending on health and education was more progressive than general health and education spending. And in Honduras household targeting by the social fund was about average among 30 targeted social programs in Latin America.

These comparisons have two salient messages. First, making sure that the benefits of social expenditures and targeted social programs are concentrated among poor households is a challenge, even among programs that are explicitly targeted. Second, community-driven programs like social funds did no worse than traditional programs in directing resources to the poor, and often did better.

A Call for Targeting More Resources to the Neediest Districts and Households

Measures that might further improve poverty targeting include:

- *Reducing access to resources by better-off regions.* When the Peru social fund restricted access by urban areas, targeting results improved considerably. However, there may be tradeoffs between targeting and other objectives—for example, between achieving more precise geographical targeting and scaling up to a larger national program.
- *Introducing targeting procedures for identifying the poorest communities within districts or municipalities.* Advances in poverty maps and collaboration with local authorities are promising areas for development.
- *Removing from the investment menu items that tend to involve greater leakage of benefits to the nonpoor.* Piped sewerage is a good example of a poorly targeted investment.

Do Social Funds Deliver High-Quality, Sustainable Investments?

The study looked at the track record of operations and maintenance in facilities that have been operating for between one and four years after a social fund investment, based on site visits. The study also examined two cross-cutting issues that affect sustainability, namely whether investments reflect local priorities and whether citizens have been actively engaged in the process of identifying and executing these small-scale investments.

Impact evidence showed that the facilities in which social funds invest can be at least as sustainable as similar facilities if not more so. The majority of the infrastructure appeared to be well constructed and operating adequately, and levels of maintenance were equivalent or better than comparators.

Even well-built and maintained schools and health clinics cannot improve welfare unless they receive needed inputs—teachers and books, medical staff, and medicines. In general, social fund projects were able to mobilize inputs, particularly for schools. Compared with similar institutions, schools and health centers that had received social fund investments enjoyed equal or better availability of staff and of such key inputs as textbooks and medicines. Social fund facilities also often had more volunteers.

Despite these successes, problems remain. Systemic shortages of key inputs were apparent in social fund and comparator facilities alike, especially in the health sector, where clinics often lacked adequate access to staff, medicines, and supplies. These results underscore the limitations of relying on social funds alone to improve welfare. Similarly, limited cost recovery in water projects reveals a sectorwide problem in ensuring a solid financial basis for water systems.

Household surveys and focus group interviews confirmed that local investments by social funds largely reflect community priorities. In addition, communities tend to be very involved in the identification of investments, and only slightly less involved during their execution. During execution, between one-third and two-thirds of citizens report participating, depending on the country, usually by contributing to the project's management or by donating labor, materials, or cash.

The initial involvement appears to have carried through to some level of continued community support during operations. In Honduras, 92 percent of schools had formed maintenance committees, and in Zambia 50 percent of communities had health center maintenance committees. Local financial support was more likely in social fund–assisted infrastructure, including greater support to parent-teacher associations in Zambia, more active fundraising in Nicaragua's schools, and financial support from beneficiary households in Armenia.

Sustainability

The study's findings point to several opportunities for improving the sustainability of social fund–financed services:

- *Work with line ministries to ensure essential inputs.* Line ministries have provided adequate staffing but have sometimes fallen short in supplying other inputs, such as textbooks in schools and essential medicines in clinics. This reflects broader sectoral problems in the allocation of budgetary resources: most spending by social sector ministries still goes for personnel, with little allocated to drugs, textbooks, or maintenance of facilities.
- *Improve technical quality.* Some problems with sustainability stem from deficiencies in the initial technical design of the infrastructure project. This is the case particularly for rehabilitated water systems with original design flaws, but also for new facilities. For more complex systems, such as piped water supply and sewerage, allocating sufficient resources for feasibility studies is essential.

- _Develop more formal systems for community-led maintenance of facilities._ Social funds typically support the creation of local maintenance committees, which have been able to provide routine maintenance and repair of simple infrastructure. These committees should receive formal recognition and clear responsibilities, particularly for facilities owned and operated by local governments or line ministries.
- _Rely on local governments to support social infrastructure._ Local governments, because of their access to resources and better knowledge of local services, may be better able than central agencies to ensure the sustainability of services. If local governments had the resources to match their increased responsibilities, they could make a big contribution to sustainability.
- _Base investments on users' willingness to pay, and provide adequate training in operation and maintenance._ For services such as water supply, for which the community is expected to finance operation and maintenance through user fees, consumers should be fully aware of the recurrent costs. Also critical is training in how to administer a community-managed system.

Do Social Funds Affect Living Standards?

The key conclusion from this research is that in every country studied, social fund investments in small-scale social infrastructure led to increased access to and utilization of services and gains in basic welfare, including higher primary enrollment and educational attainment, improved health of infants and children, and increased availability of water and sanitation services.

Education Impacts

Social fund investments improved the quality of school infrastructure, including more and better classrooms, sanitary facilities, and usually access to safe water. The impact evaluations found that a rise in staffing accompanies the improvements in infrastructure in all cases.

These infrastructure investments led to higher primary enrollment rates in Armenia, Nicaragua, and Zambia but not in Bolivia and Honduras. In Peru two case studies (using different data sources, study populations, and methodologies) reached different conclusions. A national analysis showed enrollment gains, while an evaluation of programs in rural areas found enrollment growth among the poorest but not overall.

These differences in country outcomes may be due to measurement difficulties, type of education investments, and/or rural-urban difference. Where enrollment rates are already high, any changes resulting from a social fund investment will be difficult to capture statistically (particularly if the changes are small) without extremely large samples.

The impact on enrollment rates may also depend on the type of investment. Rehabilitating existing infrastructure without increasing the size or number of classrooms is likely to have a smaller effect than constructing new classrooms that increase the number of places for students. The social funds studied finance both types of investment, and the data did not allow their differentiation by relative weight in the social funds' portfolios. And case study results suggest a tendency for generating enrollment impacts mainly when investments in schools are urban based. This is consistent with capacity constraints (and population growth) concentrated in rural areas.

Social fund investments improved educational attainment in all countries, except Bolivia, underscoring gains in educational efficiency. In Bolivia, the only country to include academic achievement test scores as part of the impact analysis, no difference between social fund and control group students was perceived.

Health Impacts

Impact analysis results showed that social fund investments led to better-quality infrastructure and services. Social fund health centers had better access than comparators to medical equipment and furniture in all cases except Honduras. Their physical conditions were typically better, with more medical rooms and better access to water and sanitation, although not to electricity. The staffing of social fund health centers was as good as or better than that of comparators, although staffing levels in both sometimes fell below recommended norms. Availability of essential drugs and supplies was generally better in social fund facilities, although all facilities had difficulty securing adequate amounts of essential drugs.

These improvements generally led to greater use of the centers, overall or for critical services. The growth in the use of critical services was often concentrated among women and children, with improvements in measures such as institutional births and the treatment of children with diarrhea. In the one case where mortality effects could be measured, that of Bolivia, social fund investments in health centers cut infant mortality rates in half. This result, based on analysis of baseline and follow-up data, remained large and significant over three different estimation strategies, and the impacts were concentrated among frequent users of social fund–financed health centers.

Water and Sanitation Impacts

Social fund investments in water systems improved households' access to piped water in all cases where this outcome was measured. Coverage rates were higher in urban than in rural areas. The improvements reduced infant and child mortality significantly in both Bolivia and Peru, and they lessened the frequency of illness in Armenia and the incidence of stunting (low height-for-age) in Nicaragua. There was no health impact in Honduras, perhaps because the focus there was on rehabilitating existing urban systems rather than expanding coverage. Households also benefited from the reduced distance to water afforded by social fund investments in Bolivia, Honduras, Nicaragua, and Peru.

Most of the social fund water systems were still operating, and doing so fairly reliably, several years after the investment was made. Still, some systems have design flaws and technical problems, and there is some evidence that the problems increase over time.

Sewerage systems financed by social funds were generally operating well and were adequately maintained. But connection rates were low in Honduras, Nicaragua, and Peru, reflecting cost and other disincentives that discourage households from connecting to the systems. Perhaps as a result of the low connection rates, households in communities benefiting from social fund investments in sewerage showed no health gains. The small sample sizes may also have influenced the results.

Social fund investments increased access to latrines in beneficiary communities in Honduras and Nicaragua. They reduced the incidence of diarrhea in Honduras and of acute diarrhea (dysentery) in Peru but had no effect on diarrhea in Nicaragua.

Strengthening the Welfare Impact of Social Fund Investments

Several strategies could help strengthen the impact of social fund investments:

- *Manage the tradeoff between maximizing impact and minimizing recurrent costs.* Many of the social funds studied have limited the construction of new health centers and new class.rooms and schools to ease the recurrent cost burden on line ministries. Although this strategy may improve the prospects for sustainability, it may also limit the potential gains in household welfare.
- *Include all the necessary components in investments.* Restricting investments to specific aspects of service provision can limit their potential impact. Including hygiene and administrative training in community-managed water projects helps ensure that citizens can use and maintain the services effectively. Providing health centers with radios and motorcycles, as was done in Bolivia, can strengthen their outreach, improving utilization and health outcomes.
- *Plan for widespread service coverage in a community.* Although investments in latrines and sewerage benefit individual households, ensuring

that a critical mass of community members has access to such services can maximize their health impact.

How Cost-Efficient Are Social Funds and the Investments They Finance?

Cost comparisons were complicated by large variations in unit costs and in the scale, location, and quality of projects, as well as by incomplete reporting. That said, social funds did have much lower overhead expenses, on average, than other agencies carrying out similar social investments. However, the study found that social funds did not always have lower unit costs than comparators, although there was much variation across countries and sectors.

Involving community members in implementing and supervising projects generally led to savings. Where social funds allowed greater community control over decisions and resources, unit costs were lower (by 25 to 40 percent) and community cofinancing was higher than in other programs. Where social funds worked through private contractors and government intermediaries, unit costs tended to be higher.

The study identified several opportunities for increasing the cost-efficiency of investments in social infrastructure:

- *Transfer the responsibility for managing contracts and control over financial resources to the local level.* If local responsibility is accompanied by sufficient supervision and technical assistance, local groups may be able to lower unit costs.
- *Require counterpart contributions from communities.* Combined with community management, this may result in more appropriate levels of technology chosen and greater attention to cost savings.
- *Control cost escalation during construction,* particularly where the social fund is working directly with private contractors. Where social funds had higher unit costs than comparators, cost escalation appears to have occurred during construction.
- *Apply life-cycle costing, where feasible, to systems and buildings.* Lower unit costs are not desirable if they result in substandard quality and reduced life span of basic infrastructure. Investments that have higher unit costs but that extend a facility's life span and may reduce maintenance costs should be compared with alternatives that have lower unit costs but a shorter life span.
- *Establish national policies on community cost sharing and define appropriate ranges of unit costs.* The wide variation in unit costs and in the contributions expected from communities calls for national policies to ensure consistency across programs and regions. Greater transparency in costs

among programs would promote adoption of the most efficient means of investment.

- *Greater input and participation by communities can improve the impact and sustainability of investments.* Program operators often view community participation as "cost," since consultation and training are required if communities are to take control of identifying and implementing small-scale investments. But as the impact evaluation confirmed, participatory processes have many potential benefits, including investments that match community needs, lower unit costs, and greater utilization and sustainability of services.

What Role Should Social Funds Play in the Future?

Social funds' mandates have expanded over time. Each of the social funds in the case study countries began in response to economic crisis or transition. All were considered temporary at their inception. All have endured and adapted. Today, governments around the world are using social funds to address longer-term poverty reduction. As mandates have grown, so have expectations of impact. Short-term goals of creating temporary employment and shoring up dilapidated local infrastructure have given way to long-term objectives of ensuring sustainable service delivery and, more recently, strengthening local institutions and organizations by building social capital and supporting decentralization.

This evolution has not always been linear, nor will it be in the future. Instead, it will depend on country circumstances and broader policy objectives. During national emergencies, social funds will still need to respond quickly, using systems distinct from those aimed at long-term impacts.

The study's findings on social funds' impact, sustainability, cost-efficiency, and success in reaching poor people point to ways of strengthening their design and adjusting their basic operating procedures in order to enhance their long-term development impact:

- Moving from "first come, first served" to participatory local planning to identify investment proposals
- Shifting from a narrow focus on infrastructure, in which the primary goals are rapid delivery and employment generation, to a focus on service delivery, aimed at greater development impact
- Moving from tracking the delivery of inputs and outputs to tracking the achievement of development objectives, including long-term improvements in basic welfare
- Heightening attention to policies and investments aimed at improving the sustainability of services.

Within this evolution, social funds are clearly a complement to, not a substitute for, effective sectoral policies, nor should they try to fulfill all the investment financing needs of all poor communities. Much of the impact and sustainability of social fund investments relies on effective strategies for service delivery under the mandate of other institutions, particularly line ministries and local governments.

Ideally, social funds advance sectoral goals through community-level investments, working in tandem with local governments, NGOs, communities, and other development agents to serve the broader national objective of poverty reduction. In pursuing this objective, the challenge ahead is to find the best balance between community-led initiatives and national policies in the implementation of effective poverty reduction strategies.

Introduction

THIS VOLUME IS THE PRODUCT OF A STRONG INTEREST, shared by numerous stakeholders, in assessing the targeting, impact, sustainability, and efficiency of social funds. The research reported on here utilizes innovative evaluation techniques to fill gaps in global knowledge about the performance of these funds, with the aim of strengthening the empirical basis for discussions and policies concerning them.

This is the first cross-country study of social funds to measure impacts and targeting using household surveys—in many cases, national Living Standards Measurement Study surveys. The methodology allows for sector-specific findings in education, health, and water and sanitation. The study answers outstanding questions concerning the degree to which line ministries have honored their commitments to provide for staffing and other recurrent expenditures associated with social infrastructure, and it offers insights into the ability of community groups to identify, execute, and maintain local investments. Finally, it compares the cost-efficiency of social funds with that of other investment mechanisms.

Social Funds: An Innovative, Community-Based Tool

Social funds are financial mechanisms that depart from traditional approaches to development by enabling communities and local institutions, rather than central governments, to take the lead in identifying and carrying out community-level investments. Designed in response to crises and to the perceived ineffectiveness of many traditional top-down programs, these investment funds are one of the development community's first large-scale attempts to implement a bottom-up model based on locally generated initiatives. Social funds complement broad macroeconomic and sectoral policies in developing countries' efforts to reduce poverty, much as regional development funds and community development block grants have been employed in Europe and in the United States to support local development initiatives.

The effectiveness of social funds in helping governments improve the well-being of their populations remains largely unmeasured. Few studies of social funds have examined their development impact with respect to reaching poor households, enhancing households' access to social services, or affecting beneficiaries' health and education outcomes. The absence of evidence is conspicuous, considering the role of social funds as one of the primary community-level poverty reduction tools available to governments and development agencies. The research reported here was initiated to address this gap.

The report covers new territory by evaluating the ability of social funds to improve household welfare. To do so, it employs rigorous impact evaluation methodologies to assess the effect of the investments. Using household survey data complemented by facility-level data, the methodologies compare the outcomes for communities that undertook social fund investments with those for control or comparison groups that did not benefit from a social fund investment but that often received other types of assistance from the public sector, nongovernmental organizations (NGOs), or the private sector. These comparison groups establish the counterfactual state of what would have happened without the social fund investment. The outcomes are measured several years after the social fund intervention, making analysis of sustainability issues possible.

This report is the first cross-country analysis of household-level data to assess the efficacy of social fund poverty targeting by comparing the poverty levels of social fund beneficiaries with national poverty distributions. The study looks closely at the distributional outcomes of government social fund programs and, where information exists, compares social fund outcomes with those of other programs with similar goals.

In addition to studying the distributional aspects of social funds, the report analyzes efficiency from a number of perspectives. It first examines in depth the cost-efficiency of social funds relative to other similar interventions, laying out the difficulties of undertaking such an analysis. It next assesses the administrative efficiency of social funds in comparison with other agencies that carry out similar social investments. Finally, the study looks at the length of time it takes for investments to be executed.

The study built on extensive collaboration among social funds, World Bank teams, and national and international researchers. Six countries were chosen for the case studies: Armenia, Bolivia, Honduras, Nicaragua, Peru, and Zambia. Each case study benefited from the involvement of the government of the country, donor institutions, the World Bank, and academia. The results presented in this report are based on the work conducted in the case study countries by evaluation teams. Box 1 lists the individual country reports that serve as the basis for the evaluation.

The evaluation involved broad participation by World Bank staff, academics, and personnel from a variety of institutions in the case study countries. In each country, local social fund officials, national statistical offices, consulting firms, universities, and NGOs worked with World Bank staff and consultants to design the evaluations, collect the data, and analyze the results. This collaboration allowed researchers to tailor their analysis to the interests of the specific country and to build local research capacity. Many other multilateral and bilateral partners contributed to the work; the government of Norway provided resources for the overall study.

In selecting the cases, researchers chose countries where an impact evaluation was under way or could be conducted relatively easily by piggy-backing on a planned and already financed national household survey. In Bolivia a World Bank research grant had supported the collection of baseline data for an impact evaluation in the early 1990s. In Peru the large household survey already included appropriate questions on the social fund, so that the fund's impact could be analyzed using the existing data. In Honduras a separate survey was designed to complement the annual national household survey. Armenia, Nicaragua, and Zambia built the impact evaluation into the Living Standards Measurement Surveys that were being implemented.

The selection process for defining those countries to be included in the study, and the fact that evaluations already existed or could be easily introduced, helped ensure that there was no bias in the selection of case study countries. The evaluations were not initiated or carried out by the social funds themselves; thus, the inclusion of a given fund does not stem from its greater capacity or eagerness to have its performance evaluated.

To ensure objectivity in data collection, analysis, and results, agencies outside the social fund carried out the evaluations in each country. In most of the country-level cases, however, key social fund staff were fully engaged in the design and execution of the study and in the development of the recommendations stemming from the evaluation. Their involvement was critical in ensuring the analytical relevance of the evaluation and the policy impact of the findings.

On the basis of the methodology developed in the cases presented in this report, social fund impact evaluations are being carried out in a number of

Box 1 Country Case Evaluation Studies

The evaluation reports listed here were the principal background studies for the cross-country analysis. (Unless otherwise specified, the documents were produced by the World Bank, Washington, D.C.)

Armenia
- Babajanian, B. 1999. "Armenia Social Investment Fund II Project: Cost-Effectiveness Analysis."
- Chase, Robert S. 2002. "Supporting Communities in Transition: The Impact of the Armenian Social Investment Fund." *World Bank Economic Review* 16 (2): 219–40.

Bolivia
- Newman, John, Menno Pradhan, Laura Rawlings, Geert Ridder, Ramiro Coa, and Jose Luis Evia. 2002. "An Impact Evaluation of Education, Health, and Water Supply Investments by the Bolivian Social Investment Fund." *World Bank Economic Review* 16 (2): 241–74.
- Urquiola, Miguel. 2000. "Analisis de costos del fondo de inversión social." Consultant's report for the Latin America and Caribbean Region, Human Development Department.
- Pradhan, Menno, Laura Rawlings, and Geert Ridder. 1998. "The Bolivia Social Investment Fund: An Analysis of Baseline Data for Impact Evaluation." *World Bank Economic Review* 12 (3): 457–83.

Honduras
- ESA Consultores. 2000. "Estudio de costo-eficiencia del Fondo Hondureño de Inversión Social."
- Walker, Ian, Rafael del Cid, Fidel Ordoñez, and Florencia Rodríguez. 1999. "Ex-Post Evaluation of the Honduran Social Investment Fund (FHIS 2)." Produced by ESA Consultores, Tegucigalpa, for the Latin America and Caribbean Region, Human Development Department.

Nicaragua
- Araujo, E., C. Hurtado, and R. Lema. 2000. "Analisis complementario de costo-eficiencia del Fondo de Inversión Social de Emergencia de Nicaragua." Social Investment Group, Managua.
- GB Consultores. 2000. "Estudio de costo-eficiencia del programa de inversión social en Nicaragua: phase 2."
- Pradhan, Menno, and Laura Rawlings. 2002. "The Impact and Targeting of Social Infrastructure Investments: Lessons from the Nicaraguan Social Fund." *World Bank Economic Review* 16 (2): 275–95.

(Box continues on the following page.)

Box 1 (continued)

- World Bank. 2000. "Nicaragua: Ex-Post Impact Evaluation of the Emergency Social Investment Fund (FISE)." Report 20400-NI. Prepared by L. Rawlings, M. Pradhan, B. Özler, and others.

Peru
- Alfaro, J., and F. Soto. 2000. "Analisis de costo-eficiencia de los fondos de inversión social: el caso de Perú." Prepared for the Human Development Network, Social Protection Unit.
- Instituto Apoyo. 2000. "Determinants of Project Success: Case Study of FON-CODES." Monograph. Lima.
- Instituto Apoyo. 2000. "Sexta evaluación ex-post del FONCODES: evaluación de impacto y sotenibilidad." Lima.
- Paxson, Christina, and Norbert R. Schady. 2002. "The Allocation and Impact of Social Funds: Spending on School Infrastructure in Peru." *World Bank Economic Review* 16 (2): 297–319.

Zambia
- Chase, Robert S., and Lynne Sherburne-Benz. 2000. "Impact Evaluation of the Zambia Social Fund."
- Dowdall, L. 2000. "Zambia Primary School Study: Final Report." Group 5 Consulting Engineers. Working paper prepared for the World Bank Human Development Network, Social Protection Unit.

---

other countries, including Belize, the Arab Republic of Egypt, Jamaica, and Yemen. This will further enrich the knowledge base on social funds and on techniques for their evaluation.

Objectives of the Study

The study seeks to answer four questions that summarize the fundamental issues in the international debate about the capacity of social funds to improve beneficiaries' living conditions:

- Do social funds reach poor areas and poor households?
- Do social funds deliver high-quality, sustainable investments?
- Do social funds affect living standards?
- How cost-efficient are social funds and the investments they finance, compared with other delivery mechanisms?

By applying rigorous evaluation techniques to representative samples of beneficiaries in answering these questions, this study casts new analytical light on hypotheses about the relative advantages and limitations of the social fund model.

Context of the Research

The findings and lessons from this research reflect a specific moment in the evolution of six social funds and therefore may not fully predict the future impact of current investments. The evaluation assesses subprojects identified and implemented between 1993 and 1999, a period when longer-term objectives—such as increasing access to and utilization of basic services—began to supplant the funds' original emergency mandates. The time period selected allowed enough elapsed time following the implementation of the social fund subprojects to make measurement of impact and sustainability possible.[1] The evaluation does not consider the effects of social fund projects on employment or on income generation—the original objectives of the first generation of social funds, which were introduced in Latin America.[2] It also does not discuss the effect of social fund investments on capacity building—a more recent emphasis of social funds seeking to assist decentralization and community development.[3]

The nature and extent of the impacts of the newest generation of social funds are likely to differ from those observed in the case studies. The case studies do not reflect the current investment portfolios, which are more likely to be integrated with local government programs, pay more attention to sustainability criteria, and contain intensive training components. Thus, the six cases are not representative of the universe of social funds, nor does the study support any broad conclusions about the impacts of social funds everywhere.

Outline of the Report

This report sets out the findings from the cross-country analysis of six social funds in the areas of poverty targeting, impact, sustainability, and cost-efficiency. The findings highlight the comparative strengths and weaknesses of social funds as they evolve from emergency disbursement tools to longer-term development mechanisms. The report is organized as follows:

---

[1] The terms "subproject" and "microproject" are used to denote the specific community-level investments financed by social funds.

[2] See Jorgensen, Grosh, and Schacter (1992) for an evaluation of the employment impact of the Bolivian social fund.

[3] See Parker and Serrano (2000) for a review of social funds and decentralization.

- Chapter 1 presents an overview of social funds, a description of the six case studies, and findings from existing studies.
- Chapter 2 describes the study's approach and the methodological issues.[4]
- Chapter 3 discusses whether social funds reach poor areas and poor households.
- Chapters 4, 5, and 6 present evidence on the impact and sustainability of social fund investments in the education, health, and water and sanitation sectors, respectively. Household-level and facility-level surveys allowed researchers to probe not only the quality and sustainability of the infrastructure that social funds financed but also the utilization rates and the changes in specific measures of living standards that have resulted from these investments.
- Chapter 7 explores community dynamics, looking at issues of preferences and participation that may influence the ultimate impact and sustainability of investments.
- Chapter 8 compares the unit costs of social fund investment and overhead expenses with those of other investment mechanisms, including other central agencies, local governments, and NGOs.
- Chapter 9 discusses the overall findings, key design issues for impact evaluations and for social funds, and general lessons concerning social funds as part of government poverty alleviation strategies.

---

[4] Chapter 2 presents an overview of the methodologies used in the study, and the appendix reviews the approach used in evaluating impacts by sector. The individual country case studies (listed in box 1) provide more detailed information on evaluation methodologies and analysis.

1

Overview of Social Funds

THIS CHAPTER DISCUSSES THE CONCEPT OF SOCIAL FUNDS, a financial mechanism that differs from traditional approaches to development in that it allows communities and local-level institutions, rather than central governments, to take the lead in identifying and executing community-level investments in a number of sectors. The scope, scale, and operational procedures of the six social funds studied are outlined. An overview of the evaluation literature on social funds places the research presented in this study within the broader context of decentralized, community-based development strategies.

Definitions and Characteristics

Social funds can be generally defined as "agencies that finance small projects in several sectors targeted to benefit a country's poor and vulnerable groups based on ... demand generated by local groups and screened against a set of eligibility criteria" (Jorgensen and Van Domelen 2000: 91). They have become a popular development tool because of their approach toward empowering local decisionmaking and their reputation as a quick and agile mechanism for getting resources to communities.

The first social fund was established in Bolivia in 1987 as a temporary response to the social effects of an economic crisis and the accompanying adjustment process. The concept spread quickly as other countries sought to ease the social impact of economic crises. Social funds have now been established in most countries in Latin America and have spread around the world, to Africa, the Middle East, Eastern Europe, and Asia. By May 2001, the World Bank had invested about $3.5 billion in social funds through more than 98 investment operations in 58 countries.[1] These social funds had also attracted more than $4.5 billion from other international agencies, as well as domestic financing from governments. Despite these sizable investments, social funds remain a small part of poverty and social protection activities in most countries. Total expenditures typically amount to less than 1 percent of gross domestic product (GDP), and the funds, in all, are equivalent to only 2 percent of World Bank disbursements in recent years (World Bank 2002).

As social funds have proliferated and have been adapted to different country circumstances, their objectives have become increasingly diverse. Within countries, social funds have evolved to meet changing conditions over time. Established in many countries in response to economic crises, social funds started out by emphasizing employment creation. Because of their ability to attract external resources and rapidly deliver small-scale investments, most social funds have seen their mandates expand to longer-term development needs, particularly investments in social sector infrastructure. Many now support capacity building and participatory processes in local governments. Today, social funds represent a diverse set of instruments across countries. Despite their variety, they generally share a number of common characteristics:[2]

- *Social funds are second-tier agencies.* Social funds do not directly execute investments. Instead, they are second-tier financing agencies that appraise, finance, and supervise investments carried out by other agencies—typically, local representatives of line ministries, local governments, NGOs, or community groups.
- *Social funds offer a choice of multisectoral investments.* Social funds typically offer implementing agencies a wide range of choices for the investment to be financed. Some funds have a relatively restricted menu focused on social infrastructure and services. Others offer a wider selection, including economic and productive investments and microcredit and social assistance programs. And still others have begun to experiment with "negative" menus—short lists of noneligible items—leaving greater scope for what *can* be financed.
- *Investment is demand-driven.* Social funds rely on project proposals submitted by a variety of local actors, generally including local governments, NGOs, line ministries, and community groups.

---

[1] Social Funds Database, World Bank Social Protection Website, <http://worldbank.org/sp>.
[2] The discussion of the institutional characteristics of social funds in this chapter draws on Wietzke (2000); see also Jorgensen and Van Domelen (2000).

- *Social funds have operational autonomy and employ modern management practices.* Social funds reside in the public sector but operate like private firms. Because they were created in crisis situations, most of them were granted exceptional status, either as autonomous agencies or with operational autonomy under existing ministries. This autonomy extends to such areas as personnel policies (remuneration, hiring, and firing) and systems for contracting projects and disbursing funds. To counterbalance their operational autonomy, social funds must submit to independent audits and to public and donor scrutiny to ensure strict accountability and transparency. Social funds are typically managed by a board of directors consisting of key ministers and representatives of civil society. They are usually subject to the same budgetary and auditing requirements as other government programs.

General Debates about the Model

Because of their institutional structure and operating procedures, social funds may have efficiency advantages over traditional investment programs of line ministries. And because they promote local identification of priorities and community participation in the implementation of small-scale investments, they may foster improved ownership and sustainability and, ultimately, enhanced impact. These attributes have placed social funds squarely in the debate about appropriate delivery mechanisms for channeling resources to poor communities. This discussion relates to institutional architecture issues regarding second-tier agencies and the modernization of public sector management and to broader debates about the efficiency and equity of decentralization and the shifting of control to communities.

Attention has focused partly on social funds as a service delivery model that involves public-private collaboration in the provision or production of services, with significant autonomy, competitive recruitment, and streamlined procedures.[3] The results from the general evaluation literature on such approaches to public sector management have been inconclusive regarding experience in developing countries (Batley 1999; Polidano 1999). The findings show some improvements in efficiency, mixed effects on equity, and large

---

[3] Such approaches are usually identified as "new public management" (Dunleavy and Hood 1994). As described on the World Bank's Administrative and Civil Service Reform Thematic Group Website, new public management (NPM) suggests structural or organizational choices that promote decentralized control through a wide variety of alternative service delivery mechanisms, including quasi markets in which public and private service providers compete for resources from policymakers and donors. One reform area that illustrates many NPM principles is the creation of semiautonomous agencies for service delivery (Aucoin 1996).

variance in program performance, depending on specific design features and the country context. Concerns have been expressed that the autonomy and good performance of social funds may undermine the will to reform sectoral ministries over the long term (Tendler 2000; World Bank 2002). In addition, social funds may either support or weaken local governments (Parker and Serrano 2000), depending on whether they work with them or bypass them, and depending on institutional design and country circumstances.

There is a vast literature on the potential efficiency and equity effects of decentralization of resources and responsibilities to local governments. The advantages credited to decentralization are based on the assumption that information at the local level is better, making it possible to allocate public goods in the best way. Local officials can be held more accountable for their performance, and the incentive structure tends to reward better service delivery because of proximity to the end users and the dynamics of exit and mobility (Tiebout 1956; Hirschman 1970; Inman and Rubinfeld 1997). At the community level, the general literature on participation indicates improved service delivery, greater sustainability, better satisfaction of citizens' preferences, and more efficient use of resources when citizens are directly involved and control is vested locally (Ostrom, Schroeder, and Wynne 1993; Jimenez and Sawada 1998; Katz and Sara 1998). For poverty programs, there is some evidence that local allocation of resources may improve targeting (Galasso and Ravallion 1999; Alderman 2002).

But decentralization also has potential pitfalls, including macroeconomic disequilibria, corruption, and increased red tape (Prud'homme 1995; Tanzi 1996; Gurgur and Shah 2000). It may widen the gulf between rich and poor people and regions; for example, Putnam, Leonardi, and Nanetti (1993) observe that in Italy the more developed areas have been able to take greater advantage of decentralization. Abraham and Platteau (forthcoming) argue that decentralization of development programs to communities carries the serious risk of elite capture: unaccountable members of the elite may hijack development efforts, particularly when there is a high degree of social and economic differentiation within the community. Yet a case study of five communities in Jamaica that received social fund financing found that the investment process was pushed and activated by local leaders who seemed to be doing it for reasons that benefited the community; the community seemed satisfied by the choice (Rao and Ibáñez 2001).

This study will help shed some empirical light on the broader claims about decentralization and reform of the state as they apply to social funds. Although the main objective of the work is to answer core questions about changes in the welfare of communities and households that benefit from social fund financing, it also examines the equity, efficiency, and sustainability of using a decentralized mechanism to finance local service delivery.

Description of the Six Case Study Social Funds

The social funds included in this study are among the oldest in their respective regions. Those in Latin America and Africa were established in the early 1990s, and the Armenia Social Investment Fund, created in 1996, was the first in the Eastern Europe and Central Asia region. The four in Latin America (Bolivia, Honduras, Nicaragua, and Peru) are the largest in the study, as measured by total and per capita annual investments (table 1.1). The Peruvian social fund invests nearly four times as much annually as the other three Latin American social funds, for a total of more than $1 billion (as of mid-2001). All four Latin American social funds have comparable per capita spending, about $5–$6 a year. The social funds in Armenia and Zambia have smaller per capita spending and finance fewer community investments per year.

All six funds have menus that define subprojects eligible for financing, with a concentration on social infrastructure. The impact evaluation focuses on schools, health centers, and water and sanitation systems, which account for the bulk of the investments.

- *Education.* All six funds finance school buildings, furniture, and basic equipment. The rehabilitation of existing infrastructure is usually favored over the construction of new facilities. The Bolivian fund also supports informal educational campaigns, rural boarding schools, and teacher training. None of the social funds finance textbooks or teachers' salaries, which are recurrent costs that are the responsibility of the line ministries. Installation of water and sanitation facilities and other basic school utilities, as well as housing for teachers, may be eligible items, depending on the location.
- *Health.* The six funds finance the rehabilitation or construction of smaller, often rural health posts and medium-size centers. All of the funds provide basic equipment and furniture, and some provide an initial complement of medical supplies. The funds in Bolivia, Honduras, and Peru support health and nutrition campaigns. None of the funds studied finance salaries of health care workers or the recurrent costs of drug supplies.
- *Water and sanitation.* All six funds finance water and sanitation (sewerage and latrine) investments. The Armenian and Peruvian funds also support local environmental rehabilitation and waste disposal.
- *Economic infrastructure.* All of the funds except the one in Bolivia finance basic economic infrastructure such as rural roads, bridges, and marketplaces.
- *Social assistance.* The funds in Bolivia, Honduras, and Peru finance certain types of social assistance projects such as nutrition and school breakfast programs.

Table 1.1 Basic Information on the Case Study Social Funds

Agency	Armenia Social Investment Fund (ASIF)	Bolivia Social Investment Fund (FIS)[a]	Honduras Social Investment Fund (FHIS)	Nicaragua Emergency Social Investment Fund (FISE)	Peru Fund for Social Compensation and Social Development (FONCODES)	Zambia Social Recovery Project (SRP)
Year created	1996	1991	1990	1990	1991	1991
Total investment (millions of U.S. dollars)	13	345	300	191	1,120	41
For the years	1996–2000	1991–2000	1990–2000	1991–98	1991–99	1991–97
Average annual investment (millions of U.S. dollars)	3	35	30	24	124	6
Average per capita annual investment (U.S. dollars)[b]	0.86	5.80	6.00	6.00	5.00	0.60
Average number of community projects financed in a year	65	439	1,500	752	4,514	107
For the years	1996–2000	1991–97	1990–2000	1991–98	1991–99	1991–97

[a] In 1991 the FIS replaced the Emergency Social Fund (ESF), which was created in 1987.
[b] Total investment divided by total national population.

- *Productive projects.* The funds in Armenia, Honduras, Peru, and Zambia support productive projects, including irrigation and other productive investments. Those in Bolivia and Zambia finance vocational training campaigns.

All but one of the six social funds are legally autonomous institutions, established under either the president's or the prime minister's office. (The Zambia Social Recovery Project is under the Ministry of Finance and Planning.) Most funds have established regional offices to devolve certain functions to the local level. Their personnel policies differ from those of the regular civil service. They finance but do not directly carry out projects, relying on a variety of local actors for implementation.

The Project Cycle and Implementation Arrangements

Each social fund divides the project cycle into standard steps that allow the processing of hundreds or thousands of small-scale investments each year. The stages of the project cycle are poverty targeting, promotion and needs identification, appraisal, implementation, operations and maintenance, and monitoring and evaluation.

POVERTY TARGETING. In allocating resources, most of the social funds regularly use poverty maps, which indicate levels of poverty by geographic area. The funds generally establish goals for allocations to the poorer areas identified by the maps. They also use the menu of eligible investments to direct resources to low-income populations by financing the types of project that are relevant to the poor and screening out projects likely to be used by the nonpoor. For most of the social funds, community outreach and capacity building are integral parts of their targeting strategies, and they try to ensure that poor and remote communities are aware of the programs.

PROMOTION AND NEEDS IDENTIFICATION. It is important to underline that social funds do not preselect the communities where investments are to take place or the type of investment to be done. Program participation relies primarily on the communities' interest in seeking financial support from the social fund and their ability to take advantage of such support.[4]

---

[4] This demand-driven process may introduce a selection bias in the evaluation of social funds' impact, based on differences in the underlying characteristics of communities that are successful in accessing funds versus those that are not. Methodologies for addressing this potential selection bias in evaluating impacts are discussed in chapter 2.

To inform communities about the availability of funding and the eligibility criteria for programs, all of the social funds conduct information campaigns on the radio and in the print media. Some reinforce these efforts with direct visits to communities by field promoters. The social funds in Bolivia, Honduras, and Nicaragua increasingly rely on local governments to promote their activities within municipalities.

APPRAISAL. All of the social funds in the sample follow a two-step appraisal procedure in which a project proposal passes a desk appraisal and a field appraisal before being forwarded for approval by boards of directors. The social funds assess proposals against standard appraisal criteria specified in operational manuals. The appraisals cover technical feasibility, cost-effectiveness, social assessments, institutional arrangements, operations and maintenance arrangements, and beneficiary contributions.

IMPLEMENTATION. Projects are executed through arrangements with private contractors, by the beneficiary communities, or under contracts with NGOs. The social funds provide financing directly to the agency, community group, or private sector contractor executing an investment. By reducing the steps involved and the number of layers through which funds flow, social funds may offer improved efficiency and a reduction in opportunities for waste, fraud, and corruption.

During construction, local supervisors ensure technical quality, under the supervision of social fund staff or private engineers. Communities also monitor implementation.

OPERATIONS AND MAINTENANCE. The social funds have adopted various institutional arrangements to ensure continued operation and maintenance of projects after the initial investment. Arrangements for maintenance often differ across sectors, but there is increased reliance on decentralized arrangements.

MONITORING AND EVALUATION. All the social funds use management information systems to monitor performance in resource allocation, project implementation, and other areas. Most routinely carry out evaluations—mainly beneficiary assessments and technical audits.

Beneficiary assessments typically explore qualitative aspects of project implementation and the dynamics between social funds and communities, local governments, and other local agents. To ensure transparency and credibility, the social funds contract the evaluations to independent agents such as NGOs, consulting firms, and university researchers. The social funds in

Armenia, Nicaragua, Peru, and Zambia perform beneficiary assessments regularly, each year or every other year.

The technical audits are also conducted fairly regularly, by internal monitoring departments or by private engineers. These audits monitor the technical quality of the infrastructure, the application of design standards, and the effectiveness of the supervision system.

Capacity Building and Coordination with Stakeholders

The case study social funds have adopted different institutional frameworks for mediating relationships with stakeholders—primarily, line ministries, local governments, and communities. Social funds and line ministries typically develop framework agreements to coordinate their work, specifying areas of cooperation and collaboration. Local governments have come to play a more important role as decentralization has gained momentum in some countries, resulting in the development of more elaborate mechanisms for coordinating with social funds. These arrangements vary widely among countries. Of the case study countries, Bolivia, Honduras, and Nicaragua work most closely with the local governments' investment planning process.

Social funds commit to following line ministry technical norms, and line ministries (or local governments, or NGOs, depending on the case) pledge to cover any recurrent costs associated with the social fund investment, where appropriate. Line ministries are given authority on a no-objection basis over each subproject presented to the social fund for financing.

The role of civil society, particularly community groups, differs greatly among the social funds. The funds in Armenia, Peru, and Zambia rely on community groups as the primary agents in selecting and implementing projects; those in Bolivia, Honduras, and Nicaragua give a larger role to local governments.

Beyond coordinating with key stakeholders, social funds also work to build stakeholder capacity in certain areas. The approach has varied among countries and over time within countries. Much capacity building takes the form of learning-by-doing, actively involving local agencies in identifying, executing, and operating and maintaining projects. In addition, social funds sponsor or directly carry out training for community groups, local governments, and line ministry staff on approaches and procedures for identifying and implementing investments. More recently, this training has focused on enhancing the sustainability of investments once social fund financing ends.

Zambia: The social fund trains local government (district) officers in project implementation.

Findings from Earlier Studies

Social funds have been subject to a significant amount of review and evaluation. Most of this has been qualitative or anecdotal in nature, and much of it has focused on theoretical assumptions about what may happen or on the mechanism itself rather than on the specific outcomes in communities and households benefiting from social fund investments. This section summarizes some of the key research findings to date regarding employment impacts, expansion of access to services, poverty targeting, and other areas pertinent to this evaluation.[5]

Measuring Workers' Gains

Most of the social funds in existence a decade ago focused on short-term benefits such as creating temporary employment, stabilizing delivery of social services, and addressing large backlogs in social infrastructure investments. The evaluations that were carried out emphasized either the type and scale of the temporary employment generated or the main quantitative outputs

---

[5] In a separate review of social funds, the World Bank's Operations Evaluation Department (OED) carried out qualitative and quantitative fieldwork in 20 communities in 4 countries (Jamaica, Malawi, Nicaragua, and Zambia) to explore issues related to participation, social capital, and sustainability (World Bank 2002). Because of the small number of social fund communities visited (three to five per country), these results are not representative of the social fund portfolios in the countries studied. Nevertheless, the findings are cited in this study as additional information. The OED used the country case studies and an earlier (October 2001) draft of this report as the principal basis for its review of the poverty targeting, impact, and cost-efficiency of social funds.

(number of kilometers of roads repaired, number of schools rehabilitated, number of water supply systems built, and so forth). On employment impacts, an econometric study that profiled workers in a subset of urban projects in Bolivia found that the Emergency Social Fund did indeed provide jobs to the poor: 25 percent of those employed through the fund were in the poorest population decile; 77 percent were in the poorest 40 percent of the income distribution; and the employment almost doubled the workers' weekly earnings (Newman, Jorgensen, and Pradhan 1991a, 1991b). An analysis in Peru that covered both urban and rural areas found that 57 percent of workers were below the poverty line and 36 were in extreme poverty (Goodman and others 1997). In the cases reviewed, social fund employment creation represented less than 1 percent of the total labor force (Stewart and van der Geest 1995; Goodman and others 1997; Lustig 1997). This is low in comparison with some of the large-scale employment guarantee schemes and massive public works programs that have been implemented in countries such as India and Chile (Stewart and van der Geest 1995; Cornia 1999; Tendler 2000).

Expanding Access to Services

Evaluations have been universally favorable concerning the ability of social funds to deliver small-scale infrastructure with relative efficiency (Goodman and others 1997; Frigenti, Harth, and Huque 1998; World Bank 2002). This performance is attributed to modern management practices, streamlined procurement, and the involvement of community groups and the private sector in implementation. However, there has been little information generated on the impact with respect to the quality and utilization of services and the ultimate effect on household welfare. Desk reviews of project documents and anecdotal evidence have raised concern about sustainability in such areas as staffing of schools and health centers and continuity of services from water and sanitation investments (World Bank 1997a; Tendler 2000), but there has been little systematic field research to shed empirical light on this question.

Reaching the Poor

Depending on the country, social funds seek to have an impact on poor communities, underserved regions, populations affected by economic and social crisis, or poor households. In the initial emergency phase, targeting concerns were largely focused on providing temporary income support through construction jobs. Now the emphasis is on where these small-scale investments are being made and on the poverty level of the populations using the services. Because the model social fund requires that communities organize themselves (or have designated representatives in the form of NGOs and local governments) and that they take the initiative to determine their needs and present proposals, critics have hypothesized that poor households and communities will be unable to participate (Tendler 2000: 17).

Initial targeting evidence seemed to support this proposition. Using some of the basic poverty maps available at the time, evaluations found that better-off regions and provinces were receiving more financing per capita (Jorgensen, Grosh, and Schacter 1992; World Bank 1997a). The researchers pointed out, however, that two factors confounded these results. First, because the maps were not very disaggregated, investments in apparently wealthy regions could nevertheless be reaching poor communities and households within those regions. Second, the measurements were taken early, in social funds' emergency phase, when investments were concentrated in urban areas for the sake of employment impacts and more remote rural areas had yet to enter fully into the program. Decisively answering the targeting questions would require more disaggregated national poverty maps, household-level data, and a longer time span of data to permit observation of more recent tendencies—all elements of the present study.

2

Methodology

THIS CHAPTER OUTLINES THE METHODS AND DATA used to conduct the case studies. An overview of the evaluation methodology describes the techniques applied in assessing success in poverty targeting, the impacts on facilities and household welfare, participation, and cost. The chapter provides details on the methodologies applied to generate the counterfactual for the impact evaluation, including the selected application of baseline data and randomized control designs, and summarizes the data sources, sample sizes, costs, and time frame for each case study. Lessons on designing and carrying out social fund impact evaluations are drawn.

Overall Approach to Study Questions

Despite the many desk studies and country reviews undertaken by the World Bank and other agencies, until the evaluations presented in this study were carried out, little research had been devoted to evaluating social funds' performance across countries with respect to their poverty targeting, their impact on household welfare, their ability to foster sustainable investments, and their cost-effectiveness compared with other mechanisms. The absence of such research has been conspicuous, since social funds are among the primary community-level poverty reduction tools available to governments and development agencies.

This study was initiated to fill the gaps in knowledge about the impact of social funds. It is the first cross-country study to assess the efficacy of social funds in targeting resources to the poor by comparing the poverty levels of individual social fund beneficiaries with national poverty levels—in many cases, using a household sample survey of beneficiaries and comparing their poverty measures with those of nonbeneficiaries surveyed by a national Living Standards Measurement Study (LSMS) survey.[1] The study also marks the first attempt to rigorously assess the effects of social fund investments on household welfare using a variety of impact evaluation methodologies (see box 2.1; see also table 2.1, below). These methodologies were used to compare outcomes in communities that undertook social fund investments with outcomes in control or comparison groups that did not, thus establishing the counterfactual of what would have occurred in the absence of the investment.

The impact evaluation work carried out in this study does not explicitly compare the outcome of social fund investments with an alternative demand- or supply-side intervention. (The cost-efficiency of providing similar investments through alternative means is, however, examined in chapter 8.) In each case study country, a counterfactual was constructed using a control or comparison group that did not benefit from a social fund investment but that often received other types of investments from the public sector, NGOs, or the private sector. The comparison is thus not between a social fund investment and no investment. Rather, it is a measure of the net effect (if any) of the social fund *beyond* what was taking place in the comparator communities and households. Even though this study was not undertaken as a direct comparison of various uses of development investment resources to achieve a particular outcome, the results provide a benchmark against which to measure the effectiveness of alternative future interventions.[2]

Research Questions

The study evaluated the poverty targeting, impact on living standards, sustainability, and costs of social funds in six countries—Armenia, Bolivia, Honduras, Nicaragua, Peru, and Zambia. The evaluations sought to answer four core questions, using the following approaches:

- *Do social funds reach poor areas and poor households?* The study assessed the ability of social funds to reach the poor at two levels, geographic and household. At the geographic level, it analyzed the distribution of social fund investments across districts ranked by poverty level. At the

---

[1] For further information on LSMS surveys, see Grosh and Glewwe (2000).

[2] A rigorous impact evaluation of which alternative intervention is most suitable for achieving a particular development goal would ideally involve random allocation of the alternative interventions across separate treatment groups. This type of evaluation has rarely been undertaken because of the amount of resources and social engineering required.

Box 2.1 Impact Evaluation Methodologies

The main methods of impact evaluation encompass *experimental designs,* based on random assignment of the intervention, and *quasi-experimental designs* (also known as nonexperimental designs), which use methods other than random assignment to generate the counterfactual. They also include estimation strategies, which are often applied in impact evaluations. With the exception of reflexive comparisons, each of the methods described in this box was used in at least one of the case country studies (see table 2.1).

Experimental, or randomized control, designs use random assignment to allocate a good or service to part of the target population (the treatment group) while withholding it from others (the control group). Experimental designs are considered the most methodologically rigorous for impact evaluation, since randomization ensures that, on average, the treatment and control groups are statistically equivalent in all characteristics, observed and unobserved. They therefore provide a means of controlling for selection bias.

Randomization can be difficult to implement: it has to be built into a program at its inception, and it is often subject to criticism because of withholding the program from some eligible candidates, although this is true for any program not reaching full coverage of its target population. Inadequate sample sizes or changes during project implementation that deviate from the random selection can undermine experimental designs and other designs using baseline data.

The other methods discussed here are classified as quasi-experimental designs.

Matched comparisons, or constructed controls, compare the treatment group with a group that has not received the intervention but that is otherwise as similar to the treatment group as possible, as measured by observable characteristics. The match can be conducted before or after the intervention. This is the most common type of evaluation methodology.

Propensity score matching uses the probability of receiving a project intervention (predicted by the propensity score) to match a comparison group with the treatment group. The propensity score is calculated using observed characteristics of the treatment group, and the treatment group's score is then matched with the score of a comparison group that did not receive the intervention. The closer the propensity score of the comparison group is to that of the treatment group, the better is the match. This method is often used when a treatment group is included (sometimes through oversampling, to ensure a statistically representative sample) within a large survey using the same questionnaire, allowing researchers to use the larger survey to generate the comparison group from those who did not receive the intervention.

(Box continues on the following page.)

Box 2.1 (continued)

To control for unobservable characteristics, the comparison group is often selected-from the same region as the treatment group, although this does not ensure that all selection issues are addressed (Dehejia and Wahba 1998; Jalan and Ravallion 1998).

Double difference, or difference in differences, compares a treatment and comparison group before the intervention (first difference) and after the intervention (second difference). Difference-in-differences estimates can be applied in both experimental and quasi-experimental designs. They require baseline and follow-up data from the same sample treatment and comparison groups.

Instrumental variables are used in statistical analysis to control for selection, since they influence program participation but do not affect outcomes. The instrumental variable identifies exogenous variation in program participation, recognizing that program placement is not random but purposive. It is often difficult to identify good instrumental variables, and use of this technique requires knowledge of the program, as well as data on program placement and selection.

Reflexive comparisons are based on baseline and follow-up surveys of program participants, without the use of a comparison group. Since program participants serve as their own comparison group in the period before the intervention, econometric modeling must be applied to account for exogenous influences. Reflexive comparisons are best used when sufficient preprogram and postprogram data are available to analyze factors exogenous to the intervention that influence the treatment group.

Source: Adapted from Freeman and Rossi (1993); Grossman (1994); Baker (2000).

---

household level, it compared data from sampled households in communities undertaking social fund investments with national poverty distributions to assess the poverty levels of citizens receiving the social fund investment.

- *Do social funds deliver high-quality, sustainable investments?* Surveys were administered to more than 1,200 schools, health centers, and water and sewerage facilities to assess the quality of the physical infrastructure financed by the social fund and the sustainability of those investments. For the evaluation of sustainability, the surveys paid particular attention to the provision of inputs complementary to the social fund infrastructure, such as staff, materials, and maintenance. The assessments usually included comparisons between facilities that had been financed by social funds and comparable facilities that had not been.
- *Do social funds affect living standards?* The study used household survey data from treatment and comparator groups to determine how social funds affect households' access to basic services and the health and

educational outcomes. It compared households in communities that had undertaken social fund projects with similar households in communities that had not, using a variety of evaluation methodologies to establish the counterfactual required for impact evaluation.

* *How cost-efficient are social funds and the investments they finance, compared with other delivery mechanisms?* Using unit cost data, the study examined whether relying on social funds to build or rehabilitate facilities is cost-effective compared with using alternatives such as line ministries or NGOs. It also assessed the efficiency of social funds on the basis of administrative costs and the time taken to execute projects.

In some cases survey data and results from qualitative assessments allowed the study to explore whether social fund investments reflect community priorities and involve communities in project design and implementation, but this was not a main focus. The study also reports on the results of research into the determinants of project success in Peru, including the role of community participation and social capital.

In each country the issues listed above were examined by focusing on those sectors in which social fund investments were concentrated in the mid- to late 1990s. Each country case study examined education and health projects, and some assessed water and sanitation projects. The data in the table below show the share of total investment absorbed by these sectors in each social fund considered during the years covered in the evaluation. (The appendix to this volume summarizes the methodologies applied, by sector.)

Country case study	Percentage of social fund spending on infrastructure in the education, health, and water and sanitation sectors
Bolivia	100
Zambia	95
Honduras	84
Armenia	82
Nicaragua	81
Peru	62

Finally, in most cases the study covered the entire national portfolio of projects, although in Bolivia and in the Peru study by Instituto Apoyo (2000b), the evaluation focused on selected rural areas.

Evaluation Methodology

This section reviews the methodologies applied in the evaluation to carry out the poverty targeting assessment, facility-level analysis, household impact evaluation, and cost studies. The evaluation designs, estimation techniques, and indicators vary considerably from country to country, reflecting data availability and the focus of the country case studies. These differences, while responsive to specific country needs, complicated the comparability of the country studies.

Evaluating Poverty Targeting

The study measured the benefit incidence of social fund investments at two levels: household and geographic. For households, the study used the data collected by the household surveys administered for the study and compared them with a national distribution of poverty based on general survey data (usually, a living standards survey or, for Honduras, a national income and expenditure survey) collected at the same time as the social fund survey data. At the geographic level the study used social fund administrative data and available information on the geographic distribution of poverty. The data for the geographic analysis covered all categories of the project (beyond the education, health, and water and sanitation projects examined for the impact evaluation) and extended over the life of the social fund, not just the time frames selected for the impact evaluation. These differences in data sources and methodologies prevented direct comparison of the household and geographic targeting results.

At the geographic level the targeting analysis examined the distribution of social fund investments across districts or municipalities according to poverty level. Districts or municipalities were ranked by poverty level and were then weighted by population. The first decile therefore corresponds to the 10 percent of the population in the poorest districts and the last decile to the 10 percent of the population in the richest districts. The use of deciles helped determine the relative distribution of social fund resources across poor and less poor areas of the country and allowed cross-country comparison.

Each country case study used preexisting country poverty measures to assess social fund targeting at the geographic level. The variability across countries in the type of poverty measure (usually consumption, income, or basic needs) and in the level of disaggregation (district or municipality) of the measures complicated intercountry comparison.[3]

---

[3] Armenia uses as a poverty measure per capita consumption, aggregated by province; Bolivia, a composite index of human development; Honduras, a composite poverty index that reflects malnutrition and access to water and sanitation; Nicaragua, an index based on malnutrition, access to water, and the district's share of displaced population following the civil war; Peru, a composite index of unmet basic needs that includes access to schooling, electricity, water, sanitation, and adequate housing, as well as measures of chronic malnutrition and illiteracy; and Zambia, an indicator based on the percentage of the population living below the national poverty line, defined as the cost of the basic food basket plus 30 percent to account for nonfood expenditures.

At the household level, the targeting analysis compared the distribution of the poverty levels of social fund beneficiaries with the national distribution of poverty based on income or consumption measures. The analysis achieved comparability by:

- Using the same income- or consumption-based measure of poverty in the social fund household survey as was used in the household surveys from which the national measures of poverty were calculated
- Ensuring that the survey data from the social fund households were collected at the same time as the national survey data.

Researchers used the representative sample of social fund beneficiaries (randomly selected for the impact evaluation) to carry out the benefit incidence analysis, after adjusting the sampling weights for any differences produced by the sample stratification by project type.

The household-level analysis also allowed researchers to measure the social funds' success in poverty targeting against the national poverty lines in the countries where these had been set. This comparison calculated the percentage of social fund resources going to those below the poverty line and to those below the extreme poverty line.[4] Finally, in some countries the data allowed researchers to distinguish between the social funds' targeting of potential beneficiaries (all households with access to a given investment) and actual beneficiaries (households that, for example, send a child to a school that has benefited from a social fund project).

Evaluating Facilities

To assess the quality and sustainability of social fund investments and to further investigate the impact evaluation results, almost all country teams carried out studies of a random sample of facilities that had benefited from social fund projects matched with a sample that had not. Social fund and comparator schools were surveyed in all countries; health centers were surveyed in all cases except Armenia and Peru. Water systems were surveyed in Armenia, Honduras, Nicaragua, and Peru, and sewerage systems in

---

[4] Poverty measures were constructed differently in the individual case study countries (see chapter 3). Full and extreme poverty lines are most commonly defined using consumption measures specific to individual countries (and, occasionally, to regions within countries). A person is considered poor if his or her annual expenditure falls below the full poverty line—the level of annual per capita consumption sufficient to attain minimum caloric requirements and basic nonfood items such as clothing and transport. A person is considered extremely poor if his or her annual expenditure falls below the extreme poverty line, that is, the level of annual per capita consumption of food at which an average person satisfies the minimum caloric requirements.

Honduras, Nicaragua, and Peru. In each case data were collected from key informants in the sampled facilities and from administrative records on staffing and utilization.

Social fund and non–social fund facilities were selected as part of the first-stage sampling in each country, using methodologies that ensured their comparability. In Nicaragua and Zambia facilities were matched according to geographic proximity and type of facility, using as the comparator facility for each social fund facility the closest facility of a similar type in a nearby district that did not have an overlapping catchment area. In Bolivia facilities were matched according to population census data and facility characteristics within the study regions. In Armenia and Honduras, and for a second set of projects in Zambia, communities with "pipeline" projects—projects similar to those sampled for the evaluation that had been approved but not initiated—served as comparators. In the Chaco region of Bolivia the study used an experimental design that randomly generated treatment group and control group schools.

Baseline data collected from the administrative records of social fund and non–social fund schools and health centers provided an opportunity to conduct difference-in-differences analysis (see the discussion in box 2.1). Except in Bolivia, where facility and household data were collected through a baseline survey before the social fund investment, no complete baseline data were available for the study. Instead, the study used information from facilities' administrative records on the types of service provided and the utilization of the facilities starting one year before the social fund intervention. Researchers gained insights into the possible effects of the social fund investments by comparing the changes in indicators over time for social fund and non–social fund facilities.

In most countries the small number of facilities surveyed limited the ability to draw general conclusions about the universe of social fund facilities. The overall evaluation therefore reviews trends across countries but attributes significant impacts to analysis of household survey data alone, while treating the results from the facilities data as case studies.

Evaluating Household Impact

Impact evaluations assess changes that can be attributed to a particular program or policy. Other types of program assessment, such as organizational reviews and process monitoring, neither consider causal relationships between the intervention and observed outcomes nor estimate the size of the effects of the intervention. Causal analysis, the hallmark of impact evaluations, is essential for understanding the role of alternative interventions in reducing poverty (Freeman and Rossi 1993; Baker 2000; Prennushi, Rubio, and Subbarao 2000).

Impact evaluations ask what the status of the beneficiaries would have been without the intervention. To determine this, researchers estimate a hypothetical state, known as the counterfactual, which they compare with the actual, observed state of the treatment group that has received the intervention.

Researchers usually estimate the counterfactual by constructing control or comparison groups that are as similar as possible to the treatment group of beneficiaries except that they have not received the intervention. Comparison groups are generated by using before-and-after techniques (reflexive comparisons); pairing those with and without the intervention (matched comparisons); or randomly selecting the treatment and control groups from equally eligible potential program recipients (randomized control). These approaches are summarized in box 2.1.

There is a rich literature on the relative merits and drawbacks of various evaluation approaches (Freeman and Rossi 1993; Grossman 1994; Heckman, Lalonde, and Smith 1999; Baker 2000). Each method is valid only so long as certain assumptions hold. At the heart of the challenge posed by evaluation research is the problem of selection bias, the term applied to elements that may influence outcomes. Examples can include elements that are difficult to measure such as community motivation, social capital, and organizational capacity.

All impact evaluations face the issue of how to control for selection bias, but social funds pose a particular challenge. Projects financed by social funds are generally developed and proposed by communities or by local agents acting on behalf of communities, and communities are free to select from a menu of project types that can be proposed for social fund financing. Most social fund–financed investments are public goods available in a community, not private goods provided directly to households, which means that utilization is contingent on individual or household preferences and capacities to access the investments provided. These dynamics complicate the estimation of the counterfactual, given the range of selection issues at play, which are driven by both household and social fund preferences and capacities. These same issues make the random assignment of a social fund investment to a specific community or household impossible, ruling out the application of a straightforward experimental design.

Despite these difficulties, the studies presented in this volume marshaled a variety of evaluation designs, including randomized control designs and propensity score matching—approaches generally recognized as valid in the impact evaluation field. Each country case study team chose an evaluation design that made optimal use of available data and resources, and each team used control or comparison groups to generate a counterfactual.

Beyond these experimental and quasi-experimental designs, the evaluation made use of analytical techniques, which are often employed in impact evaluations, particularly to control for selection issues and exogenous influences that can affect program outcomes. These techniques range from multivariate analysis applied in a regression framework to specific tools used to address selection issues such as instrumental variables. Table 2.1 presents the impact evaluation designs and estimation strategies used in each case country evaluation.

The study teams relied mainly on matched comparisons, in which they looked for differences between a treatment group of social fund beneficiaries and a comparison group with similar characteristics that did not implement a social fund project. The technique used in constructing the matched comparison varied across countries, and several studies applied more than one approach.[5] This type of analysis is the best available when baseline data do not exist and random allocation of the intervention is not feasible, as was the case everywhere except in Bolivia.

The social fund evaluations in Honduras, Peru, and Zambia used pipeline projects to establish a counterfactual. Communities that had received a social fund intervention were matched with those selected to receive one in the future. This technique allowed researchers to address the inherent difficulty of matching communities on the basis of observed characteristics; communities able to organize themselves to prepare a social fund project probably share special, unobservable social dynamics that are difficult to measure in surveys. In this respect the pipeline approach may be the best technique, short of randomization, for addressing selection bias. The technique provided the added benefit of generating baseline data on facilities and communities due to receive a social fund investment in the future. The new approach, first applied in the Honduran social fund evaluation, deserves further consideration, given its potential for establishing systematic impact evaluations.

Propensity score matching was used in several cases where data were available for constructing a comparison group. In Armenia, Nicaragua, and Zambia the national household poverty surveys allowed researchers to construct a comparison group with propensity scores similar to those of the treatment group through the use of a model for predicting participation in a social fund project. In Bolivia it was possible to construct a comparison group by using the large surveys generated for the social fund study, particularly the health survey, which was based on a random sample of households in the sampled provinces.

---

[5] The matching was carried out at different levels (community, facility, and household), using a variety of techniques, depending on the country case. Except where pipeline projects and randomization were used, the matching was carried out on the basis of observable characteristics that were not subject to change as a result of the social fund intervention. These characteristics were drawn from a variety of sources, depending on country case availability, including census data and administrative data from line ministries.

Table 2.1 Impact Evaluation Designs Applied in the Case Study Countries

Country	Evaluation design	Treatment group	Comparator group	Estimation strategies	Complementary evaluations
Armenia	• Propensity score matching	• Random sample of households drawn from the complete set of communities with completed social fund projects	• Propensity score matched communities, stratified to account for higher probability of participation in Yerevan, earthquake zones, and conflict zones	• Probit estimates for propensity score matching	• Facilities survey • Qualitative beneficiary assessments
Bolivia	• Matched comparison with similar communities • Propensity score matching • Randomized control design in education evaluation in Chaco region	• Random sample of eligible communities selected to receive social fund projects, stratified by type of project • Random assignment of promotion of social fund education projects in Chaco region	• Matched non–social fund facilities and communities based on facilities and community characteristics using project and population census data • Similar households using propensity score matching, within same region, selected from health survey	• Bounds estimates • Instrumental variables • Probit estimates for propensity score matching • Difference in differences	• Facilities survey • Water quality test • Mathematics and language achievement tests • Cost study

(Table continues on the following page.)

Table 2.1 (continued)

Country	Evaluation design	Treatment group	Comparator group	Estimation strategies	Complementary evaluations
			• Communities that were not selected in random assignment of education projects in Chaco region		
Honduras	• Matched comparison with pipeline communities	• Random sample of social fund projects and corresponding households, stratified by type of project	• Social fund pipeline projects and corresponding households matched by sector of social fund investment	• Multivariate analysis	• Facilities survey • Qualitative beneficiary assessment • Cost study
Nicaragua	• Matched comparison with similar communities • Propensity score matching	• Random sample of social fund projects and corresponding households, stratified by type of project	• Matched non–social fund facilities and corresponding households based on geographic proximity and characteristics of facilities • Similar households using propensity score matching within same region, selected from national LSMS survey	• Probit estimates for propensity score matching • Difference in differences	• Facilities survey • Qualitative beneficiary assessment • Cost study

Peru 1 (Paxson and Schady 2002)	• Matched comparison between geographic areas with high and low levels of social fund investment	• Geographic areas with high levels of social fund investment in education	• Geographic areas with low levels of social fund investment in education	• Multivariate analysis • Difference in differences • Instrumental variables	• Facilities survey • Cost study • Social capital study
Peru 2 (Instituto Apoyo 2000b)	• Matched comparison with pipeline communities	• Random sample of social fund projects and corresponding households, stratified by type and size of project	• Social fund pipeline projects and corresponding households, matched by district or province and sector of social fund investment	• Multivariate	
Zambia	• Matched comparison with pipeline communities • Propensity score matching	• Random sample of social fund projects and corresponding households, stratified by project type and location	• SF pipeline projects and corresponding households • Similar communities, using propensity score matching within same region, selected from national LSMS survey	• Probit estimates for propensity score matching	• Facilities survey • Qualitative beneficiary assessment • Cost study

In Bolivia an experimental design was used to evaluate the impact of education projects in the Chaco region. Communities were randomly selected for active promotion of the offer to participate in a social fund education project. Although this was not a direct random assignment of the intervention, the random offer of participation was sufficient to generate a valid experimental design (Newman and others 2002).[6]

In addition to the main evaluation designs, the case study teams employed a variety of estimation strategies to examine the evaluation results, with rich variation from country to country. These approaches included the use of instrumental variables, difference-in-differences techniques, case control methods, and bounds estimates.

This volume concentrates on the results and policy implications of the research and does not discuss at length the evaluation designs and analytical approaches used in the case studies. Detailed information on the methodology is available in the country case reports and in related academic articles, listed in the Bibliography and Box 1.[7]

Approaches to Impact Evaluation in the Country Case Studies

Each case country evaluation used a different evaluation design and estimation technique to analyze the impact of the social fund investments, and most employed more than one approach (see table 2.1). The choice of methodology was contingent on the available data, the research areas identified as priorities in each country, and the resources available for the evaluation.

ARMENIA. The impact evaluation of the Armenian social fund studied the fund's investments in schools and water supply projects and relied on propensity score matching. An LSMS survey provided information about communities where the social fund had not operated, and a separate impact evaluation survey of social fund beneficiaries was administered to a random selection of households in communities in which the social fund had completed an education or water supply project. Communities in the social fund survey were matched to those in the LSMS survey, using propensity score estimates. Differences between the social fund treatment households and the LSMS control households indicated the impact of the social fund.

The early operations of the Armenian social fund were focused on rehabilitating schools in three areas: the capital city of Yerevan, the zone affected

---

[6] The use of both an experimental design and a matched comparison design with and without propensity score matching in evaluating the impact of education investments in Bolivia allows for the comparison of a range of evaluation approaches (see Pradhan, Rawlings, and Ridder 1998; Newman and others 2002).

[7] Several of the academic articles from the country case study evaluations have been published in the *World Bank Economic Review*, vol. 16, no. 2 (2002).

by the 1988 earthquake, and the region affected by civil conflict. As a result, the oversampled households surveyed for the impact evaluation represented communities in highly unusual circumstances. Although propensity score matching techniques were used to correct for the potential biases, the national LSMS survey did not cover a large number of households in these geographic areas. The research team conducting the evaluation concluded that the methodological difficulties affected the robustness of the evaluation and that they helped explain why few of the differences between social fund and comparator schools and communities were statistically significant. Nor did facility-level matching adequately capture the important differences between social fund schools and other schools.

BOLIVIA. The impact evaluation of the Bolivian social fund focused on education, health, and water projects in 5 rural provinces in the Chaco region and in a sample of 17 provinces in other rural areas. (Bolivia has 111 provinces.) No national household survey was available that would allow researchers to piggyback through oversampling or to assess poverty targeting at the household level. Instead, researchers applied a tailored evaluation. As a result, the Bolivian case study was the most comprehensive and robust, but also the longest and costliest.

Bolivia was the only case study in which both baseline and follow-up data were available for facilities and households. It was also the only case study that used an experimental design—one of the most robust evaluation methodologies (Grossman 1994)—along with other designs. And it was the only one that applied water quality tests and student achievement tests. The Bolivian evaluation also included a cost study and facilities surveys.

For most of the impact analysis, the Bolivian case study applied propensity score matching methodologies, using the large random sample of households from the health survey to generate comparison groups. In addition, researchers applied bounds estimates to evaluate the range of program impacts in education, and hazard functions and life table estimates to assess the effects of health projects on under-five mortality (Newman and others 2002).

In the Chaco region the case study introduced an experimental design through random allocation of the offer to participate in an education project to equally eligible communities, after identifying the most needy and least needy communities (Pradhan, Rawlings, and Ridder 1998).

HONDURAS. The evaluation of the Honduran social fund examined the impact of social fund–financed primary education, rural health, water, sewerage, and latrine projects. Lack of an appropriate survey precluded the oversampling of social fund beneficiaries from a larger household survey and the use of propensity score matching techniques to construct a comparison group.

Instead, the study team developed a series of data collection instruments tailored to the evaluation, including household and facilities surveys, a qualitative assessment carried out in conjunction with the impact evaluation, and a cost study. The Honduran case study was the first to construct a comparison group by using pipeline projects.

NICARAGUA. The Nicaraguan evaluation examined the impact of social fund primary education, rural health, water, sewerage, and latrine projects. The evaluation took advantage of the national 1998 LSMS household survey, oversampling social fund beneficiaries and matching them to similar non-beneficiaries by using propensity scores. It also used another approach for estimating the counterfactual in health and education investments: matching social fund facilities (and the corresponding households) to the "nearest neighbor" non–social fund facilities with similar characteristics. This second approach was carried out at the sample design stage. Administrative data on program coverage were used to guide the matching of social fund and non–social fund facilities on the basis of geographic proximity and the size and characteristics of the facilities (Pradhan and Rawlings 2002).

The evaluation also included a qualitative beneficiary assessment applied in a subsample of communities selected for the impact evaluation; a facilities evaluation based on detailed surveys applied to social fund schools, health posts, and water and sanitation systems and to non–social fund schools and health posts; and a cost study. The use of these different evaluation approaches, particularly for generating the counterfactual, lent perspective and robustness to the evaluation.

PERU. Two separate studies were conducted. The Paxson and Schady evaluation (2002) analyzed existing national household surveys on household living conditions (the 1994 and 1997 Peru LSMS surveys and a 1996 household survey conducted by the Peruvian National Statistical Institute) without oversampling for social fund beneficiaries. For the impact evaluation, the researchers combined the household survey data with administrative data on social fund expenditures by region, using regional identifiers in the household survey to assess educational outcomes by region. The study also used multivariate analysis and instrumental variables to control for selection. The pragmatic approach employed in this evaluation was possible because of the existence of an unusual combination: a large-scale social fund having many education projects, and a large national household survey, representative at the district level, that included a question on whether the household was a social fund beneficiary. Although the approach used kept costs low, the analysis was limited to an assessment of targeting and the district-level impact of social fund education projects.

The Instituto Apoyo (2000b) evaluation and its accompanying household survey were designed to assess the welfare impact of rural social fund projects in education, water, sewerage, latrines, and electrification. As in Honduras and Zambia, researchers constructed the counterfactual by using pipeline projects as comparators. A module for facilities was included in the household survey to obtain information on social fund and non–social fund schools, water and sanitation facilities, and electric utilities. The evaluation also included a cost study. The sample size of the household survey, combined with the study's rural focus and the extent of both the social fund investments and Peru's indigenous population, allowed researchers to assess the impact of the social fund in indigenous areas—a feature unique to this case study.

The different data sources, evaluation approaches, and questions addressed in the two evaluations of the Peruvian social fund yielded a rich array of findings. Each study reached different conclusions, notably regarding the impact of the social fund on school enrollments—thus underscoring the limitations of any one evaluation method and the influence that data sources and evaluation methods can have on determining outcomes.

ZAMBIA. The Zambian evaluation considered the impact of social fund–financed health and primary education projects, taking advantage of the 1998 Living Conditions Monitoring Survey, an LSMS-style national household survey fielded to study poverty. The evaluation oversampled social fund beneficiaries and matched them to similar nonbeneficiaries, using propensity scores. It also used pipeline projects and the corresponding households as comparators. For the facility-level analysis, the evaluation relied primarily on a "nearest neighbor" approach, matching social fund schools and health centers to the closest non–social fund school or health center with similar characteristics. Detailed surveys were applied to the social fund and comparator schools and health centers. The evaluation also included a cost study.

Of the case studies, the Nicaraguan and Zambian studies applied the most similar evaluation methodologies: both used similar methods of estimating the counterfactual for the household-level impact analysis, and both made extensive use of facilities data.

Cost Study Methodology

In each case study, country researchers compared the costs of the social fund with those of NGOs or of central or local government agencies carrying out similar investments. Each analysis included only the major sectors receiving social fund financing in that country. All of them considered

Table 2.2 Cost Study Sample Frames and Methodologies

				Nicaragua[a]			
Item	*Armenia*	*Bolivia*	*Honduras*	*I*	*2*	*Peru*	*Zambia*[b]
Project category							
Social fund projects	128	2,238	1,123	11	33	40	1,150
Comparator projects	264	—[c]	65	27	10	27	301
Approach used							
Desk review	Yes	Yes	Yes	Yes	Yes	Yes	Yes
Field inspection	No	No	No	Yes	Yes	No	Yes[d]

[a] Two studies were carried out in Nicaragua: (1) Bermudez (1999), and (2) Araujo, Hurtado, and Lema (2000).
[b] Estimated number of schools upgraded. Cost estimates were averages based on standard school plans of each program.
[c] Standard plans from an NGO school construction program were reviewed.
[d] Field inspections were carried out in nine of the sampled projects; the other projects were assessed through desk reviews alone.
Source: Country case reports, as cited in the Bibliography and Box 1.

education projects; whether health, water, and sanitation projects were included depended on the social fund's focus and on data availability.

Each case study identified comparator institutions and reviewed the unit costs (cost per beneficiary, per square meter of construction, per latrine, etc.) of standard investments. In some cases researchers visited project sites to judge subjective factors such as the quality of construction. Table 2.2 shows the number of social fund and comparator projects reviewed in each country case study and the countries in which field inspections were conducted.

Analysis of Participation, Perceptions, and Priorities

The study examined the interaction between community social dynamics and social fund success, but it did not apply a specific methodology to probe this area because it was not a central focus of the research. Several case studies, however, used focus groups, key informant interviews, and other qualitative data collection techniques to assess communities' participation in social fund projects, their perceptions of the projects, and the priority they gave to them (box 2.2). In addition, questions on these subjects were included in the household and facility surveys in almost all the case study countries.

Data Sources and Sample Sizes

The data sources used for the country case studies are summarized in table 2.3. Table 2.4 presents sample sizes for each study.

Box 2.2 Qualitative Assessments Reviewed

Armenia

1997 Impact Assessment Study. Included a survey of 1,102 people, a survey of 20 project sites, and focus group interviews with beneficiary groups, implementing agency staff, construction companies, and local government representatives (Development Programs, Ltd. 1997).

1999 Sociological Study. Included a survey of 1,190 people, a survey of 20 project sites, and focus group interviews with beneficiary groups, implementing agency staff, construction companies, and local government representatives (Development Programs, Ltd. 1999)

Bolivia

1995 Perception of the Benefits of FIS Projects. Covered 95 projects selected from the impact evaluation baseline survey; conducted focus group interviews with or surveys of community members, community representatives, and line ministry staff (Coa 1995).

Honduras

1999 Ex-Post Evaluation. Conducted 30 focus group interviews in 15 communities with households selected from those in the impact evaluation household survey (Walker and others 1999).

Nicaragua

1998 Qualitative Evaluation of FISE Beneficiaries. Included a survey of 43 projects, a survey of 256 individuals, and 24 focus groups on projects implemented in 1993–96. The surveys were administered to local government staff (12 percent of respondents), line ministry staff (27 percent), former workers on social fund projects (13 percent), local beneficiaries (40 percent), and contractors (9 percent) (IDEAS 1998).

Peru

1997 Fourth Ex-Post Evaluation. Covered 300 projects completed in 1994 and surveyed 2,800 community members, beneficiaries, project committee members, and works operators or social fund zone chiefs (Instituto Apoyo 1997).

1999 Fifth Ex-Post Evaluation. Covered 150 projects completed in 1996–97 and surveyed 1,100 community members (Instituto Apoyo 1999).

2000 Sixth Ex-Post Evaluation. Covered 165 water projects completed in 1996–99 and surveyed 990 households (Instituto Apoyo 2000c).

Zambia

1994 Beneficiary Assessment III. Covered 21 projects (15 rural and 6 periurban), with subteams of four people spending six days at each site. Included 28 focus group

(Box continues on the following page.)

Box 2.2 (continued)

interviews, 30 ordinary group discussions, and semistructured interviews with 45
beneficiaries (University of Zambia, Participatory Assessment Group, 1994).
1997 Beneficiary Assessment IV. Covered 12 projects, using a methodology similar to
that of the 1994 beneficiary assessment (University of Zambia, Participatory
Assessment Group, 1997).
1998 Beneficiary Assessment V. Covered 19 projects, using a methodology similar to
that of the 1994 beneficiary assessment (University of Zambia, Participatory
Assessment Group, 1998).

Data Sources

Each country case study made use of a variety of data drawn from the following sources:

- *Household surveys.* Household data on beneficiaries were often collected by adding questions to an existing national LSMS household survey, oversampling beneficiaries, and creating comparison groups from
  households that had not benefited from a similar social fund intervention.[8] In Bolivia and Honduras and in the Instituto Apoyo (2000b) study
  in Peru, however, household surveys were designed and applied for the
  sole purpose of the impact evaluation.
- *Facilities surveys.* Surveys collected information on the staffing and
  operation of schools, health centers, and water and sanitation systems
  (depending on the scope of the study). These surveys were applied to
  facilities that had received a social fund investment and, usually, to
  similar facilities that had not. The study used a separate survey for
  each type of project.
- *Qualitative assessments.* Several country case studies included qualitative assessments that sought the opinions and perceptions of beneficiaries and other stakeholders. These studies complemented the
  quantitative data collected through household surveys, which were
  used primarily for the targeting and impact analysis. In Honduras and
  Nicaragua the qualitative assessments were designed as part of the
  impact evaluation, and the fieldwork was carried out in a subset of communities sampled for the impact evaluation. In Armenia, Peru, and

---

[8] LSMS surveys, which are designed to study poverty and welfare, include many of the variables of interest for the evaluation of welfare impact (see Grosh and Glewwe 2000). All of the
LSMS surveys used in the study were nationally representative and were based on random
samples of households in the case study countries.

Table 2.3 Data Sources Used in the Country Case Studies

Country and coverage	Types of projects evaluated	Time frame of projects evaluated	Data sources
Armenia National	Primary and secondary education Water supply Irrigation[a]	Projects completed 1994–97	1996 national LSMS household survey 1996 impact evaluation oversampling household survey 1997 facilities survey Social fund administrative data
Bolivia Five provinces in the Chaco region (rural) Seventeen provinces in other rural areas[b]	Primary education Health[c] Water	Projects completed between 1993 baseline survey and 1997 follow-up survey	1992 census data 1993 baseline and 1997–98 follow-up impact evaluation household survey 1993 baseline and 1997–98 follow-up facilities survey 1998 water quality test 1998 educational achievement tests for mathematics and language 1999 cost study Social fund administrative data
Honduras National	Primary education Rural health	Projects completed 1994–98	1998 impact evaluation household survey 1998 facilities survey

(Table continues on the following page.)

Table 2.3 (continued)

Country and coverage	Types of project evaluated	Time frame of projects evaluated	Data sources
	Water		1998 qualitative beneficiary assessment
	Sewerage		1999 cost study
	Latrines		Social fund administrative data
Nicaragua National	Primary education	Projects completed January 1994–June	1998 national LSMS household survey
	Rural health	1997	1998 impact evaluation oversampling household survey
	Water		1998 facilities survey
	Sewerage		1998 qualitative beneficiary assessment
	Latrines		2000 cost study
			Social fund administrative data
Peru I (Paxson and Schady 2002) National	Primary education	Projects completed 1992–98	1994 national LSMS household survey
			1996 Peruvian National Statistical Institute household survey
			1997 national LSMS household survey
			Social fund administrative data

| **Peru 2**
(Instituto Apoyo 2000b)
Rural areas in departments
with more than 200 projects,
including a representative sample
of indigenous communities | Primary education
Water
Sewerage[c]
Latrines
Electrification[c]
Irrigation[a] | Projects completed
1996–99 | 2000 impact evaluation household survey
2000 cost study
2000 determinants of project success study
Social fund administrative data |
| **Zambia**
National | Primary education
Health[c] | Projects completed
1991–97 | 1998 national Living Conditions Monitoring Survey
1998 impact evaluation oversampling household survey
1998 facilities survey
1999 cost study
Social fund administrative data |

Note: LSMS, Living Standards Measurement Study.

[a] Included only in the cost study, not the impact and targeting assessment.

[b] Bolivia has 111 provinces.

[c] Included only in the impact and targeting assessment, not the cost study.

Table 2.4 Household and Facility Sample Sizes Used for Targeting and Impact Evaluation, Treatment and Comparator Groups Combined

	Household survey sample size		Facilities survey sample size[a]			
Country case study	Social fund survey[a]	National survey	Education	Health	Water	Sewerage
Armenia	2,260	3,600	53	n.a.	60	n.a.
Bolivia[b]	7,300	n.a.	139	146	n.a.	n.a.
Honduras	2,320	n.a.	24	21	24	12
Nicaragua	1,310	4,040	48	40	24	12
Peru 1 (Paxson and	n.a.	18,000	n.a.	n.a.	n.a.	n.a.
Schady 2002)[c]		3,500				
		3,500				
Peru 2 (Instituto						
Apoyo 2000b)[d]	5,120	n.a.	141	n.a.	335	44
Zambia	2,950	13,500	68	30	n.a.	n.a.
Total	21,260	46,140	473	237	443	68
Totals for all surveys	67,400		1,221			

n.a. Not applicable.

Note: Latrine projects were sampled in Peru, Nicaragua, and Honduras as part of the household survey but are not reported, since no separate facilities survey was applied. In Bolivia water projects were included in the analysis, but there was no separate water facilities survey.

[a] In Armenia, Nicaragua, and Zambia the social fund survey consisted of the application of a national household survey questionnaire to a sample selected for the social fund study.

[b] The reported sample size is from the 1993 baseline survey in Chaco and other rural areas. Households and projects were resurveyed in the 1997–98 follow-up survey. Households that could not be located were replaced.

[c] The Paxson and Schady evaluation collected no primary data, instead using social fund administrative data crossed with household survey data from the 1996 Peruvian National Statistical Institute (INEI) household survey (18,000 households), the 1994 Peru Living Standards Measurement Survey (3,500 households), and the 1997 Peru Living Standards Measurement Survey (3,500 households).

[d] The Instituto Apoyo study also sampled 74 electrification projects and 9 irrigation projects, but these were not analyzed as part of this study.

Zambia beneficiary assessments were carried out as part of routine monitoring and evaluation activities (see box 2.2).

- *Cost studies.* To assess unit costs and processing efficiency, the study compared social fund projects with similar projects carried out by other agencies in each of the six countries. Administrative data, site visits by engineers, and standard design and cost estimates were all used in the cost studies. (see table 2.3).
- *Social fund administrative data.* All country case studies used information from social fund databases on the geographic distribution, expenditures, and composition of social fund projects. In several cases the targeting and impact assessments also used poverty map data.

Sample Size and Design

The household and facilities surveys used in the study generated data for both treatment and comparator groups from more than 65,000 households and 1,200 schools, health centers, and water and sanitation projects (see table 2.4).

In each of the case study countries the evaluation was based on a random sample of social fund projects and a random sample of households in the area of influence of the sampled projects. The sampling followed a simple two-stage procedure. In the first stage projects were randomly selected from the social fund portfolio, which was stratified by type of project. In the second stage a random sample of households was selected from the area of influence of the facilities that had benefited from the sampled project.

In each country the household sample of social fund beneficiaries was representative by type of social fund project and was generalizable to the universe of social fund beneficiaries. These representative household samples allowed conclusions to be drawn about the targeting and impact of all social fund investments of the kind being examined. By contrast, the samples used in the facilities surveys were not always designed to be representative by type of project, and often the facility-level results are not generalizable to all social fund projects. The facility and household data were the main source of information for the targeting, impact, and quality assessments.

The range of sample sizes across the case study countries reflects the availability of national survey data and the focus of the particular evaluation. Honduras had one of the smaller samples collected for the social fund study; the sample size of 2,320 households was not designed to be large enough to capture changes in school enrollment rates. One of the larger sample sizes (25,000 households) is found in the Paxson and Schady (2002) study in Peru. That study drew on a combined sample from three general-purpose household surveys, none of which was designed for the purpose of evaluating the social fund. The sample size in Bolivia (7,300 households) reflected the emphasis on collecting data to measure under-five mortality—a relatively rare event requiring large samples to identify project impact. The large (5,120 households) sample size from the rural-focused Instituto Apoyo (2000b) study in Peru allowed an impact evaluation of projects carried out in areas inhabited largely by indigenous people.

Costs and Time Frame

The costs of the impact evaluations and targeting analyses based on household surveys averaged about 1 percent of the World Bank loan or credit in each case study country, excluding the costs of counterpart teams from the social funds and of the national household surveys (table 2.5). Thus, the cost

Table 2.5 Estimated Costs of Impact Evaluations and Targeting Analyses (percent, except as otherwise specified)

			Breakdown of evaluation costs			
Country	Estimated cost of evaluation (U.S. dollars)[a]	Cost as percentage of IBRD loan or IDA credit[b]	World Bank			Data collection
			Travel	Staff	Consultants	
Armenia	111,000	0.6	28	18	35	18
Bolivia	878,000	1.4	3	15	13	69
Honduras	263,000	0.9	3	12	53	32
Nicaragua	449,000	0.8	5	33	8	56
Peru 1 (Instituto Apoyo 2000b)	350,000	0.4	0	0	100[c]	—
Peru 2 (Paxson and Schady 2002)	33,000	0.0	0	82	16	0
Zambia	174,000	0.9	8	52	16	24
Average	323,000	0.7	7	30	27	36

— Not available.

Note: The data exclude the costs of the cost studies, which ranged from $15,000 to $25,000.

[a] Excludes the cost of local counterpart teams not financed from the loan or credit and the cost of gathering the national survey data (includes only the cost of oversampling the social fund study).

[b] Cost of the evaluation as a percentage of the International Bank for Reconstruction and Development (IBRD) loan or International Development Association (IDA) credit to the client government for the period of financing corresponding to the projects considered in the evaluation. The relative cost data are meant to be indicative, as the evaluation was often financed from sources other than the loan or credit.

[c] The lump-sum contract with a local research firm did not disaggregate costs between consultants and data collection.

Source: World Bank administrative data.

of obtaining evidence on the impact of a social fund's projects often accounted for only a small part of the overall financing of the social fund.[9]

The costs of the impact evaluations depended on the availability of existing data and the scope of the evaluation and ranged from about $33,000 for the Paxson and Schady (2002) study in Peru to almost $900,000 for the evaluation in Bolivia. Data collection was usually the most expensive component, accounting for more than a third of the evaluation costs, on average. As the Bolivian case study illustrates, collecting both baseline and follow-up data raised the costs. Data collection costs were also higher where new survey instruments were designed and where, as in the Bolivia, Honduras, and Instituto Apoyo (Peru) studies, all of the data for the evaluation were collected as part

---

[9] In addition to the World Bank, sources of social fund financing often include other multilateral agencies, bilateral donors, government resources, and in-kind contributions from beneficiaries in the form of land and labor.

of the evaluation effort rather than being drawn from existing household surveys. The remaining costs were concentrated mainly in evaluation design and analysis activities carried out by World Bank staff and consultants.

In the least expensive evaluation, by Paxson and Schady (2002) in Peru, a World Bank economist and an outside consultant analyzed existing data, incurring no data collection costs or field expenses. The most expensive evaluation, that in Bolivia, carried out baseline and follow-up surveys of both households and facilities. The evaluation also included water quality tests and scholastic achievement tests in mathematics and language. Since no other household and facilities data were available, the collection of data had to be fully financed as part of the evaluation.

The timing of the impact evaluations varied, depending on the evaluation design. Again, Peru and Bolivia provide a study in contrasts. Whereas the Paxson and Schady evaluation in Peru took only a few months, the Bolivian evaluation lasted nearly a decade. The Bolivian social fund was the first to use an impact evaluation based on a household survey, and it began development of the study design in 1991; baseline data were collected in 1993. A follow-up household survey was administered in 1997–98, and analysis of the results has only recently been completed.

Implications

The conclusions from this chapter can be grouped into two general areas: lessons regarding the evaluation methodology applied, and recommendations on the operational aspects of conducting the studies. Chapter 9, which presents the conclusions of this report, also offers recommendations for future directions in evaluating social sector projects. These lessons and recommendations are based on the material reviewed in this volume, the experiences of the country case study teams, and the in-depth analytical work presented in each country case report.

Lessons on Methodology

Covering as they did a wide variety of approaches and evaluation designs, the case studies generated a number of lessons:

- *Using multiple approaches strengthens evaluation results.* The use of a variety of approaches for establishing the counterfactual in the impact analysis and the inclusion of other types of evaluations (such as qualitative assessments and facilities studies) helped lend robustness and depth to the evaluation results. In Honduras and Nicaragua, applying qualitative methods in a subsample of the communities selected for the impact evaluation added useful depth and nuance. These qualitative analyses were supported by solid understanding of the respondents' socioeconomic environment, garnered from the household survey data.

- *Using communities that have been approved for future project funding ("pipeline communities") to establish the counterfactual is a promising approach for carrying out program evaluations and establishing an impact evaluation system.* This approach allows researchers to address a variety of selection issues—such as community motivation and aspects of the social fund screening process—that may not be controlled for in information on observable characteristics from survey and administrative data. Moreover, the data on the pipeline group can serve as a baseline in future studies, helping to establish an efficient impact evaluation system.

- *Randomization of the offer to participate in a project can be sufficient to generate a valid experimental design.* The impact evaluation of education projects in Bolivia's Chaco region demonstrated that randomization of project promotion (rather than of the projects themselves) can provide a solid basis for a randomized control design. This is a promising lesson for social policy research, since individual behavior can often alter the composition of designed treatment and control groups. When budget constraints prevent programs from reaching all potential beneficiaries, randomization (through a lottery, for example) should be considered as a method for selecting beneficiaries. Random selection of treatment and control groups also provides a transparent mechanism for selecting program participants.

- *Focusing on key measures and on the sample design is critical to ensuring that an evaluation can answer the questions that it addresses.* Researchers should undertake power calculations to estimate the sample sizes needed to measure impacts at the design stage of the evaluation. Measuring some outcomes can be challenging and expensive. In Bolivia, for example, measuring changes in under-five mortality required relatively large samples, since the death of children under five is a relatively rare event. In Honduras the study team decided not to measure school enrollment as an outcome because the sample sizes required to pick up a measurable difference between treatment and comparison groups would have had to be very large, given the relatively high primary enrollment rates.

Operational Recommendations for Evaluation

A review of the experience with the impact evaluations in the six case study countries points to several operational recommendations for conducting evaluations of social programs:

- *Focus on the evaluation at the beginning of the project.* Planning the evaluation in the early stages of project design will provide a wider range of options, including the opportunity for randomization. In addition, the cost and time frame of an evaluation will define its boundaries and should therefore be assessed at the beginning of the design stage. The cost and time frame depend largely on the breadth and depth of the evaluation, its design, and the availability of survey data.

- *Look for opportunities to piggyback on planned household surveys.* Using existing household surveys for the targeting and impact analysis is often more operationally feasible and cost-effective than carrying out an independent survey. The combination of oversampling project beneficiaries from a general household survey and using propensity score matching techniques to generate a counterfactual is a useful approach to impact evaluation. Moreover, it can provide a basis not only for impact evaluation but also for household-level incidence analysis. A caveat is that the evaluation team may have only limited control over the content of the questionnaires applied in the survey and the quality of the fieldwork and data processing. If the incidence of the program and the sample size of the survey are large enough to generate results without oversampling beneficiaries—as was the case for education projects in Peru—piggybacking even without oversampling beneficiaries allows researchers to carry out impact evaluations at little cost.

- *Secure the support of stakeholders from the program under evaluation to help ensure the relevance of the evaluation.* This type of collaboration is critical to ensuring that an evaluation will be used to inform program design and implementation. In addition, if program administrators and government policymakers are to be convinced that such evaluations are worth the price of forgoing some investments in communities, the studies need to focus on issues that these officials consider priorities.

- *Coordinate with other donors.* Coordination among donors can facilitate the design and financing of the evaluation as well as the follow-up of the results. Coordination is also important in order to avoid duplication of evaluation efforts, to rationalize the financing of evaluations, and to foster collaboration in supporting the implementation of policy changes suggested by the evaluation results.

- *Take advantage of routine data collection.* To better assess facility-level impacts, social funds should routinely gather baseline data from projects as part of the appraisal and should collect follow-up data from representative samples of social fund projects to monitor the changes that have occurred since the investment. These efforts would provide much of the basic data needed for routine evaluation of the progress of social funds, which could be complemented by impact evaluations focusing on new models or practices.

- *Respect and be aware of the critical links between program administration and evaluation.* Evaluations can be strengthened by being closely aligned with program administration, as the random allocation of projects supporting an experimental evaluation design illustrates. Conversely, divergence between the focus of the evaluation and program administration—in timing, design, and other aspects—can undermine evaluation efforts.

3

Performance in Poverty Targeting

THE DATA FROM THE STUDY SHOW THAT SOCIAL FUNDS are successful in reaching the poor. The geographic distribution of social fund expenditures was progressive in all of the countries studied, with poor districts receiving more per capita than wealthier districts and the very poorest districts receiving shares exceeding their shares of the population. Geographic targeting has improved over time in all six social funds. The high levels of investment in some of the poorest areas refute the idea that such areas are systematically incapable of accessing resources from demand-driven programs. In most cases, however, the overall distribution of resources at the household level was only mildly progressive. Positive discrimination toward poor households was best achieved by latrine and health projects; sewerage projects tended to benefit the better off. Comparisons with other programs showed that social funds' geographic and household targeting compared favorably with that of other targeted social programs, as well as with general social spending and municipal-level transfers.

Research Focus

Although social funds were originally designed to address the social costs of economic adjustment, they have more recently been viewed as a tool for reaching populations that public investment programs have historically underserved. Most social funds now explicitly aim to reach poor communities, although they do not target specific households. Most engage in geographic targeting, with a preference for proposals from poorer communities or with notional allocation targets based on poverty maps.[1] The types of investment eligible for financing, such as primary schools, basic health facilities, and basic water and sanitation, are those that may be more likely to be used by lower-income groups. Moreover, research on targeting at the margin suggests that since the better off usually already have access to basic services, any investments that increase coverage will tend to be pro-poor (Lanjouw and Ravallion 1999).

The cross-country analysis seeks to answer the following core questions regarding poverty targeting performance:

- Have social fund resources benefited poor areas?
- Have social fund resources benefited poor households?
- What does the evidence suggest with respect to targeting within districts and among potential versus actual beneficiaries?
- How do these outcomes compare with those of other public expenditures?

Geographic Targeting Performance

All the social funds in the study have a broad national presence, and virtually all districts or municipalities in the six countries have received some social fund financing. In Peru, however, the social fund has recently focused on rural areas, where poverty is more concentrated.

To assess the extent to which social funds targeted resources to poorer districts and municipalities, the study used a poverty ranking of districts or municipalities in each country to construct population deciles. Because each country uses a different measure of poverty at the district or municipal level, the absolute levels are not directly comparable across countries, but the relative findings do show the degree to which resources went to the worse-off districts in each country.

The size of the geographic units used in the study, which were based on the units used in current social fund poverty maps, varied greatly by country

---

[1] Social funds do not usually identify areas that are lacking in any one particular type of social infrastructure; that is, they do not direct spending on schools to the areas with the lowest enrollment rates. Rather, they target on composite indicators of poverty, whether unmet basic needs or income/consumption measures. Typically, there is a good overlap between populations without access to basic services (such as health facilities and primary schools) and poverty levels. The more general measures of poverty are preferable for resource allocation purposes, since social funds do not decide ex ante what the type of intervention should be in a specific community.

Table 3.1 Units Used in Analysis of Geographic Targeting

Country	Unit	Number of units	National population	Population of largest unit	Population of smallest units
Armenia	Marz	11	4,000,000	1,200,000	69,000
Bolivia	Municipality	265	6,000,000	716,000	400
Honduras	Municipality	294	5,000,000	625,000	800
Nicaragua	Municipality	147	4,000,000	938,000	600
Peru	District	1,818	25,000,000	591,213	140
Zambia	District	57	10,000,000	1,100,000	34,000

Note: In some countries the number of units has varied over time. The table uses the most recent estimates.

(table 3.1). The largest units were in Armenia, where a *marz* (similar to a province) may contain up to 1.2 million people. The Latin American cases had the smallest districts and municipalities, some with as few as 140 people. The larger the unit, the greater the likelihood of variations in poverty levels within a unit; thus, targeting performance could vary solely on the basis of the geographic level of analysis. The variation in the size of geographic units limits the direct comparisons that can be made among countries and should be taken into consideration in assessing results. Because of potential income heterogeneity within districts and municipalities, geographic targeting information is only a proxy measure for whether resources benefit poor communities and households. This is particularly true for major urban areas, since cities generally appear to be the least poor districts of any country. In Honduras, for example, Tegucigalpa accounts for most of the richest three deciles of the population by municipality.

The prevalence of poor people even in relatively better-off areas complicates the interpretation of geographic targeting results. For example, urban Lusaka, with 10 percent of Zambia's population, is that country's wealthiest district—but it is also home to 4 percent of the nation's poor. Under the lens of geographic targeting analysis, any social fund spending in Lusaka will appear to favor a better-off area, even though the poor people who live there may benefit from the intervention.

Cumulative Results

The distribution of social fund expenditures to date has been generally progressive. Poorer districts or municipalities tended to receive more per capita than did better-off areas, and the poorer half of the population received more

Table 3.2 Cumulative Geographic Distribution of Social Fund Resources by Population Decile

Decile	Armenia, 1996–99	Bolivia, 1991–98	Honduras, 1991–98	Nicaragua, 1991–98	Peru, 1992–98	Zambia, 1991–98
I (poorest)	10.7	10.8	14.5	14.7	25.3	9.8
2	13.2	13.6	10.7	14.4	21.2	10.6
3	12.4	15.2	11.4	12.8	19.2	14.9
4	12.0	13.0	9.0	11.4	12.3	8.6
5	9.4	11.0	10.0	10.6	8.3	8.6
6	5.7	11.9	10.4	10.7	4.9	13.5
7	5.7	8.0	8.0	8.3	3.2	8.4
8	6.9	7.6	5.0	6.9	3.0	10.6
9	10.1	6.0	15.1	5.5	1.9	6.4
10 (richest)	13.9	2.8	6.0	4.7	0.7	8.6

Source: Armenia, World Bank data; Bolivia, Social Investment Fund database; Honduras, Social Investment Fund database; Nicaragua, Emergency Social Investment Fund database; Peru, Paxson and Schady (2002); Zambia, Social Recovery Project database.

per capita than did the wealthier half (see table 3.2). The poorest 30 percent of district population received between 35 percent (Zambia) and 66 percent of resources (Peru), and the poorest 10 percent received between 10 percent (Zambia) and 25 percent (Peru). There was no systematic bias against poor areas in access to social fund resources.

Social funds' cumulative geographic distribution of resources has generally been progressive (figure 3.1). The Peruvian social fund had the most progressive distribution, largely because of its predominantly rural focus, and those in Bolivia and Nicaragua were close behind. The Honduran social fund was slightly less progressive than the other Latin American examples, but the poorest decile of the population by municipality still received more than twice the resources per capita than the richest did. The Latin American funds use poverty maps proactively, in most cases setting spending targets for each municipality.[2]

In Zambia spending was less progressive. Like many African countries, Zambia has generally high poverty levels, with more than 65 percent of the population living below the national poverty line in three-quarters of its districts. Even in the least poor district—the capital, Lusaka—about one in

---

[2] In Nicaragua and Peru municipalities are organized into categories of low, medium, and high poverty, and targets are established for each category. In Honduras allocations are now defined for each municipality.

Figure 3.1 Cumulative Geographic Distribution of Social Fund Resources by Municipal or District Poverty Decile

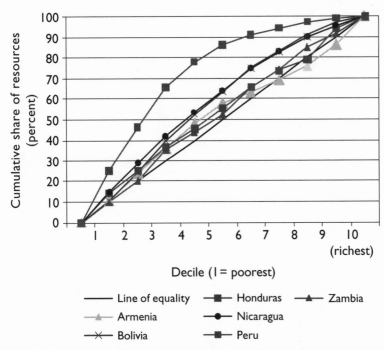

Note: The figure shows the data from table 3.2 in the form of concentration curves. The 45-degree line (line of equality) indicates a neutral distribution. Any curve above the line represents a progressive, or pro-poor, distribution; any curve below it indicates a regressive distribution.
Source: Authors' calculations.

three people lives below the poverty line. Given this widespread poverty, the Zambian social fund did not start with pro-poor geographic targeting goals but instead aimed at relatively equal distribution across districts. The richest 20 percent of districts received only 15 percent of resources, so there was some positive discrimination, basically away from Lusaka.

Armenia was the only case of regressive targeting, and that only in the wealthier districts; the allocation of expenditures among the poorest 40 percent of districts was pro-poor. The results show that it was the middle-income districts, not the poorest ones, that received less than their population share. The Armenian social fund did not use explicit geographic poverty targeting in its early years, when the goal of responding to the urgent needs for reconstruction in earthquake-affected zones tended to dilute the poverty criteria for allocating investment. In addition, evidence suggests that the geographic distribution of resources may be less important in

Armenia than in the other countries because of the high income inequality within districts.[3]

Recent Trends

The overall results cover cumulative expenditures, including the funds' early years of operation, when they focused on dealing with crises. Data for recent years show that all the case study social funds have improved their geographic targeting, shifting toward a higher concentration of expenditure in poorer districts (figure 3.2). Several factors explain these shifts:

- *Evolving goals.* Most social funds produced results very quickly at the outset, often in an environment of crisis and with an emphasis on generating temporary employment. They achieved these rapid results by focusing on the areas that were easier to reach, typically urban areas. Over time, social funds have adopted strategies for extending their reach to poorer and more remote areas to fulfill their evolving mandates.
- *Proactive outreach.* After the initial start-up period, social funds tended to intensify their outreach activities. The most important of these included information campaigns to alert communities to the programs, technical support to communities for identifying and preparing project proposals, and establishment of regional offices, which reduced the transactions costs of applying for funding for communities far from the capital city.
- *Positive discrimination.* As social funds began to receive a surplus of project proposals, and as their tools for allocating resources evolved, they could begin to make poorer areas a priority. Poverty maps, which became more refined over time, with the greater availability of disaggregated data, took on an increasingly important role in allocating resources. In Bolivia, for example, the only poverty maps available at the outset were regional or, at best, province level, and the information was outdated. Over time, better data have allowed the development of municipal-level poverty maps. In most of the case study countries social funds have been at the forefront of efforts to use these maps in allocating program resources.
- *Increase in demand responsiveness.* Demand by poor areas for social fund resources has strengthened over time. Beneficiary assessments show

---

[3] A World Bank (1999c) analysis of social assistance in Armenia found that the districts (marzes) with the highest proportion of poor also have the most severe poverty. There is, however, great inequality within districts, and the differences between districts are not sufficient to justify targeting benefits or subsidies to those with the highest poverty rates.

Figure 3.2 Change in Geographic Targeting over Time

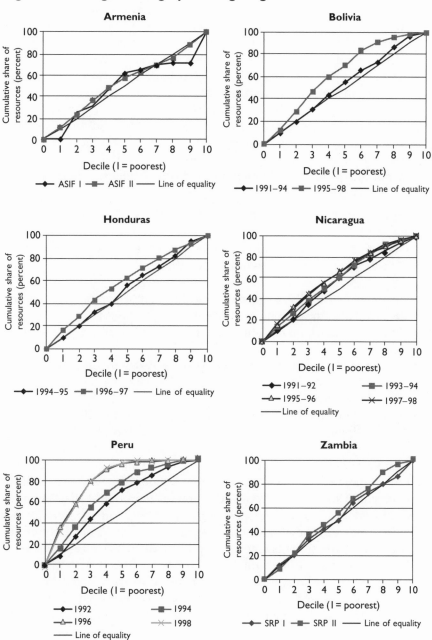

Note: ASIF, Armenia Social Investment Fund; SRP, Social Recovery Project. The 45-degree line (line of equality) indicates a neutral distribution. Any curve above that line represents a progressive, or pro-poor, distribution; any curve below it indicates a regressive distribution.
Source: Authors' calculations.

that communities are often mobilized by word of mouth and by visits to other communities. Communities with closer-knit social networks and more dynamic leaders tend to respond more quickly to the incentives provided by a social fund, while poorer communities may wait until the demonstration effect in other areas becomes convincing (Owen and Van Domelen 1998). As a result, more remote and risk-averse communities may lag in seeking program resources.

- *Exogenous factors.* In Bolivia the 1994–95 fiscal decentralization reform enabled poor municipalities to increase their demand for social fund financing (Parker and Serrano 2000). Resources became available for the use of technical specialists to assist in identifying priorities and preparing projects and for counterpart contributions.

Variation in Spending among Districts or Municipalities

Even though all districts or municipalities may have access to a social fund, the intensity of investment differs greatly among areas:[4]

- In Armenia the district (*marz*) with the highest per capita spending received 2.5 times as much as the one with the lowest.
- In Bolivia per capita investment in municipalities ranged from $0.49 to $377.05.
- In Zambia the district with the lowest per capita investment received only $0.38 per person, while the district with the highest received $22.00 per person.
- In Honduras the ratio of per capita spending in the district with the highest spending to that with the lowest was 61 to 1.

High variation in spending was also observed among the poorest districts and municipalities, with no apparent relationship between the level of poverty and the amount received. Some of the poorest districts have been very adept at accessing social fund financing, often receiving per capita investments many times the national average. In Zambia, for example, social fund investments among the poorest districts ranged from $1.60 to $12.90 per capita through the end of 1998, compared with a national average of $4.40. In Bolivia, where the national average was $33.20, the poorest municipalities received $0.50 to $197.30. Thus, the data do not support the hypothesis that the poorest areas are incapable of participating in

---

[4] This is consistent with findings from other programs based on similar demand-driven mechanisms. For example, a recent study of the demand-driven public works program Trabajar in Argentina found a progressive geographic distribution of resources overall but also considerable horizontal inequity between equally poor areas in different provinces (Ravallion 2000).

demand-driven programs. In all cases some of the poorest districts received many times the national per capita average.

Several factors may drive these disparities. First, social fund investments are "lumpy." Communities propose projects that often vary greatly in size, resulting in large differences in per capita expenditures. Second, social fund projects are not entitlements. Communities manifest varying degrees of the capacity and self-motivation needed to mobilize efforts to present viable proposals for funding, whether directly or through their intermediaries (NGOs, line ministries, and local governments), and this can give rise to large variance in spending among districts with similar poverty levels. Finally, the extensive general literature on the political economy of public spending argues that the timing, composition, and geographic distribution of expenditures in democratic regimes are based on electoral interests (Nordhaus 1975; Ames 1987; Rogoff 1990; Schuknecht 1996). In looking at the political dimension of social fund expenditures in Peru, Schady (1999) found that marginal voters, core supporters, and the poor all received a disproportionate share of social fund expenditures, leading to the conclusion that decisions about social fund financing were made on the basis of both political and technical criteria.

Household Targeting Performance

Most of the social funds in the study have explicit geographic targeting mechanisms but target resources to poor households only through the menu of eligible interventions, such as water supply, primary education, and primary health care. This mechanism may or may not lead to effective self-selection by households.

There are two ways to analyze the household targeting results. Analysis of *absolute targeting* differentiates beneficiaries between poor and nonpoor, comparing household income or consumption with national poverty lines. Because different countries use different methods to construct these poverty lines, comparisons across countries can be misleading. Analysis of *relative targeting* defines where beneficiaries fall in the national income (or consumption) distribution. While this analysis cannot specify how many beneficiaries are poor, it does show what share of beneficiaries is in the lowest income deciles. This study used both approaches.

Results may vary depending on the measure selected. Income or consumption deciles can be constructed using either the household or the individual as the unit of analysis. Household deciles are constructed by ranking each household by income or consumption, while individual or population deciles rank each person by income or consumption. Because poor households tend to be larger than nonpoor households, the poorer population deciles will contain fewer households than do wealthier deciles. Thus, in most cases results based on household deciles will appear to be more progressive than those based on population deciles. Population deciles are typically used to analyze benefits, such as primary education, that are attributed to specific individuals in a household. For services benefiting all household members, such as water and sanitation, household deciles are used. Since social funds finance both types of interventions, which measure is the correct one is debatable.

In addition, the poverty targeting of a social fund can be calculated on the basis of either a head count of beneficiaries or the relative intensity of resources going to different poverty groups. Since the targeting incidence and the distribution of resources vary by type of project, the two measures may yield different results.

Although there is no compelling reason for choosing one method over another, the study used the most conservative measure—the incidence of beneficiaries based on population deciles. As results for Honduras show, basing incidence on population deciles and the number of beneficiaries rather than on the amount of resources gives the least progressive targeting result (box 3.1). The targeting results should therefore be taken as a minimum in terms of the potential progressiveness of social fund spending.

Household-level findings correspond to the period covered by the impact evaluation. The sample frames of the impact evaluation correspond to projects completed in 1994–99, with the specific years depending on the country. The household targeting analysis does not cover the most recent years, when the most progressive geographic distribution of resources was observed.

Results Based on Poverty Lines

Social funds have benefited more poor than nonpoor households and individuals. The share of beneficiaries classified as poor ranged from 55 percent in Nicaragua to 71 percent in Zambia and to more than 90 percent in rural Peru (box 3.2).

The poor made up as large a share of the social fund beneficiaries as they did of the national population—or an even larger share. In Zambia the share of beneficiary households that were poor was about the same as the share of poor households nationwide (more than 70 percent). In Honduras, Nicaragua, and Peru the share of beneficiaries considered poor was larger than the corresponding share of the national population. Peru had the most progressive distribution: whereas half the national population lived below the poverty line, two-thirds of beneficiaries did.

This finding also holds for those in extreme poverty. In Nicaragua, Peru, and Zambia the extremely poor represented a slightly larger share of social fund beneficiaries than of the national population, and in Honduras the extremely poor accounted for 11 percent of the national population but for 16 percent of social fund beneficiaries, a difference of about 45 percent.

Box 3.1 Comparing Targeting Results in Honduras Using Different Measures

The data for Honduras shown in the table confirm that targeting appears to be more progressive when the measurement is based on households rather than individuals. Nineteen percent of beneficiary households are in the poorest household decile, but only 15 percent of individual beneficiaries are in the poorest population decile. Because social fund resources are concentrated in pro-poor projects, the incidence of resources is more progressive than the incidence of beneficiaries: 24 percent of resources goes to the poorest household decile, and 20 percent to the poorest population decile.

Distribution of Social Fund Resources and Beneficiaries by Decile, Honduras (percent)

Decile	Household deciles		Population deciles	
	Beneficiaries	Resources	Beneficiaries	Resources
I (poorest)	19.0	23.7	15.2	19.7
2	13.0	12.4	11.5	11.4
3	9.7	8.1	8.7	7.6
4	8.9	8.9	8.4	8.7
5	7.6	10.3	6.9	9.6
6	7.7	7.1	8.2	7.8
7	12.0	7.9	12.6	8.5
8	10.4	10.3	11.4	11.6
9	7.2	7.1	8.8	8.9
10 (wealthiest)	4.4	4.3	6.1	6.1

Source: Walker and others (1999); World Bank estimates.

Even though social funds benefited the poor and the extremely poor more than the nonpoor, they could not prevent the nonpoor from benefiting as well. The share of nonpoor participants ranged from 29 percent (Zambia) to 45 percent (Nicaragua). This finding shows the targeting limitations of investments in communitywide basic services. Social funds invest in infrastructure and services that benefit the broad community, and they do not use household means testing.[5] To the extent that there is income heterogeneity at the community level, leakage will occur. In addition, health centers and

---

[5] The exceptions are certain microenterprise support programs and, recently, a cash transfer program carried out by the Nicaraguan social fund (see note 7).

Box 3.2 Targeting of Social Funds to the Poor and the Poorest

The table shows the distribution of social fund beneficiaries by degree of poverty—poor and extremely poor. Armenia and Bolivia are omitted, as explained below.

Percentage of Social Fund Beneficiaries Classified as Poor

			Peru		
Item	Honduras	Nicaragua	Education	Rural	Zambia
Social fund beneficiaries					
Poor	58	55	66	94–99	71
Extremely poor	16	18	23	65–81	57
Nonpoor	42	45	34	1–6	29
National population					
Poor	54	48	50	—	72
Extremely poor	11	17	20	—	56
Nonpoor	46	52	50	—	28

— Not available.
Source: For education projects in Peru, Hentschel, Poggi, and Schady (1996); for rural projects in Peru, Instituto Apoyo (2000b); for data sources for other countries and for years, see chapter 2, table 2.3.

Armenia. Armenia is omitted from the table because its poverty line is not yet available, but beneficiary households were poorer, on average, than nonbeneficiary households. Social fund households had per capita expenditures 5 percent lower than those of comparison groups. They also had a higher likelihood of registering for unemployment benefits, often experienced more wage arrears, received social assistance at higher rates than households nationwide, and tended to spend a larger share of their total expenditures on food than non–social fund households—a robust indicator of relative poverty.

Bolivia. Bolivia is not included in the household incidence analysis because comparable data are not available. The Bolivia baseline evaluation did include descriptive information on per capita consumption to characterize households that were using facilities in which the social fund was planning to invest. The data could not be linked to national-level data on per capita household consumption because national household-level poverty data were lacking.

Honduras. The Honduras data are based on an index of unmet basic needs of households. For the purposes of this analysis, "poor" means households with one or more

---

Box 3.2 (continued)

unmet basic needs, and "extremely poor," households with three or more unmet basic needs.

Nicaragua. Data are based on the share of social fund resources. Individuals classified as extremely poor are those with consumption levels at or below the cost of acquiring the minimum caloric intake recommended for Nicaragua, and the poor are defined as those whose consumption levels equal the cost of the minimum caloric intake plus an allowance for nonfood items.

Peru. Two sources of data are available. Hentschel, Poggi, and Schady (1996), using household consumption, estimate the extremely poor population of Peru at 20 percent and the poor plus extremely poor at 50 percent. The data are based on households benefiting from education investments. Social fund beneficiaries are divided into population quintiles with the share of beneficiaries in the lowest quintile corresponding to the extremely poor and the lowest three quintiles corresponding to the poor in general. The figures in the second column, from Instituto Apoyo (2000b), are based on a sample of rural projects with poverty classification such that the extremely poor spend less than $1 per capita per day, the poor less than $2 per capita per day, and the nonpoor, more than $2 per day.

Zambia. Individuals classified as extremely poor are those with consumption levels at or below the cost of acquiring the minimum caloric intake. The poor are those whose consumption levels equal the cost of the minimum caloric intake plus 25 percent for nonfood items.

---

schools tend to be more centrally situated within districts in order to broaden access. Within a given district, communities that have such infrastructure may be better off than more remote and dispersed populations.[6]

Results Based on Income or Consumption Deciles

The distribution of benefits by income or consumption decile can be compared across countries to indicate which social funds are relatively more progressive. Variation in the absolute level of poverty, however, limits cross-country comparability. For example, the same relative distribution of benefits may

---

[6] A recent study on the targeting of a rural roads program in Vietnam found similar results, with 48 percent of beneficiaries below the poverty line, as against 40 percent for rural areas in general and 65 percent for the poorest rural communities (van de Walle and Cratty 2002).

reach more poor households in countries with greater absolute poverty. As noted, the study used the most conservative estimate, which was based on population deciles and had beneficiaries, not social fund resources, as the unit of analysis.

For most of the social funds studied, the distribution of beneficiaries at the household level was either neutral or mildly progressive—a finding consistent with that based on poverty lines. The only exception was Armenia, where beneficiaries were concentrated in the middle of the income distribution, with both the poorest and the richest deciles accounting for slightly less than their population shares. The share of beneficiaries who were among the poorest 40 percent of the population was 37 percent in Armenia, 43 percent in Zambia, 44 percent in both Honduras and Nicaragua, and 45 percent in Peru (see table 3.3 and figure 3.3).

The evidence confirms that social funds have been able to reach the poorest of the poor at the household level. Except in Armenia, the share of beneficiaries who were in the poorest quintile exceeded 20 percent. The poorest quintile accounted for 27 percent of beneficiaries in Honduras, 25 percent in Zambia, and 23 percent in Nicaragua and Peru. In Armenia this share was only 15 percent.

Social fund investments also benefited better-off households. In Armenia and Zambia the wealthiest quintile accounted for around 20 percent of

Table 3.3 Distribution of Social Fund Beneficiaries by Population Decile (percent)

Decile	Armenia	Honduras	Peru[a]	Nicaragua	Zambia
1 (poorest)	8	15	10	9	9
2	7	12	13	14	14
3	10	9	11	10	10
4	12	8	11	11	11
5	10	7	12	14	14
6	13	8	10	8	8
7	10	13	12	9	9
8	12	11	10	12	12
9	9	9	9	7	7
10 (richest)	9	6	2	7	7
Total	100	100	100	100	100

Note: The data show the distribution of the beneficiary population for the types of project studied. In all cases these accounted for by far the greatest part of social fund activity. Comparable household targeting data are not available for Bolivia. Data may not sum to totals because of rounding.
[a] Education projects only.
Source: For data sources and years, see chapter 2, table 2.3.

Figure 3.3 Household Targeting by Social Funds

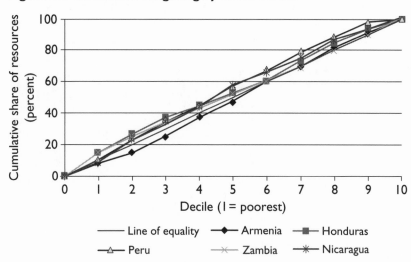

Note: The 45-degree line (line of equality) indicates a neutral distribution. Any curve above that line represents a progressive, or pro-poor, distribution; any curve below it indicates a regressive distribution.
Source: Authors' calculations.

beneficiaries. In Honduras, Nicaragua, and Peru, by contrast, the wealthiest quintile was at a greater disadvantage in accessing social fund resources, accounting for between 11 and 15 percent of beneficiaries.

Results by Type of Project

The concentration of benefits among the poor varied by type of project. In each of the three case study countries that had data on latrine investments, these projects were well targeted to the poor, with less of the benefits going to the nonpoor than for other types of social infrastructure project. In Nicaragua 73 percent of latrine beneficiaries were classified as poor, and in rural Peru 81 percent were classified as extremely poor. In Honduras latrine users tended to be poorer than other types of social fund beneficiaries. The poorest quintile accounted for 34 percent of latrine beneficiaries in Nicaragua and for 37 percent in Honduras (table 3.4). These findings reflect the essentially self-targeted nature of latrine projects, which tend to be used by the lowest-income groups.

Health centers were also relatively well targeted to poor users, although with some variation among countries. In Honduras health centers were the most progressive type of project, with almost half the beneficiaries in the

Table 3.4 Distribution of Social Fund Beneficiaries by Population Decile and Type of Project, Honduras and Nicaragua (percent)

Decile	Education	Health	Water	Sewerage	Latrines
Honduras					
I (poorest)	21.4	31.8	14.4	6.9	19.3
2	10.1	16.6	13.7	9.3	17.9
3	6.1	12.2	12.2	4.5	14.5
4	8.0	8.7	12.3	7.7	11.8
5	9.0	8.3	9.0	12.1	13.8
6	7.8	5.1	5.3	11.6	8.8
7	7.5	5.0	10.7	17.5	4.0
8	12.4	5.9	12.8	13.2	5.6
9	11.2	2.7	3.2	9.2	2.2
10 (richest)	6.4	3.8	6.3	7.9	2.2
Nicaragua					
I (poorest)	8.1	9.4	2.9	0.0	14.4
2	14.8	13.5	9.7	4.0	19.1
3	11.4	4.9	20.0	0.3	9.6
4	6.2	29.8	9.9	0.6	20.7
5	16.5	7.2	7.4	9.0	11.0
6	7.8	5.8	7.4	9.4	8.0
7	8.5	7.0	15.3	14.8	7.4
8	13.9	7.0	9.2	23.0	4.8
9	4.6	8.7	10.4	25.5	4.3
10 (richest)	8.4	6.9	7.8	13.4	0.8

Note: Based on population deciles and potential beneficiaries. Data for Honduras are based on social fund expenditures; those for Nicaragua are based on the incidence of beneficiaries.
Source: For data sources, see chapter 2, table 2.3.

poorest quintile. In Nicaragua 65 percent of health center beneficiaries were poor, and 23 percent were in the poorest quintile. The strong progressiveness of health centers in Honduras may reflect the concentration of rural centers in the sample and, for both countries, the tendency for the poor to use public health centers. Wealthier households tend to opt for private sector providers or to visit clinics with a greater array of services.

Education and water projects were generally pro-poor, although less so than latrines and health centers. In Honduras 31 percent of the beneficiaries of education projects and 28 percent of the beneficiaries of water projects were in the poorest quintile. In Nicaragua water and education investments were only mildly pro-poor, with benefits distributed across the poverty spectrum. For both types of investment, as with other community infrastructure, all those in the community have access, with no screening or means testing for participants.[7]

Sewerage investments were regressive, benefiting the better-off proportionally more than other types of project. In Nicaragua very few beneficiaries of sewerage projects were in the bottom 40 percent of the income distribution, and only 9 percent were classified as poor. The same general finding holds for Honduras, where sewerage investments were the only regressive type of project expenditure, with beneficiaries clustered in the fifth through the eighth income deciles. These findings reflect the nature of the investment: sewerage systems require concentrated populations that already have access to piped water.

Comparison of Targeting by Social Funds and Other Programs

The optimal result of a poverty-targeted program would be for only the poor to benefit—but that is rarely the case. In the absence of perfection, the relative performance of different programs and financing mechanisms is of interest. One possible comparator for social funds would be other programs with the same basic objective of addressing deficits in social infrastructure. Another would be a country's social safety net and other targeted social programs.

Yet another criterion for comparing the targeting outcomes of social funds might be ministry expenditures in health, education, and other relevant sectors. Grosh (1994) posits this as a reasonable basis for comparison; even though public primary health and education programs have different goals than many targeted programs, they can provide a minimum benchmark for the incidence of benefits that should be expected of targeted programs. In other words, we would expect targeted programs to perform better than universal programs. In some instances it might be relevant to compare social funds with municipal transfers. In Bolivia, for example, the current policy discussion foresees eventually merging the social investment fund into the system of general fiscal transfers to local governments.

One of the main constraints on program comparisons is lack of comparable data. Targeting data are not routinely collected for all government expenditures. The most appropriate comparisons would be those that use

---

[7] The Nicaragua Social Investment Fund recently launched a pilot conditional cash transfer program aimed at encouraging poor families to send their children to school and to use health center services. The program uses a blend of geographic and household targeting strategies. Initial results show that over 60 percent of beneficiary families are in the lowest three deciles of the national household income distribution (IFPRI 2002a, 2002b), as against about 40 percent for the school infrastructure program. Such demand-side programs can help reach poorer groups and complement the provision of school places through construction programs.

the same poverty classifications and data sources. In the absence of such information, international experience may provide some general insights, although in interpreting them, the usual caveats about different country circumstances and the often significant variations in methodologies and data apply.

Geographic Targeting

The geographic allocation of resources by social funds appears to be more pro-poor than that by other government programs in the two countries where comparable data are available, Peru and Bolivia. In Peru researchers generated comparable data for three programs: the social fund (FONCODES), another national social infrastructure program (INFES), and a targeted national nutrition program (PRONAA). In Bolivia, where the social fund now serves as a cofinancing agent with municipal governments, the study contrasted the geographic allocation of social fund expenditures with that of municipal government expenditure, including spending from general fiscal transfers.

In the three programs studied in Peru, the social fund had the most pro-poor geographic distribution of expenditures. In 1995 it allocated 20 percent of its resources for educational infrastructure to the poorest district decile, compared with about 8 percent for PRONAA and 7 percent for INFES (figure 3.4). The social fund also compared favorably with general government spending on basic education. A 1999 study found that the government's allocation of per capita spending on basic education was regressive, with higher spending in better-off departments. By contrast, the social fund's geographic allocation of educational resources was pro-poor (World Bank 1999d).

In Bolivia the social fund had a pro-poor expenditure pattern, while general municipal transfers were concentrated in the better-off municipalities. The poorest municipalities, accounting for 42 percent of Bolivia's population, received 63 percent of social fund expenditures in 1993–99 but only 22 percent of total municipal expenditures in 1996 (table 3.5). Thus, social fund transfers were three times as likely to reach a poor municipality as were general fiscal transfers. This finding implies that merging social fund resources into Bolivia's general system of fiscal transfers would worsen the targeting outcome for those resources if no specific targeting guidelines are set.

Household Targeting

Thanks to national household surveys, a broader set of comparisons was available for household targeting results. Existing data allowed the comparison of

Figure 3.4 Geographic Poverty Targeting by the Social Fund and Two Other Social Programs, Peru, 1995

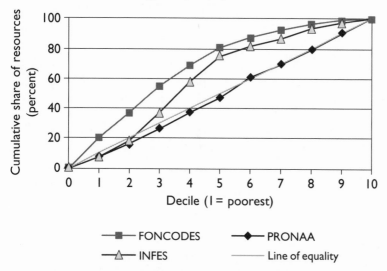

Note: FONCODES is the social fund; INFES, the national social infrastructure program; and PRONAA, a targeted national nutrition program. The 45-degree line (line of equality) indicates a neutral distribution. Any curve above that line represents a progressive, or pro-poor, distribution; any curve below it indicates a regressive distribution.

Source: Authors' calculations.

Table 3.5 Distribution of Social Fund and Municipal Expenditures among Municipalities Ranked by Poverty, Bolivia (percent, except where otherwise specified)

Poverty index	Number of municipalities	Share of total population, 1992	Share of social fund expenditures, 1993–99	Share of municipal expenditures, 1996
80 or more (poorest)	264	42	63	22
60–79	30	16	15	11
Less than 60 (wealthiest)	17	42	21	67

Source: World Bank (2001a).

household targeting results for social funds with those for other social programs in Armenia and Peru, with benchmark expenditures on health and education in Nicaragua, and with international experience with targeted social programs.

Table 3.6 Distribution of Social Program Benefits among Households by Decile, Armenia, 1998 (percent)

Social program	1	2	3	4	5	6	7	8	9	10
Social fund	8	7	10	12	10	13	10	12	9	9
Pensions	10	9	11	11	10	11	10	11	9	8
Disability benefits	11	9	10	12	13	9	9	13	7	7
Child allowances	14	11	10	10	10	11	10	9	9	6
Unemployment benefits	11	15	9	15	14	7	12	5	8	4
Student stipends	5	11	8	4	10	12	9	19	15	7
State transfers (total)	10	9	11	11	10	11	10	11	9	8
Humanitarian aid	3	5	6	9	10	11	10	13	13	20

Source: World Bank (1999c).

In Armenia the distribution of resources by most targeted social programs, including the social fund, is neutral. The social fund performs in the middle of the range for national social assistance programs. As shown earlier, beneficiaries of the social fund are distributed relatively evenly across the income spectrum. This flat distribution, however, is typical of many of the targeted social assistance programs in Armenia, even those able to screen individual beneficiaries (table 3.6). The social fund's distribution is similar to that of state social transfers, pensions, and disability benefits; it is less pro-poor than the distribution of child allowances and unemployment benefits; and it is more progressive than the distribution of humanitarian aid and student stipends.

In Peru the social fund had the most pro-poor distribution among three types of support to local school infrastructure.[8] As measured by the

---

[8] Compared with all social expenditures in Peru (including health, housing, education, and infrastructure and antipoverty programs), the social fund is better at reaching the poor. A World Bank poverty study (World Bank 1999d) found that only 17 percent of national social spending reached the poorest quintile but that 23 percent of the social fund's education spending did. Whereas 21 percent of national social spending benefited the richest quintile, this was true for only 2 percent of the social fund's education spending. The social fund and the nutrition program PRONAA had larger shares of beneficiaries and higher coverage rates (more than 15 percent) in the bottom 40 percent of the income distribution than did other targeted social programs, including nutrition programs, housing credits, productive programs, and other social infrastructure programs. According to the World Bank study, the social fund's performance in reaching poor households compares favorably with that of NGO programs in the country, and it has significantly less leakage to the better off.

Figure 3.5 Household Targeting by the Social Fund and Two Other Social Programs, Peru

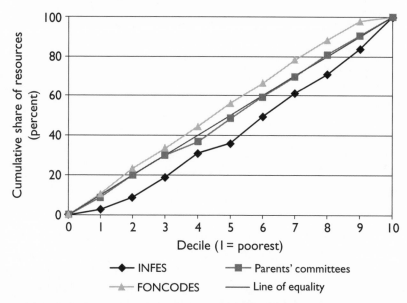

Note: FONCODES is the social fund, and INFES is the national social infrastructure program. The 45-degree line (line of equality) indicates a neutral distribution. Any curve above that line represents a progressive, or pro-poor, distribution; any curve below it indicates a regressive distribution.
Source: Authors' calculations.

distribution of beneficiaries by income decile, the social fund (FONCODES) was more likely to reach poor households than the national social infrastructure program (INFES) or investments by local parents' committees (figure 3.5). Whereas investments by parents' committees were fairly evenly spread across the income distribution, investments by INFES tended to benefit the better off, perhaps because the program includes secondary schools.

In Nicaragua social fund spending on health and education was more progressively distributed than general health and education spending. Data from the 1998 LSMS survey show that the poorest quintile accounted for 23 percent of beneficiaries of social fund spending on education but for only 11 percent of general education spending (table 3.7). Similarly, social fund spending on health projects was more pro-poor than general health spending, with 58 percent of the beneficiaries of such projects in the poorest 40 percent of households, compared with 41 percent for general health spending. (Unfortunately, the 1998 expenditure data were not disaggregated between primary and higher levels of services.)

Table 3.7 Distribution of Education and Health Benefits by Quintile, Nicaragua, 1998 (percent)

Sector and program	1 (poorest)	2	3	4	5
Education					
Social fund beneficiaries	23	18	24	22	13
General education spending	11	14	20	21	35
Distribution of primary students (1993)	18	22	23	21	16
Health					
Social fund beneficiaries	23	35	13	14	15
General health spending	18	23	22	19	18

Source: For comparators, Li, Steele, and Glewwe (1999); World Bank (2001c). For the social fund, see chapter 2, table 2.3.

International experience with targeted social programs varies widely by type of program, type of benefit, and country circumstances. Evidence from Latin America and the Caribbean suggests that social funds are probably in the middle of the range for targeted social programs. In one of the few systematic reviews of the targeting performance of social programs designed to reach the poor, Grosh (1994) evaluated 30 programs in Latin America, including food stamps, student loan programs, income support programs, and day care and targeted nutrition support. Most of these programs include individual and household means testing and thus should screen out nonpoor beneficiaries more effectively than community infrastructure programs such as social funds. Grosh found a range of 15 percent (for student loans in Jamaica) to 57 percent (for Chile's unified family subsidy) of beneficiary households among the poorest quintile of households. For the Honduran social fund (the only case study program for which comparable household-based deciles were constructed), the incidence of beneficiary households in the poorest quintile was 37 percent, about the middle of the range.

Targeting within Districts

To analyze the poverty level of beneficiary households within districts, the average poverty level of households benefiting from social fund investments in a specific district is compared with the average poverty levels for that district. Only the Peruvian data are sufficient to give robust results at the district level using this method. One drawback of the analysis is the relatively large sizes of the districts, which often encompass several communities.

Figure 3.6 Intradistrict Targeting by the Social Fund and Two Other Social Programs, Peru

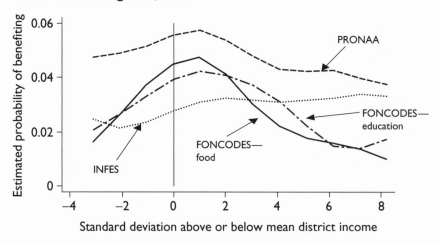

Standard deviation above or below mean district income

Note: FONCODES is the social fund; INFES, the national social infrastructure program; and PRONAA, a targeted national nutrition program.
Source: Paxson and Schady (2002).

This makes it difficult to distinguish whether the results for targeting are attributable to success in reaching poorer or less poor communities within a district or to income heterogeneity within communities themselves.[9]

Within districts in Peru, households with an income higher than the average district income are more likely to benefit from social fund (FONCODES) education investments and food programs than those that are below the district average. Figure 3.6 shows that households slightly above the district average are more likely to benefit but that as incomes rise, this tendency drops precipitously. This tendency is similar to (or is more accentuated in) the other social programs, INFES and PRONAA.[10]

The Peruvian social fund appears to be more successful at reaching relatively poorer households within wealthy districts than relatively poorer

---

[9] Data available for Peru show considerable heterogeneity in the intradistrict distribution of welfare, pointing to the potential for benefits to leak to better-off households. For example, Paxson and Schady (2002) report that only 24 percent of the variance in income between inter-district and intradistrict components is explained by differences across districts and that three-quarters of the variance comes from differences in per capita income within districts. This heterogeneity may make it less likely that reaching poor districts means that poor households will be reached.

[10] Since this finding is based on intradistrict incomes, even the "wealthiest" households within a given district may fall below the poverty line.

Figure 3.7 Intradistrict Targeting by the Social Fund and Two Other Social Programs, by District Income Group, Peru

"Better-off" districts

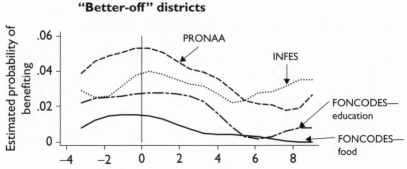

Standard deviation above or below average district income

"Worse-off" districts

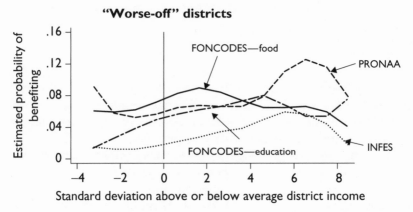

Standard deviation above or below average district income

Note: FONCODES is the social fund; INFES, the national social infrastructure program; and PRONAA, a targeted national nutrition program. "Better-off" and "worse-off" districts are those with FONCODES indices below and above 15, respectively, according to the poverty map.
Source: Paxson and Schady (2002).

households within poor districts. As presented in figure 3.7, in better-off districts the likelihood of benefiting from a social fund (FONCODES) investment declines as average income for that specific district increases. In the poorest districts the pattern is reversed for all of the programs studied; the likelihood of benefiting from a program increases with income, although only slightly so for the social fund. This likelihood is perhaps better explained by the tendency to locate investments around more concentrated populations in the most dispersed rural districts. Another possible explanation for the lower likelihood of participation by the poorest households within the poorest districts is that poorer families may not access basic services (by sending their children to school, visiting health centers, or hooking up to sanitation systems) because of affordability and other demand-side factors.

Analysis of Potential versus Actual Beneficiaries

Since social fund subprojects are identified and prepared at the local level on the basis of local expressions of interest and priorities, there is a possibility that local elites will "capture" program benefits in their own interests. In this scenario, wealthier interest groups within a community, through powerful citizens or through their proxies in local government and NGOs, manipulate the identification and selection of investments to implement subprojects that will benefit them more than the community as a whole. Targeting evidence could reveal such capture by showing whether benefits accrue disproportionately to the wealthier households within a community. In more heterogeneous areas, the risk of elite capture may be greater (Galasso and Ravallion 2000).

In the analysis discussed here, potential beneficiaries are defined as households that live within the radius of influence of a project and could potentially use the services provided, and actual beneficiaries are households that report actual use of the service. For example, some neighborhood households that are potential beneficiaries of sewerage investments have not connected to the sewerage line and so are not actual beneficiaries. The same holds for primary education (some households with access do not send children to school) and for health centers (community members may not attend the clinic). To illustrate, figure 3.8 shows concentration curves for actual and potential beneficiaries in Honduras and Nicaragua for education, health, and sewerage projects. Overall, no clear pattern emerges, as the findings vary by country and sector:

For *education* projects in both Nicaragua and Honduras, the concentration curve for direct beneficiaries is more pro-poor than for potential beneficiaries. In other words, the poor are more likely to benefit from education investments than the population in general within communities executing education projects, contradicting the elite capture argument. In both countries these findings reflect the generally universal coverage of primary education, even among lower-income populations. The greater concentration of direct beneficiaries among poorer households may also be explained by their greater likelihood of having school-age children.

In *health* investments there is no significant difference between the poverty levels of potential and actual users. In Honduras health projects are pro-poor, with virtually no difference between potential and direct beneficiaries. In Nicaragua there is a very slight tendency within the very lowest income quintile for potential users to be slightly more represented than

Figure 3.8 Household-Level Poverty Targeting by Sector, Social Funds in Honduras and Nicaragua

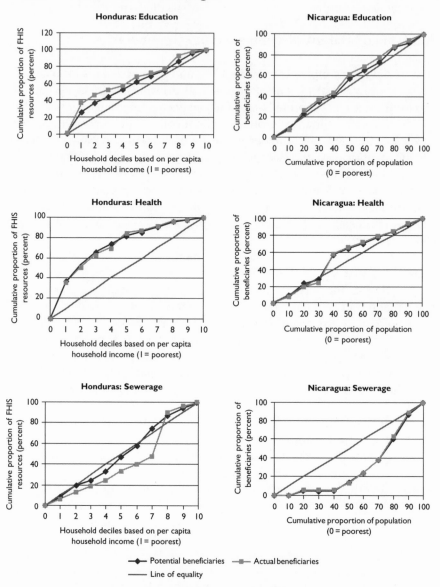

Note: FHIS, Honduran Social Investment Fund. The 45-degree line (line of equality) indicates a neutral distribution. Any curve above that line represents a progressive, or pro-poor, distribution; any curve below it indicates a regressive distribution.
Source: Authors' calculations.

actual users, but this may simply mirror health status. Overall, the concentration curves for the two are very similar.

In the two countries where *sewerage* was studied, the study reached distinct conclusions about differences in targeting outcomes between direct and potential beneficiaries. In both countries, however, the incidence of sewerage expenditures is regressive, benefiting proportionately more higher-income households than poorer ones. In Nicaragua there appears to be little difference between the poverty levels of potential and direct beneficiaries. In other words, social fund sewerage systems tend to serve better-off neighborhoods, and within those neighborhoods there is no distinction in poverty levels between those households that use the system and those that do not. By contrast, in Honduras, although the households with potential access also tend to have higher incomes in general, within those neighborhoods there is a marked tendency for the wealthier households to connect to the system. This parallels some of the qualitative evidence from Honduras on the perceived high cost of connecting to the system, which would be prohibitive for poorer households.

Implications

The institutional design features of the social funds affected targeting outcomes both positively and negatively. Efforts to reach poor populations improved geographic targeting results in all cases. The use of poverty maps and targets to progressively allocate resources across districts helped realize the central government and donor preference that resources reach poor areas without distorting the essentially demand-driven nature of the programs. In several cases, however, poorer areas were only slightly favored. In addition, where social funds used more open menus, these may have resulted in greater leakage of benefits to better-off areas and households, as was true for sewerage investments in Honduras and Nicaragua.

The targeting evidence provides no support for the hypothesis that demand-driven mechanisms are unable to reach the poorest of the poor. In all cases the poorest districts received the largest per capita allocations. Moreover, the poorest households typically received at least the average amount of per capita social fund spending—if not more—although there were some notable exceptions in the sewerage sector. There is no evidence that, within the areas of influence of a project, better-off households tend to capture more benefits (with the exception of sewerage in Nicaragua).

The social funds in this review have operated on a "first come, first served" basis while employing additional promotional efforts to encourage demand from lagging districts. This system has been successful in generating demand well beyond the capacity of social fund resources and in building an incentive structure that rewards community initiative. But it also results in a great deal of discretion in allocating funds and thus in a high variance in the amount spent in each district. Several social funds, such as the Honduran program, have recently begun to set annual allocations for each municipality to provide a more balanced distribution and promote local planning efforts. This system also reduces the potential for applying political criteria to the selection of projects.

More progressive geographic allocations may help redress historical underfunding in poorer areas. Experience shows that poverty maps should be used not only to track the distribution of resources to ensure regional balance but also to channel resources toward poorer areas. The aggressiveness of such targeted allocation varies among the social funds studied: those in Armenia and Zambia use relatively neutral targets, while some in Latin America place greater weight on distributing resources to poorer areas. Social funds that wish to remain national in scope will, however, always have less progressive geographic targeting results because of the inclusion of urban areas. To counteract this tendency, investments in urban areas should be limited to specific poor neighborhoods to reduce the risk of leakage of benefits in this heterogeneous environment. Newer, more disaggregated poverty maps that can identify the poverty levels of communities will be very useful in supporting this task.

Better local coordination can improve the identification of poor communities in both wealthier and poorer districts. For poor communities that still have difficulty in accessing resources, additional measures may be needed to improve equality in results. These measures may include providing early assistance for community organization, waiving requirements for counterpart funding by communities, and extending technical assistance.

Further research is needed to better determine the implications of income heterogeneity within and between communities for programs that seek to support the poor through communitywide infrastructure. Such research should focus on the potential gains from disaggregating poverty data below the municipal or district level in order to better locate concentrations of the poor. Since many programs use only geographic targeting, the findings of this research would have implications beyond the social fund community.

There may be a tradeoff between improved household targeting and the use of more open menus of eligible investments. As a targeting tool, social funds have defined menus featuring basic services more likely to be demanded by the poor. This strategy is supported by household targeting results showing significant differences in outcomes among different types of project. Further restricting menus to improve targeting results would eliminate some of the potentially positive attributes of greater choice for communities, yet more open menus may allow better-off households and communities to capture benefits. At the very least, for investments that tend to benefit the better off, the development of more rigid screening criteria, including the introduction of data on income levels of potential beneficiary households, may help reduce leakage.

There is a potential complementarity among social funds, demand-side interventions, and more targeted social assistance. A well-targeted program of social infrastructure can provide the basis for targeted subsidy programs. For example, social fund interventions could complement subsidies for schooling of the children of the very poorest, health subsidies or insurance schemes for the poor, or targeted interventions such as the provision of school lunches or nutritional supplements through health centers. Unlike infrastructure projects, these interventions can directly target resources to households or individuals rather than provide broad community benefits. But even programs aimed at encouraging targeted households to send their children to schools and clinics depend on the availability of good-quality education and health infrastructure.

4

Education

THIS CHAPTER REVIEWS THE IMPACT of social fund investments in education carried out in each of the six case study countries, primarily for constructing and refurbishing schools. It describes findings concerning the impact of social funds on the quality of school infrastructure, the availability of key noninfrastructural inputs, and the outcomes for student enrollment, educational performance, and sustainability. The analysis shows that, overall, social fund schools have better infrastructure than comparator schools, leading to an expansion of the schools' physical capacity and to better access to basic services such as water and electricity at schools. The infrastructure investments have been accompanied by a corresponding increase in the availability of complementary noninfrastructural inputs such as textbooks and teachers, indicating that there has been the necessary coordination between the social funds and other actors—primarily ministries of education—responsible for providing those inputs. In half of the cases, social fund interventions in education improved enrollment rates and educational efficiency in the communities receiving the investment beyond those experienced in comparator schools. Other outcome measures were assessed in some of the country cases; they indicate positive impacts of social funds on dropout rates and attendance but not on repetition or achievement.

Research Focus

Social funds aim to improve access to education through investments in the quality and capacity of school facilities. Although social funds have operated for more than a decade, few studies have gathered the empirical evidence needed to determine whether the funds have achieved this goal and whether the improvements have affected beneficiaries' educational status.

The following fundamental questions formed the core of this study's assessment of the effectiveness of interventions in education by social funds:

- Are the infrastructure investments in schools leading to sustainable improvements in quality and availability?
- Do line ministries or other sources provide teachers, textbooks, and other necessary noninfrastructural inputs to accompany the investments in infrastructure?
- Do communities use the schools that the social fund builds and refurbishes?
- What is the final impact of social fund investments on beneficiaries' educational status?
- Are the social fund investments sustainable?

This chapter examines five aspects of the impact of social fund education projects:

- Quality and expansion of school infrastructure
- Provision of complementary materials and staff, including desks, textbooks, and teachers
- Impact on school size, using data from school records
- Impact on enrollment, attainment, and other educational outcomes, using household data
- Sustainability of the investments.

All country assessments include enrollment and attainment data, but the availability of other outcome measures, such as absenteeism and academic achievement, varies from country to country.[1] This chapter reports all available indicators from each of the case studies, summarizes the main findings, and discusses the implications of the research for social fund operations.

Evidence concerning the impact of education projects is particularly relevant given the prominence of school infrastructure investments in most social fund portfolios. In all countries participating in this impact evaluation study, education represents a larger share of investments than any other type of subproject (table 4.1).

---

[1] Measures of educational attainment pertain to the amount of education accumulated (or likely to be accumulated). They include age-for-grade, accumulated years of education, and the gap between a student's ideal and actual age-for-grade.

Table 4.1 Education Project Component of Total Social Fund Investment

Country	Period	Percentage of total spending for education projects
Armenia	1996–2000	35
Bolivia	1994–98	50
Honduras	1991–98	57
Nicaragua	1991–98	57
Peru	1992–98	27
Zambia	1991–98	76

In the country cases studied, social fund investments constituted an important share of national investments in education. In Bolivia between 1991 and 1997, 21 percent of all schools in the country benefited from a social fund investment.[2] In Nicaragua (1991–99) social fund investments in education accounted for 49 percent of all national public education investments. In Honduras (1994–97) social fund investments built an estimated 58 percent of new schools and 61 percent of new classrooms. Peru's social fund (1992–98) financed over 10,000 education subprojects worth $12.2 million. In Zambia (1991–98) the social fund rehabilitated 16 percent of the existing stock of primary schools. In many countries, including some of the case study countries, social funds have surpassed line ministries as the principal financers of investments in the construction, expansion, and rehabilitation of schools.

Impact on Infrastructure

This section presents the results of the school facility surveys carried out in a sample of social fund schools and in a comparison group of non–social fund schools in the case study countries. The results of the social fund investment in school infrastructure (and, in some cases, in school equipment) reflect the direct output of the social fund investment, as distinguished from the longer-term impact.

Social fund investments have clearly improved the physical condition of schools. Schools that have received a social fund investment have more classrooms—and, in most cases, higher-quality classrooms—than other

---

[2] In Bolivia during during the period 1991–97 the Social Investment Fund built or rehabilitated 4,619 classrooms—an average of 577 a year—while the National School Construction Agency (CONES), in the 22 years following its establishment, built 3,900 classrooms, an average of 177 a year.

A Zambian school before and after a social fund investment.

schools (table 4.2). In Bolivia social fund investments raised the share of classrooms in good condition from 25 to 58 percent, increased the average physical space available per student from 1.54 square meters to 3.28 square meters, and reduced the number of students per classroom from 28 to 19. In non–social fund schools the share of classrooms in good condition remained almost unchanged, and the space per student rose slightly, from 1.49 square meters to 1.87, but the number of students per classroom rose from 25 to 28. In Honduras social fund schools have, on average, 2.5 more classrooms than non–social fund schools. In Nicaragua social fund primary schools have an average of six classrooms; in non–social fund schools the average is under five. More parents in Nicaragua reported improvements in the quality of infrastructure and classroom furniture in these schools than in non–social fund schools (84 versus 29 percent; see also box 4.1). In Zambia non–social fund schools were twice as likely to hold classes outdoors as were social fund schools.

Table 4.2 Physical Condition of Social Fund and Non–Social Fund Schools, Case Study Countries in Latin America

Country and Item	Social fund school	Non–social fund schools
Percentage of classrooms in good physical condition[a]		
Bolivia	58	27
Honduras	44	38
Peru	68	44
Percentage of households reporting improvements in school infrastructure		
Nicaragua	84	29

[a] As measured by engineers' ratings of classroom conditions as good, adequate, or bad.
Source: For Bolivia, Honduras, and Peru, engineers' evaluations as reported in country-specific school surveys; for Nicaragua, household surveys.

Box 4.1 A Parent Speaks about the Importance of Social Fund Investments in School Infrastructure

For me the school has been a great project, enormous. Before we had a little school made of planks and everything would get wet right down to the books. . . . Now we are doing well, but we need more support in maintaining the school.

—*From a focus group discussion, Las Lagunetas, Nicaragua*
(IDEAS 1998)

Table 4.3 Access to Safe Water and to Electricity in Social Fund and Non–Social Fund Schools (percent)

Country	Social fund schools	Comparator schools	Net difference
Access to safe water[a]			
Armenia	100	96	4
Honduras[b]	77	91	−14
Nicaragua	87	64	23
Peru	67	32	35
Zambia	81	76	5
Access to electricity			
Armenia[c]	100	96	4
Bolivia[d]	20	17	3
Honduras[b]	54	64	−10
Nicaragua[c]	56	23	33
Zambia[c]	60	32	28

Note: No data were available on access to water for Bolivia and on access to electricity for Peru.
[a] Well water, piped water inside or outside the building, or water from a standpipe.
[b] None of the education projects sampled in Honduras included water or electricity components.
[c] During school hours.
[d] Lower-bound impact estimate after statistical matching.
Source: For data sources and years, see chapter 2, table 2.3.

Social fund interventions have improved schools' access to safe water in Armenia, Nicaragua, Peru, and Zambia but not in Honduras (table 4.3). In Armenia access to piped water was high for both social fund and comparator schools, but 54 percent of social fund schools had continuous access during school hours, while only 33 percent of comparator schools did. In Honduras social fund investments did not significantly raise a school's probability of having access to safe water—a predictable result, since the schools sampled did not receive provision of water as part of the social fund investment.

Social fund schools had uniformly better access to sanitation services in all the countries where this outcome was studied (that is, omitting Peru). In Nicaragua social fund schools had an average of 3.2 latrines, compared with 2.3 in non–social fund schools; in Honduras the ratio was 5.4 to 4.3. In Bolivia the share of schools with access to sanitation services increased by 29 percent as a result of the social fund intervention. In Zambia the number of students per ventilated pit latrine was reduced significantly.

The availability of electricity in schools depended on its availability in the community. Significant improvements in access to electricity were noted in Nicaragua and Zambia. The apparent improvement in Nicaragua may at least in part reflect better local availability of electricity; 81 percent of communities with social fund schools had electricity, while only 57 percent of comparator communities did. In Armenia access to electricity was very high in all sampled schools; in rural Bolivia it was very low. In Peru few communities receiving or about to receive a social fund school project had access to electricity. In Honduras comparator schools had better access to electricity, but the comparator schools were drawn from the social fund pipeline; thus the difference may reflect the social fund's movement toward better-off schools as it assumes a national role as the main provider of school infrastructure.

Although social funds have generally improved the availability of basic services in schools, problems remain in several countries. Only 35 percent of social fund schools had piped water installations in Nicaragua, and in Armenia only 54 percent had regular water service during school hours—an indication of supply problems in the local water system. In Honduras, where social fund schools had worse access to water and electricity than the comparator schools, 31 percent of school survey respondents reported problems in project construction or installation, and participants in focus groups urged the social fund to pay more attention to water provision in school projects.

Impact on the Availability of Equipment, Furniture, and Textbooks

Social fund schools' access to basic noninfrastructural materials such as furniture and textbooks was similar to or better than that of non–social fund schools. In some cases social funds provided basic furniture such as desks and chalkboards as part of the school investment. The results point to reasonable coordination between social fund investments in infrastructure and materials and between investments by social funds and line ministries.

In several countries social fund interventions improved the situation with respect to desks for students and teachers (see tables 4.4 and 4.5). In Bolivia the number of desks per student more than doubled, reducing the ratio of students to desks from 2.6 to 1.2, while the ratio remained largely unchanged in non–social fund schools. The average number of teachers' desks per classroom

Table 4.4 Students per Desk, Bolivia, Honduras, and Zambia

Country	Social fund schools	Comparator schools
Bolivia	1.2	1.6
Honduras	0.9	1.1
Zambia	1.7	2.5

Source: For data sources and years, see chapter 2, table 2.3.

Table 4.5 Availability of School Furniture, Zambia

Indicator	Social fund schools	Comparator schools
Students with a desk (percent)	60*	40
Rural	67*	40
Urban	53	40
Classrooms with teacher's desk and		
chair (percent)	50*	10
Rural	70*	10
Urban	44*	15
Chalkboards per classroom	1	1

*Difference is significant at the 10 percent level.
Source: For data sources and years, see chapter 2, table 2.3.

also rose significantly, from less than 0.2 to close to 0.6 in the Chaco region. In Armenia social fund schools had an average of 1.5 more student desks and chairs in good condition per classroom than did comparator schools. In social fund schools in Armenia, 74 percent of classrooms had a teacher's desk in good condition, and 89 percent had an adequate blackboard; in comparator schools the figures were 65 and 72 percent, respectively.

The supply of basic learning materials was at least as good in social fund schools as in non–social fund schools, and sometimes better. In Armenia social fund schools consistently had more maps and more charts for language, mathematics, and science. In Bolivia students in social fund schools had an average of 4.1 textbooks, compared with 2.4 for students in non–social fund schools. There was little difference in Honduras and Nicaragua.

Impact on Staffing, School Size, and Student-Teacher Ratios

An increase in staff accompanied the improvements in infrastructure, so that social fund schools had staffing patterns similar to or better than those of non–social fund schools:

- In Nicaragua the number of teachers in social fund schools rose by 20 percent over the period studied, significantly more than the increase in non–social fund schools.
- In Zambia social fund schools had, on average, almost twice as many teachers (30) as non–social fund schools (16).
- In Peru social fund schools gained an average of 1.2 teachers and 1.6 grades and were 15 percent more likely to offer at least one secondary school grade.
- In Armenia social fund schools had, on average, 1.4 more teachers, although all the schools were relatively large (with 63.2 teachers in social fund schools and 61.8 in comparator schools).
- In Honduras student-teacher ratios were similar in social fund and comparator schools.

Although no evidence was found of a decline in staffing levels in non–social fund schools, no conclusions can be drawn about the effect of social fund investments on the overall distribution of teachers in the education system. The data needed to reach conclusions about the impact of social funds on the crowding-in or crowding-out of teachers within the school system were not available.

Number of Students

In all the case study countries, social fund investments led to an increase in the number of students enrolled (table 4.6).[3] In Bolivia, however, matriculation increased more in non–social fund schools, and in Armenia the difference was small and was not statistically significant.

In Honduras social fund investments resulted in an average increase in matriculation of 18 students per school (40 percent), while in non–social fund schools matriculation increased by less than 2 students (6.5 percent). Most of the social fund schools sampled offered afternoon shifts, while only 30 percent of the comparison group did. All of the sampled social fund schools were used as community meeting places, one rural school was being used for adult literacy classes, and another housed a day care center.

---

[3] School size measures assess the number of children matriculated in a sample of schools using schools' administrative records (as opposed to enrollment rates, which use household survey data to examine the percentage of children going to school). In all countries except Peru, the study examined changes in school size using before-and-after school-level matriculation data by retrieving information from sampled schools' administrative records for a period before the social fund investment. This provided a basis for the application of difference-in-differences analysis to look at the changes in school size reported in table 4.6.

Table 4.6 Change in School Size (percent)

Country	Social fund schools	Comparator schools
Armenia	6	—
Bolivia	7	26
Honduras	40	7
Nicaragua	20	−1
Peru	40	—
Zambia	17	−2

— Not available.

Note: For all countries except Armenia and Peru, the table reports the percentage change in enrollment based on a comparison of preinvestment and postinvestment data collected in social fund and comparator schools. For Armenia and Peru, it reports ex post comparisons of the size of social fund and comparator schools.

Source: For data sources and years, see chapter 2, table 2.3.

Table 4.7 Student-Teacher Ratios

Country	Social fund schools	Comparator schools
Armenia	11	10
Bolivia	20	22
Honduras[a]	34	34
Nicaragua	24	24
Peru	28	32
Zambia[b]	47	48

[a] Morning shift.

[b] Includes teachers working a double shift.

Source: For data sources and years, see chapter 2, table 2.3.

In Zambia social fund schools received more applications than non–social fund schools (514 compared with 159) and had much lower acceptance rates (35 percent compared with 65 percent). While matriculation increased in social fund schools, it stagnated or fell slightly in the comparison group, mirroring the national trend in recent years of declining primary school enrollment.

Student-Teacher Ratios

The rise in school size was generally accompanied by a corresponding increase in the number of teachers, resulting in student-teacher ratios in social fund schools that were similar to or better than those in non–social fund schools (table 4.7). In Nicaragua the increase in teachers surpassed that in school size, leading to a decline in student-teacher ratios. In Zambia social fund schools grew more than the comparators, but so did the number of teachers, resulting in similar student-teacher ratios. In Bolivia, too, the ratios were similar, as a result of a decline in the ratio for social fund schools between 1993 and 1998 and a slight increase in the ratio for non–social fund schools. In Honduras both social fund and non–social fund schools had student-teacher ratios in line with national norms in the morning shifts but higher ratios in the afternoon shifts. In Armenia student-teacher ratios increased slightly in social fund schools.

Impact on Educational Outcomes

Analysis of household survey data found that social fund investments in education had mixed effects on enrollment rates and other measures of educational performance, depending on the country and the measure used.

Enrollment Rates

Social fund investments led to higher enrollment rates in Armenia, Nicaragua, and Zambia but not in Bolivia or Honduras (table 4.8). The two studies in Peru reached different conclusions about the social fund's impact

Table 4.8 Net Primary Enrollment Rates (percent)

		Comparator communities	
Country	Social fund communities	Pipeline match	Propensity score match
Armenia	87	79[*]	84
Bolivia	83[a]	83[a]	—
Honduras[b]	89	89	—
Nicaragua	92	87[**][c]	82[**]
Peru(rural)[d]	90	90	—
Zambia	78	71[**]	75
Urban	86	78[*]	82[*]
Rural	70	69	67

[*] Difference is significant at the 10 percent level.
[**] Difference is significant at the 5 percent level.
— Not available.
[a] Enrollment rate for 1993 baseline in Chaco using randomization; 1997 comparison showed no significant difference for either the Chaco region or for other rural areas, using various methodologies.
[b] Data refer to gross enrollment.
[c] "Nearest neighbor" statistical match.
[d] Social fund beneficiaries experienced a 0.9 percent increase in enrollment rates, but the difference was not statistically significant (Instituto Apoyo 1999).
Source: For data sources and years, see chapter 2, table 2.3; for information on methodology, see appendix I.

on enrollment, probably because of differences between the studies' level of analysis.

The measure of enrollment varied slightly from country to country, depending on the survey data available and the analysis conducted. Most evaluations examined the net enrollment rate (the percentage of children in a given age group enrolled in school). The ages used corresponded to the primary school age, generally 7–12. In Peru the study also considered secondary schools and school-age children up to age 15.

In Nicaragua the net primary enrollment rate was 5–10 percentage points higher in social fund than in non–social fund communities, depending on the comparison group. Female enrollment rates were 4 percentage points higher than male rates, a difference not observed in non–social fund communities (box 4.2).

In Peru the Paxson and Schady study (2002) concluded, on the basis of national survey data, that increased school attendance was directly correlated with the social fund resources that an area received: the districts that received the most resources for school improvements achieved the largest gains in primary school enrollment rates.[4] The Instituto Apoyo study (2000b), which covered only rural areas, concluded that the probability of children age 6–14 being enrolled in school did not increase significantly as a result of social fund investments. That study found, however, a significant, positive impact on school enrollment among households in extreme poverty: for this group, living on less than $1 a day, social fund investments in education raised the probability of being enrolled in school by almost 2 percent. For indigenous communities, the study found that although the number of students attending social fund schools increased by an average of 34, the social fund investment did not have a significant impact on enrollment rates (box 4.3).

The school-level matriculation data from the facilities surveys and the enrollment data from the household surveys point to the same results: in most of the case study countries, social funds have made an important contribution to increasing access to education. In Bolivia there was a very small increase in school size and a small, but not significant, increase in enrollment. In Nicaragua and urban areas of Zambia the large increase in the size of social fund schools is reflected in the significant changes in enrollment rates. In Peru social fund schools experienced an increase in size and enrollment at the district level (Paxson and Schady 2002) relative to comparators and among specific population groups, including households in extreme poverty (Instituto Apoyo 2000b). In Honduras the social funds had an effect

---

[4] In the Paxson and Schady study (2002) the data used to examine the impact of social fund investments on school outcomes are based on a survey question asking whether a child attends school. The survey did not ask about matriculation or absenteeism. The attendance results are therefore included in the discussion on enrollment.

Box 4.2 Poverty and Gender Aspects of the Impacts of Social Fund Investments in Education in Nicaragua

The Nicaraguan country study analyzed the impact of social fund investments in primary education by consumption quintile and gender. The analysis found that:

- The impact on enrollment is larger for girls.
- The improvements in the education gap are greater for poor children.
- Boys are slightly more likely than girls to begin primary school at an earlier age as a result of social fund investments.

Impact of Living in the Area of Influence of a Social Fund Primary School, Nicaragua

Indicator and category of community	Quintile[a]					Gender	
	I (poorest)	2	3	4	5	Male	Female
Net primary enrollment rate (percent)							
Social fund communities	82.8	96.1	96.4	94.7	90.2	90.0	93.9
Matched communities	85.9	86.9*	97.9	82.0*	84.6	87.1	87.4*
Propensity score matched communities	69.2*	93.3	85.1*	73.9*	89.1	82.4*	81.7*
Education gap (years)							
Social fund communities	1.8	1.4	1.7	1.3	0.6	1.6	1.3
Matched communities	2.2*	2.0*	1.5	1.5	0.7	2.1*	1.3
Propensity score matched communities	2.6*	2.0*	1.8	1.7	0.6	2.1*	1.7*
Enrolled in correct grade for year (percent)							
Social fund communities	16.8	23.6	25.4	24.8	55.3	21.8	31.5
Matched communities	12.4	19.5	36.7	27.0	48.2	22.9	28.2
Propensity score matched communities	4.5*	9.1*	21.2	43.1	66.4	17.1	27.9
Age in first grade (years)							
Social fund communities	8.1	7.7	8.0	7.3	8.9	8.1	7.8
Matched communities	9.1	7.8	8.3	7.8	8.0	8.9	8.2
Propensity score matched communities	8.7	8.0	7.1	9.8	11.0	8.7	8.3

* Difference is significant at the 10 percent level.
[a] Based on the national distribution of per capita consumption as observed in the Living Standards Measurement Study survey.
Source: Pradhan and Rawlings (2002).

Box 4.3 Indigenous Communities and Social Funds: Lessons from Education Investments in Peru

The Peruvian social fund carries out the majority of its education projects in indigenous communities (63 percent at the time of the evaluation in 2000). This allowed the evaluation to explore whether social fund investments in education have a different effect in indigenous than in nonindigenous communities. The study found that in indigenous communities social fund investments in school infrastructure led to an increase in school size but that these investments did not lead to changes in attainment or absenteeism, as they did in the general population. A number of other differences were found between indigenous and nonindigenous communities:

- *Participation and social capital.* Slightly more indigenous than nonindigenous communities had local organizations (91 versus 87 percent). The mix of organizations varied. Religious groups were more prevalent in nonindigenous communities, and community-based organizations were more prevalent in indigenous communities. In nonindigenous communities parents' associations were more likely to be involved in infrastructure projects, children's educational activities, and health campaigns. In indigenous communities parents were more likely to be involved in community activities at the school, such as festivals and commemorative events.
- *Infrastructure inputs and physical sustainability.* In indigenous communities social fund investments in school infrastructure increased the share of classrooms in good physical condition by 36 percent. Unlike the outcome for social fund schools overall, these investments did not change a school's probability of having direct access to potable water or additional classrooms.
- *Noninfrastructural inputs and utilization.* Social fund investments in indigenous communities raised matriculation by an average of 34 students per school, just as in schools overall. The investments also allowed the addition of 1.3 grades. They did not affect the average number of teachers or the probability of access to a secondary school grade, as they did for social fund schools countrywide.
- *Enrollment and educational performance.* Consistent with the pattern for social fund schools as a group, social fund investments in education had no impact on enrollment rates in indigenous communities. But, in contrast with the general findings, the investments also had no impact on attainment (accumulated years of education) or on absenteeism in indigenous communities.

Source: Instituto Apoyo (2000b).

---

on school size, but there was no corresponding impact on enrollment. Primary school enrollment rates in Honduras were, however, already high in relation to the sample size used in the impact evaluation, and the study team did not expect to find an effect on enrollment. (But see box 4.4 for a local assessment of the subtler effect of social fund investment.)

Box 4.4 Comment on the Social Fund's School Investments, Honduras

Well, I think that the children study today in a better environment and because they are in a nice classroom, they put more care into learning, they are freer to do that. Before, they used to walk in tight groups and now they move about more freely and go out happily to play. The classroom looks nice and it stands out in the community. It is a good piece of work, yes.... In the old school there were a lot of dropouts among the older kids, now all the children are still coming. About 30 adults are attending the literacy course.

—*Community leader, La Empalizada, Honduras (Walker and others 1999)*

The results also suggest that it may be more difficult to increase enrollment in rural than in urban areas. The two case studies based on rural data (that in Bolivia, and the Instituto Apoyo 2000b study in Peru) found no significant impact, and the case study in Zambia found no impact in rural areas. By contrast, national data from Armenia and Nicaragua and urban data from Peru and Zambia showed significant impacts on enrollment.

Educational Attainment

Most of the case studies found that social fund investments led to gains in educational attainment. The studies examined various measures of educational attainment, including age-for-grade, accumulated years of education, and the gap between a student's ideal and actual age-for-grade, all of which assess educational efficiency. Age-for-grade measures are a good indicator of late entry, performance, and repetition. Children who are in the appropriate grade for their age are a sign of an efficient school system, since the system must finance fewer years of schooling to bring the children to a given level of education. Children in the appropriate grade are also less likely to drop out of school than are children who are older than the norm for the grade. Accumulated education is a conceptually similar measure because it assesses individual performance and the efficiency of the school system. It is directly linked to future earnings in the labor market and thus has long-term effects on poverty.

In Honduras, Nicaragua, and rural Zambia social fund investments had a clear, significant impact on age-for-grade measures. In Honduras the investments reduced age-for-grade by 15 percent and in rural Zambia, by 4 percent. In Nicaragua the age in first grade fell from 8.6 to 7.9 years, although no impact on age-for-grade was found beyond first grade. No effect was found in urban Zambia or in the Paxson and Schady study (2002) in Peru.

In Nicaragua social fund investments led to a reduction in the education gap (the difference between the ideal and actual age-for-grade) of 0.2–0.4 year, depending on the comparison group. In Peru the Instituto Apoyo study (2000b) found that social fund investments led to a statistically significant accumulation of 0.1 additional year of education among children age 6–14, and 0.2 year among children age 10–14.

Case studies also examined other measures of educational performance. The Instituto Apoyo study (2000b) in Peru examined school absenteeism over the previous month and found that for children age 10–14, social fund investments reduced the probability of a child's missing school as a result of illness by 4.5 percent. No significant results were found for other age groups or for other reasons for missing school. The Bolivian and Nicaraguan case studies also looked at the impact of social fund investments on absenteeism, but neither found a significant effect. Nor did the Nicaraguan study find conclusive evidence on the impact of social fund investments on repetition. The study found a positive, statistically significant impact when using the propensity score–matched comparison group: the repetition rate was 19 percent in non–social fund communities but 7.3 percent in social fund communities. Use of the geographically based–matched comparison group yielded a positive, but not statistically significant, impact. In non–social fund communities the repetition rate was 10.9 percent, suggesting that a statistically significant impact might have been detected had the sample size been larger.

In Bolivia indicators show lower dropout rates in social fund communities in both regions, but the Bolivian study (the only one to measure the impact of social fund investments on educational achievement) found no effect on achievement as measured by mathematics and language tests. That finding is generally consistent with the literature in this area (box 4.5).[5]

Sustainability

Sustainable delivery of education services depends on teachers, textbooks, desks, and other inputs generally provided by the government in public schools. But it also depends on communities' involvement in maintenance, on cost recovery, and on support from local actors.

Maintenance of school infrastructure varied across schools and countries. In most countries, including those in the study, maintenance of public

---

[5] A recent evaluation of the impact of education-related conditional cash transfers provided by Mexico's PROGRESA program shows no significant positive impacts of PROGRESA on achievement test scores after almost a school year and a half of exposure to the program (Schultz 2000).

Box 4.5   Infrastructure Inputs and Academic Achievement in Developing Countries

The finding by the Bolivian case study that social fund investments had no impact on test scores is reasonably consistent with the general literature and points to the complex factors determining student achievement. In a review of the education production function literature for the United States, Hanushek (1986) concludes that physical inputs are rarely related to variations in student achievement and that other factors, particularly family characteristics, are better predictors of student achievement. But the literature for developing countries—where infrastructure investments can often dramatically change a school's environment—do point to positive relationships between physical inputs and student achievement. Harbison and Hanushek (1992) find that in 22 of 34 education studies in developing countries, physical inputs had a positive effect on student outcomes (see the table). Velez, Schiefelbein, and Valenzuela (1993) find a similar positive relationship in 23 of 70 studies in Latin America. (The smaller share showing positive results in Latin America probably reflects the higher overall quality of school facilities in that region compared with other developing regions.) Glewwe and others (1995) find that physical inputs have a small but positive effect on student achievement in Jamaican primary schools.

Studies Showing Effects of Physical Inputs on Primary School Achievement in Developing Countries

Study	Facilities	Instructional materials
Harbison and Hanushek (1992)		
Number of studies	34	—
Positive effect	22	—
Negative effect	3	—
No effect	9	
Velez, Schiefelbein, and Valenzuela (1993)		
Number of studies	70	34
Positive effect	23	14
Negative effect	2	3
No effect	45	17

—Not available.

---

schools remains the legal responsibility of the education ministry, but communities often fill in when there is a vacuum—a common occurrence in many places. In Nicaragua levels of preventive maintenance and general repairs varied from school to school, with no clear pattern emerging for social fund relative to non–social fund schools. In Honduras social fund schools were generally cleaner, and all the social fund schools visited had a school- or community-based committee in charge of maintenance, whereas only 82 percent of non–social fund schools did.

Cost recovery also varied across countries. In Zambia students attending social fund schools were more likely to pay maintenance, parent-teacher association, and general fees than were those attending non–social fund schools. In Nicaragua the structure and application of school fees were similar in the two types of school. In Honduras social fund and non–social fund schools made similar use of fund-raising, but social fund schools were less likely to charge school fees. In the earthquake zone in Armenia households in social fund areas spent more on education than those in the comparator areas, while in the conflict zones social fund households spent less. The lack of consistent patterns in cost recovery reflects the fact that social funds generally do not set financial norms for schools.

In most cases social fund schools received more external support than did comparators. In Zambia social fund schools were more likely to have support from outside groups, particularly private benefactors. In Nicaragua social fund schools were more active in fund-raising than their non–social fund counterparts. In Honduras social fund schools were more likely to rely on benefactors' support and less likely to charge fees. In Armenia, by contrast, students in social fund schools received significantly less aid (for books and food) than those in comparator schools.

Implications

The impact evaluation results for education show that concerns about empty classrooms in social fund–supported schools have been largely unfounded: as school infrastructure has expanded, so has the number of teachers. As a result, the numbers of teachers and the student-teacher ratios in social fund schools are at least as good as, and often better than, those in non–social fund schools. This finding suggests that the mechanisms social funds have in place for coordinating with line ministries (for example, requiring ministries to guarantee the provision of teachers before an investment in the expansion of classroom capacity is made) are adequate.

Progress has been made in improving school facilities, but now social funds need to sharpen their focus on providing complete infrastructure, particularly water and sanitation services. Social funds should also require the active participation of beneficiaries and local institutions to ensure that the infrastructure provided meets local expectations. They should consider introducing a local approval process that makes final payments to contractors contingent on verification, by the community and the social fund, that the project has been fully completed.

Continued effort is needed to clarify the roles and responsibilities of stakeholders responsible for providing and sustaining social services. Although social funds, line ministries, and communities have made progress in coordinating their roles and responsibilities in education, this progress needs to continue to ensure good-quality results. For example, much of the investment by social funds has gone to rehabilitating deteriorated schools— but improved maintenance would reduce the need for rehabilitation. In most of the countries studied, social funds were able to stimulate greater community involvement in maintenance, but the "rules of the game" need to be clearly specified. Among these rules are fulfillment by line ministries and local governments of their legal mandate to ensure adequate general maintenance of school buildings.

To remove barriers to access, especially for the poorest, social funds should consider demand-side interventions and outreach campaigns that promote direct contact with households. Multivariate analysis underscores the importance of family characteristics, such as parents' education and household poverty levels, in determining educational outcomes, pointing to a possible role for demand-side incentives. Results showing the difficulty of expanding rural enrollments suggest that demand-side approaches may be even more important in remote areas.

Social funds and education ministries need to be specific about the results they want to achieve. This entails establishing goals as part of national poverty reduction strategies, monitoring and evaluating progress toward those goals, and setting forth explicit responsibilities for providing key inputs. If raising enrollment rates and increasing student achievement are established as goals for social fund investments, the government should put in place specific policies to support those goals and should collect baseline and follow-up data to track progress.

5

Health

THIS CHAPTER EXAMINES THE IMPACT of social fund investments in the health sector in the four case study countries that supported health activities: Bolivia, Honduras, Nicaragua, and Zambia. It describes the findings related to infrastructure and key inputs (equipment, medicine, and staff), utilization, impacts on household health, and sustainability. The research found that social fund health interventions had a positive impact on infrastructure quality and on the availability of medical equipment and furniture. Essential drugs and replaceable medical supplies were generally more available in social fund facilities, although all facilities had difficulty in securing adequate supplies of essential drugs. Social fund facilities were staffed as well as or better than comparators. Utilization of social fund facilities has generally increased more than that of comparators, overall or for specific critical services. In the one case in which changes in mortality rates could be measured, the social fund intervention was found to reduce significantly infant and child mortality rates, in comparison with facilities not supported by social funds.

Research Focus

This chapter examines the impacts of health sector interventions by social funds. Specifically, it seeks to answer five questions:

- Have social funds improved the quality of the facilities that they have rehabilitated or built, so that, several years after receiving social fund

support, these health facilities are of better physical quality and are better equipped with medical equipment and furniture than comparators?[1]
- Are social fund facilities worse or better than comparators in securing inputs, such as personnel, medicines, and other medical supplies, that are essential to providing quality services but are typically outside the social fund intervention?
- Has the social fund improved utilization rates? Do the physical and other improvements draw more people to use the facilities?
- What impacts do social fund interventions have on health outcomes at the household level? Is there any evidence of a reduction in such important indicators as infant or under-five mortality rates?
- How sustainable are the services provided? Do they receive the support they need from line ministries and from communities with respect to maintenance and financing, as well as staffing and essential materials?

The chapter presents the evidence from the study regarding these questions and concludes with a discussion of the implications of the findings for the future design of social funds.

Four of the country case studies—those for Bolivia, Honduras, Nicaragua, and Zambia—assessed the impact of health subprojects. (Armenia and Peru were omitted because health projects constituted a very small proportion of social fund investments in those countries. In Peru health accounted for only 2.5 percent of social fund investment between 1996 and 1999, and in Armenia no health facility investments were undertaken by the social fund during the period studied.) In the four countries analyzed, health interventions accounted for between 10 and 15 percent of the social fund's investments (see table 5.1).

Even though health interventions were not a large portion of social fund portfolios in the countries studied, the social funds nevertheless made important contributions to health investments. In Bolivia between 1991 and 1997, the social fund rehabilitated, renovated, or equipped 28 percent of the existing public health centers, and it was responsible for roughly 25 percent of all public health investment between 1994 and 1998. In 1995 the Honduran social fund's resources for health, which were channeled toward the primary network of the Ministry of Public Health, represented 15 percent of external funding for health and 5.5 percent of all resources received by the ministry. In addition to rehabilitating facilities, between 1994 and 1998 the Honduran social fund built 72 percent of all new rural health posts and 56 percent of all new urban health posts. Between 1991 and 1998, the social fund in Nicaragua accounted for a fourth of public sector health investments. Although in

---

[1] The comparators are generally government health facilities, either centrally or locally managed. In a few cases NGO-run facilities also received social fund support.

Table 5.1 Health Project Component of Total Social Fund Investment

Country	Period	Percentage of total spending for health projects
Bolivia	1994–98	14
Honduras	1994–98[a]	14
Nicaragua	1991–98	15
Zambia	1991–98	10

[a] FHIS 1 and FHIS 2.

Zambia the first social fund program had smaller coverage than in other countries, more than 660,000 community members nevertheless benefited from social fund-supported health centers.

Most of these health facilities operated primarily in poor rural areas. In Honduras most of the facilities surveyed were small facilities in rural areas. The results for Nicaragua are based for the most part on information on small rural health posts. In Zambia more than two-thirds of health facilities were rural, and in Bolivia all were rural.

Impact on Infrastructure

Overall, social fund-supported health centers had better physical facilities than did comparators—which is not surprising, since their principal objective was to improve the physical infrastructure (table 5.2). Social fund interventions had other important effects on the physical characteristics of health centers. In Bolivia the number of patient rooms increased 33 percent for social fund facilities, compared with a 54 percent decline in the comparison groups. In Zambia the number of examination rooms and delivery rooms in social fund facilities doubled, and the number of patient wards increased from an average of 2.7 to 4.1, as against a steady 2.9 for the comparators. As a result, social fund facilities in Zambia had an average of 10 medical rooms (delivery rooms, dispensary rooms, examination rooms, patient wards, and storerooms), compared with 7 for the comparators.

Access to safe water in social fund facilities was typically as good as or better than that in comparators except for Honduran facilities which were less likely to have access to wells (table 5.3). In Zambia the share of social fund facilities with safe water increased from 60 percent before the intervention to 88 percent afterward. In Bolivian and Honduran facilities supplied by piped water, there was no significant difference in access between treatment and comparison groups. Many facilities in both groups still operate without piped water—but then, most of these health facilities are in rural villages that may not have access to piped water. In Honduras about 40 percent

Table 5.2 Health Facilities in Adequate or Better Condition (percent)

Country	Social fund facilities	Comparator facilities
Honduras	97	62
Nicaragua	70	25
Zambia	94	71

Note: Not assessed in Bolivia.
Source: For data sources and years, see chapter 2, table 2.3.

Table 5.3 Health Facilities' Access to Utilities

Utility and country	Social fund facilities	Comparator facilities
Safe water (percentage of facilities with access)[a]		
Honduras		
Piped water	63	63
Well water	13	38
Nicaragua	91	83
Zambia	88	77
Sanitation		
Bolivia (percentage increase in service)	40	18
Honduras (toilets per facility)	4.1	1.0
Nicaragua (latrines or flush toilets		
per facility)	2.2	1.9
Zambia (latrines per facility)	3.4	0.6
Electricity (percentage of facilities with access)		
Bolivia	33	37
Honduras	38	63
Nicaragua		
During open hours	65	64
Available in community	74	92
Zambia	81	50

[a] Well water, piped water inside or outside the building, or water from a standpipe.
Source: For data sources and years, see chapter 2, table 2.3.

of all facilities lacked piped water, and in Nicaragua about 50 percent did. In all countries sanitation services were better in social fund-supported facilities than in comparators.

Information on the effect of social fund investments on access to electricity is generally inconclusive. Social fund-supported health facilities in Bolivia and Honduras reported having less access to electricity; those in Zambia had more access; and those in Nicaragua had about the same access as their comparators. Interpreting information on access to electricity poses several difficulties. First, many rural communities in the case study countries, especially in poor areas, have only limited access to electricity, which affects the access of the health facility. Second, facilities that operate refrigerators and other electrical equipment from off-grid energy sources may have reported that they lacked electricity. In Honduras, for example, only 38 percent of facilities reported having access to electricity, but 50 percent had refrigerators, many powered by bottled liquid petroleum gas. In Bolivia the social fund provided health facilities that lacked electricity with solar panels to power a radio, lights, and a refrigerator for storing medicines and vaccines.

Impact on Availability of Key Inputs

This section describes study findings on the availability of key inputs for health centers, including medical equipment and furniture, essential medicine and supplies, and staff.

Medical Equipment and Furniture

The availability of medical equipment and furniture in social fund-supported health facilities was generally as good as or better than that in comparators. In Bolivia the average number of beds increased significantly more in social fund facilities (from 0.5 to 1.9) than in comparators (from 0.43 to 1.16), but an index of available medical equipment in good condition was not significantly different for the two groups. In Nicaragua the 18 key pieces of furniture specified by Ministry of Health norms were consistently available in 65 percent of social fund facilities but in only 53 percent of non-social fund facilities. The basic set of medical equipment (scales, refrigerators, crutches, and the like) was available in 65 percent of social fund facilities and 60 percent of comparator facilities. In Honduras 53 percent of the social fund facilities had all 17 items from the basic list, while 59 percent of comparators did. The Zambian social fund facilities were significantly better supplied than their comparators with both medical equipment and furniture. With respect to medical equipment, even though preintervention levels were similar, after rehabilitation social fund facilities in Zambia typically had three times the number of medical trolleys and twice the number of hanging weighing scales, sphygmomanometers, sterilizers, and stethoscopes as did comparators. The results for furniture were similar to those for equipment.

Access to Essential Medicines and Supplies

In most of the case study countries, social fund-supported health facilities had a more reliable supply of medicines and other critical medical supplies provided by the ministry of health than did comparators. A large share of both treatment and control facilities in all the countries had difficulty securing a

Table 5.4 Health Facilities' Access to Essential Medicines and Supplies (percent)

Country and indicator	Social fund facilities	Comparator facilities
Bolivia		
Average increase in index of available medical supplies, 1993–97	62	23
Nicaragua		
Facilities with replaceable medical supplies available[a]	59	42
Facilities with key medicines consistently available	55	56
Honduras		
Average share of 38 basic medicines available	42	44
Zambia		
Facilities with 11 essential medicines and condoms	79	77

[a] Absorbent cotton, thermometers, urine collectors, and the like.
Source: For data sources and years, see chapter 2, table 2.3.

reliable supply of essential drugs. In Bolivia in 1993, before the intervention, social fund facilities had a smaller share of necessary medical supplies than comparators did, but the share was significantly larger by 1997, after the intervention (table 5.4).

Nicaraguan social fund facilities enjoyed significantly better availability of replaceable medical supplies than comparison facilities, which social fund staff attributed to the fund's practice of obtaining commitments from the ministry before carrying out an investment. Availability of key medicines was low for both the social fund facilities and the comparators. In Honduras and Zambia there was little difference in the availability of basic medicines, although Zambian social fund facilities ran out of chloroquine less frequently than comparators and were more likely to have condoms and Septrin (a combination of antibiotics).

Staffing

Staff numbers in social fund-supported facilities tended to increase between 1993 and 1997–98, while comparators experienced a smaller increase or a decline (table 5.5). As a result, social fund-supported health facilities are staffed as well as or better than comparators, although for both groups staffing levels are often below health ministry norms. Social funds do not

Table 5.5 Staffing of Health Facilities, 1993 and 1997–98
(average number of staff, except where otherwise specified)

Country and indicator	Social fund facilities			Comparator facilities		
	1993	1997–98	Change	1993	1997–98	Change
Honduras (percentage of facilities with staff)						
Doctor	—	9	—		0	—
Qualified nurse	—	64	—		100	—
Auxiliary nurse	—	27	—		0	—
Health promoters	—	36	—		14	—
Administrative staff	—	82	—		43	—
Nicaragua[a]						
Total staff	15.4	18.6	3.2	17.2	13.1	–4.1
Professional staff	1.0	1.4	0.4	0.6	0.5	–0.1
Zambia[b]						
Total staff	13.0	14.6	1.6	7.2	7.7	0.5
Professional staff	3.9	4.2	0.3	2.9	2.6	–0.3
Nonprofessional staff	9.1	10.4	1.3	4.3	5.1	0.8

— Not available.
Note: Bolivia was omitted because the analysis did not include detailed information on staffing.
[a] Data for Nicaragua refer to 1993 and 1997. In Nicaragua professional staff are defined as doctors, nurses, dentists, and pharmacists. Total staff includes nurse's aides and volunteers.
[b] Data for Zambia refer to 1993 and 1998. In Zambia professional staff are defined as doctors, clinical officers, public health nurses, registered nurses, and registered midwives.
Source: For data sources, see chapter 2, table 2.3.

finance staffing; thus, the findings show that health ministries do provide staffing or that attrition at social fund health facilities is lower. These findings are especially important, since adequate staffing is critical in ensuring the provision and the sustainability of health services.

In Nicaragua and Zambia staffing in social fund health posts increased significantly between 1993 and 1997, mostly as a result of increases in non-professional staff. In both countries one in three social fund facilities gained a professional staff member, while one in five comparators in Nicaragua, and one in three in Zambia, lost one. Nicaraguan social fund health posts were almost twice as likely as comparators to employ a doctor. The Honduran study had more limited information on staffing, but it did find that one social fund facility had not yet opened because of lack of staff.

The evidence suggests a trend of increased staffing in social fund facilities and reduced staffing in comparator facilities. The data and the sample sizes available did not permit exploration of whether staff members have moved from non-social fund to social fund facilities.

Impact on Health Outcomes

Household survey data were analyzed to assess short-term changes in the utilization of health centers and longer-term impacts on morbidity and mortality outcomes.

Utilization Rates

Health centers supported by social funds typically experienced significant increases in utilization rates or had higher utilization rates than comparators (table 5.6). This finding is consistent with the hypothesis that more people would use services offered by social fund-supported health centers, which typically have better-quality facilities and are better staffed. It is also consistent with the findings of other research on the links between quality and utilization (see box 5.1).

Data for analyzing utilization were available from both facilities surveys and household surveys. In the three cases where facilities information was available, the data showed an increase in utilization, especially for certain services, for certain hours that the facility was open, or for both. The household-level data, available for four cases, showed larger increases in utilization rates for social fund facilities than for comparators in two cases and equivalent increases in the other two.

In Bolivia, where only household data on utilization were available, the case study found no significant difference in overall utilization between social fund facilities and comparators in 1997, although it did find differences for prenatal care and the treatment of coughs. In communities with social fund health interventions, the share of women receiving prenatal care increased by 21 percent in 1993–97, compared with only 1 percent in the comparison groups. This finding is probably critical to the mortality outcomes reported for Bolivia in table 5.9.

In Honduras evidence from several sources points to increased utilization as a result of social fund investments. Household survey data show that social fund investments led to a 10 percentage point increase in the share of sick people seeking professional medical services. Multivariate analysis confirms that the social fund investments influenced the decision to seek medical attention.[2] Whereas 29 percent of sick people in communities with a comparator facility traveled to a health center in another village, almost all the social fund beneficiaries sought treatment at the local center, saving time and money.

---

[2] Other significant determinants were the household head's educational level, whether a patient was younger than age five, and whether the illness was respiratory (see Walker and others 1999: 58, table 41).

Table 5.6 Impact of Social Fund Investment on Household Utilization of Health Facilities, 1998

Country and indicator	Social fund households (mean)	Comparator households (mean)[a]	p-value
Bolivia (difference-in-differences estimates)[b]			
Use of public health service (not conditional on illness)	0.002	0.002	0.60
Use of public health service (conditional on illness)	0.011	0.010	0.49
Fraction of women receiving any prenatal care	0.207	0.007	0.001
Fraction of births attended by trained personnel	0.063	0.050	0.58
Fraction of cases of diarrhea treated	0.006	−0.138	−0.23
Fraction of cases of cough treated	0.031	0.113	0.08
Honduras (percentage of household survey respondents)[b]			
Seek medical attention at health post when having health problem	51	41	—
Total visiting Ministry of Health primary network	41	33	—
Visited social fund health center	35	4	—
Visited other Ministry of Health center	6	29	—
Visited Ministry of Health hospital	2	3	—
Visited private provider	6	4	—
Nicaragua (percent)			
Utilization rate	10	6	0.000
Utilization rate for children under age six	23	6	0.000
Utilization rate for children under age six with diarrhea	43	10	0.000
Women receiving any prenatal care	76	87	0.034
Institutional births	69	71	0.781
Births attended by trained personnel	98	95	0.302

(Table continues in the following page.)

Table 5.6 (continued)

Country and indicator	Social fund households (mean)	Comparator households (mean)^a	p-value
DPT vaccination coverage	87	96	0.147
Polio vaccination coverage	94	100	0.150
Zambia (percent, except for vaccinations)			
Seek treatment (not			
conditional on illness)	18	20	0.278
Urban	23	21	0.320
Rural	16	19	0.165
Seek treatment (conditional on illness)	38	49	0.005
Urban	51	53	0.402
Rural	31	46	0.005
Went to hospital (if treated)	31	46	0.012
Urban	48	55	0.259
Rural	16	36	0.014
Went to health center (if treated)	72	60	0.050
BCG vaccinations per child	1.07	1.05	0.323
Rural	1.06	1.01	0.095
DPT vaccinations per child			
(significant rural and urban)	2.99	2.67	0.000
Polio vaccinations per child (rural)	2.87	2.69	0.049
Measles vaccinations per child	0.93	1.00	0.071

— Not available.
Note: BCG, Bacillus Calmette-Guérin (vaccine for tuberculosis); DPT, diphtheria, pertussis, and tetanus.
^{a} For Bolivia, Nicaragua, and Zambia, propensity score matched comparators; for Honduras, pipeline project comparators.
^{b} Data refer to 1997–98.
Source: For data sources, see chapter 2, table 2.3.

Other analyses were conducted in Honduras to corroborate the utilization findings. In one, utilization of social fund-supported facilities was compared with utilization in all rural health posts in Honduras on the basis of data from a World Bank study (World Bank 1988). The analysis found that rural health posts supported by the social fund had 7.5 consultations per nurse per day, compared with 6.0 per day for all rural health posts. A second analysis, using Ministry of Health data, found that urban health centers supported by the social fund had an average of 54 consultations per day, compared with only 34 for all urban health centers (table 5.7).

The qualitative investigation in Honduras corroborated the finding of increased utilization. It found that the social fund health facilities have attracted more users (especially pregnant women and children) and that there were two main reasons for this: the lessening of the distance to a health

---

Box 5.1 Evidence on Supply-Side Factors Affecting Utilization of Health Care

Many studies that have examined the effects of supply-side factors in the health sector on the demand for health services and on health outcomes have found a positive relationship between improvements in the quality of service and demand for health services.

- A study in Ghana found that improving the availability of drugs would increase patients' use of public facilities by 44 percent. Increases in use resulting from other improvements were estimated as follows: better infrastructure (water and sanitation), 33 percent; better service (availability of a laboratory and the ability to vaccinate children and to provide prenatal, postnatal, and child monitoring clinical services), 25 percent; and more personnel (an increase in staffing to three), 19 percent. Making all these improvements would increase use by 128 percent (Lavy and Germain 1994).
- In Okun State, Nigeria, Akin, Guilkey, and Denton (1995) found that use of public health clinics was positively and significantly affected by facilities' physical condition, the availability of drugs, and the number of functioning x-ray machines and laboratories.
- A study of obstetric care in Cebu, Philippines, showed that the quality of services had a significant effect on use. Quality was measured by the availability of medical supplies, the practitioner's training, the availability of service, the size of the facility, and waiting time (Hotchkiss 1993).
- In Kenya the broad availability of drugs was found to be positively related to utilization of health services (Mwabu, Ainsworth, and Nyamete 1993). Lavy and others (1996) arrived at the same conclusion for Ghana.

The studies found a negative relationship between distance and the demand for services. In Kenya the distance to government health facilities was negatively correlated with utilization (Mwabu, Ainsworth, and Nyamete 1993). Lavy and Germain (1994) found that in Ghana reducing the distance to public facilities by 50 percent is associated with a 96 percent increase in patient use.

Source: Study results as presented in Alderman and Lavy (1996).

---

center, and involvement of community members as health volunteers through midwife, first aid, and other training. (See box 5.2 for comments by clients in Honduras.)

In Nicaragua the propensity score matching analysis of the household data (which statistically matched the treatment and comparison groups

Table 5.7 Average Daily Consultations in Urban and Rural Health Posts, Honduras, 1997

Location of health posts	Social fund health posts			All Ministry of Health posts
	Constructed	Restored	Total	
Urban	64.2	52.5	54.1	34.4
Rural	8.1	10.9	9.4	9.2

Note: Based on total annual visits, including for vaccinations, and a norm of 250 service days a year.
Source: Walker and others (1999): 45, table 28.

Box 5.2 Beneficiaries of Social Fund Health Posts Speak Out

Interviewer: Where did you go when you had a health problem before you had the CESAR [rural health center]?
Ana: To Langue, and it took all day.
Mariana: We suffered the sun and rain.
Esperanza: I have three kids, and I wasted a whole day.
Sonia: Suffering hunger because we went with only the two lempira to pay for the doctor's appointment.

—Women's focus group participants, Honduras

For me things have changed. Before this health post was here, we had to go to Jinotega to the health post, even for little things and the children's small illnesses.

—Comment by a beneficiary, San Antonio de Sisle, Nicaragua

---

according to key characteristics) showed significantly higher utilization of social fund facilities than of comparators both for the general population and for children under age six. For children under age six with diarrhea, the utilization rate was four times as high for social fund facilities as for the comparators. The share of women receiving prenatal care, however, was significantly lower among the population near social fund facilities.

The Nicaraguan case study also compared social fund beneficiaries with households in the closest community having a health center, without any further matching by household characteristics. This comparison showed no significant differences in utilization rates for children under age six and lower utilization rates for those age six and over in social fund facilities (7.2 percent for social fund facilities and 9.6 percent for comparators). The share of institutional births was lower among comparators than among social fund facilities (55 and 69 percent, respectively).

Table 5.8 Health Facility Utilization Overall and by Female Patients, Nicaragua, 1993 and 1997

Item	1993	1997	Difference
Mean number of daily visits			
Social fund facilities	11.3	17.0	5.7
Comparator facilities	8.8	14.0	5.2
Difference in differences			0.5
Daily visits by female patients (percent)			
Social fund facilities	58.5	65.7	7.2
Comparator facilities	60.8	64.6	3.8
Difference in differences			3.4
Visits for pregnancy and postpartum services (percent)			
Social fund facilities	13.1	14.7	1.6
Comparator facilities	10.9	13.7	2.8
Difference in differences			−1.2

Source: World Bank (2000a): table 9.1.

Analysis of the facilities data for Nicaragua showed results similar to those for the propensity score matching: utilization rates increased in both treatment and comparison facilities, although social fund health posts exhibited slightly greater and significant increases. The facilities data also showed that the percentage of daily visits made by female patients increased significantly more in social fund facilities than in comparators. Visits for pregnancy and postpartum services increased in both groups, although the increase was larger for the comparator posts (table 5.8).

In Zambia the household data on utilization showed that when seeking treatment was not conditional on illness, there was no difference in utilization between social fund facilities and comparators. When seeking treatment was conditioned on illness, households served by social fund facilities appeared less likely to seek treatment. Since the social fund facilities are in better condition, are better equipped, and are better or equally well staffed, quality does not appear to be the biggest issue.

The facilities data for Zambia showed that social fund-supported facilities remained open more hours a week than comparators (97 and 69 hours, respectively). The biggest difference was in urban areas, but rural social fund facilities also operated more hours a week than their comparators (64 versus 56 hours). While social fund facilities and their comparators devoted about the same amount of time to community outreach activities (11 and 12 hours a week, respectively), social fund facilities spent almost three times as many hours on school health programs (11 hours a week, compared with 4 for non-social fund facilities). Hours for health services for children under age five in social fund facilities increased by 15 percent between 1993 and 1998, and hours for prenatal care, by 30 percent.

This increase in hours of operation correlates with an increase in visits for certain services between 1993 and 1998. During the last quarter of 1998, social fund facilities had 567 more cases, on average, than in the last quarter of 1993, while comparator facilities treated 271 fewer cases, on average. The number of visits by children rose by 26 percent in social fund facilities but declined by 3 percent in non-social fund facilities. Social fund facilities recorded a 23 percent increase in deliveries, compared with a decrease of 11 percent for comparator facilities. Attendance for family planning almost tripled in both types of facility.

A clear finding from both Honduras and Zambia is that when households near social fund-supported health facilities seek treatment, they are much more likely than comparators to go to their local health facility rather than to a hospital. This is an especially welcome finding in Zambia, where people's tendency to bypass lower levels of health care because of perceived inefficacy unnecessarily overburdens secondary and tertiary levels of care.

Health Outcomes

The data allow for different health outcomes to be examined in different countries, including infant and child mortality rates, vaccination coverage, and the incidence of disease. Interpreting these results is often problematic because of the numerous factors contributing to the outcomes, particularly the incidence of disease. The robustness of the results is also related to the data and methodologies used in the evaluations.

The one case study able to collect robust information on mortality rates, Bolivia, found that social fund investments led to large and significant improvements in mortality rates for both infants and children (table 5.9). Social fund and comparator communities had similar infant and under-five mortality rates in 1993. By 1997, the infant mortality rate in social fund communities had dropped significantly, to half its 1993 level, but it increased in comparator communities. Under-five mortality rates also fell in social fund communities and increased in comparator communities.

Researchers verified these results using three methods: matching; construction of life table estimates for households for which survey data were available for both 1993 and 1997; and use of estimated coefficients from the construction of a Cox proportional hazard function to calculate under-five mortality rates (see Newman and others 2002 for the model specifications). Researchers also tested alternative explanations for the results, including mother's age, mother's education, family consumption per capita, availability of piped water, adequacy of water throughout the day and year, distance to water supply, presence of adequate sanitation facilities, and presence of

Table 5.9 Impact of Social Fund Investments in Health Centers on Infant and Under-Five Mortality, Bolivia, 1993–97

Indicator	Social fund communities (mean)		Propensity score matched communities (mean)	
	1993	1997	1993	1997
Infant mortality rate (per 1,000 live births)	61.5	30.8	59.8	67.2
Under-five mortality rate (per 1,000)	94.0	54.6	92.6	107.9
Deaths among children under age five (percent)	10.3	6.0	10.2	10.7
Survival among children under age five (percent)	89.7	94.0	89.8	89.3
Difference between treatment and comparison groups in proportion of children dying		Percent		
1993		−0.08*		
1997		4.7**		

* Difference is significant at the 10 percent level.
** Difference is significant at the 5 percent level.
Note: Table shows combined data for sampled districts in the Chaco region and in other rural areas.
Source: Newman and others (2002).

non-social fund improvements in water or sanitation. Even when these factors were controlled for in the analysis, the results held. Finally, researchers tested the hypothesis that if the services provided at the clinic caused the differences in mortality rates, the rates would fall more among the families that used the clinic than among those that did not. They found significantly lower mortality rates among the families that used the health clinic.

The two case studies that collected information on vaccination coverage, Nicaragua and Zambia, found that coverage by social fund facilities was generally as good as or better than that by comparators. In Nicaragua both treatment and comparison groups had high overall coverage rates for diphtheria, pertussis, and tetanus (DPT) and polio vaccinations (see table 5.6). In Zambia coverage in social fund facilities was slightly, although still significantly, higher for rural Bacillus Calmette-Guérin (BCG) tuberculosis vaccinations, DPT vaccinations, and polio vaccinations. Measles vaccinations per child were somewhat lower in areas served by social fund facilities.

The incidence of disease may say more about a social fund's targeting than about its outcomes. For example, building a health post would not affect the environmental factors determining whether children get a cough, but it might determine what happens after they get the cough. It is difficult to determine how much the incidence of disease in a community reflects the social fund's success in targeting poorer or sicker communities and how much it reflects a social fund intervention. Moreover, the chain of causality between infrastructure improvements and health outcomes is complex and may differ under different country circumstances. The time between the initial intervention and the measurement of disease incidence may make a difference; the average lapse between the initial health intervention and the impact evaluation ranges from one to four years among countries and within the same country. For this reason, no attempt is made here to link the incidence of disease with the social fund intervention. Rather, data are presented that relate to the relative health status of communities that are supported by social funds and those that are not.

The household surveys offer mixed and inconclusive evidence on disease incidence. In Bolivia there was no significant difference between treatment and comparison groups. In Nicaragua social fund communities had a higher incidence of diarrhea and respiratory infections compared with the propensity score matching comparison group but not compared with the other comparison group. In Zambia social fund households were more likely to report that someone was sick, but less likely to report that the person had diarrhea.

Aside from the present study, several studies in Africa have shown that changes like those brought about by the case study social funds—reduced distance to clinics, improved quality of services, more weekly hours of child health care, and increased prenatal care—contribute significantly to health outcomes (box 5.3).

Sustainability

We have seen that social fund–supported health facilities are typically in better physical condition than comparators, are better or equally well equipped, and have similar or better staffing—all important indicators of sustainability. Other significant indicators include maintenance, financing, and community support.

Maintenance was found to be better in social fund health facilities (table 5.10). In Nicaragua the social fund facilities were much more likely to have received repairs and key preventive maintenance than comparators (table 5.11). In Zambia 50 percent of social fund facilities had committees responsible for maintenance, while only 14 percent of comparators did, and a greater proportion of social fund facilities (81 percent) carried out maintenance activities in 1998 than was the case for comparators (71 percent). Half of the social fund facilities had undertaken painting and plaster patching, but only 29 percent of the comparator facilities had done painting and 36 percent, plaster patching.

Box 5.3 Evidence on Supply-Side Factors Affecting Health Outcomes

A study of Côte d'Ivoire and Ghana found that increased distance to clinics resulted in higher child mortality rates in both countries (Benefo and Schultz 1994). Lavy and others (1996) found that in Ghana health services directly related to children (post-natal care and child growth monitoring) were significant in explaining child survival, height, and weight. Using data from the Ghana Living Standards Survey, the study found that the number of weekly hours for child health care had a large and significant positive impact on children's survival both in rural areas and in Ghana as a whole. If child services were available one more hour a week (a 15 percent increase), "the median survival duration of children would increase by almost 1 percent; if rural child services equaled the urban mean (11.5 hours a week), the mean survival time of rural children would increase by 9.3 percent, substantially reducing the gap between rural and urban children" (Lavy and others 1996: 349).

The Ghana study also found that the number of hours for child services had positive and significant effects on child height and weight and that greater availability of birth services significantly improved survival rates and weight-for-height in rural areas. This last finding mirrors the finding in Bolivia that increased use of social fund–supported facilities (especially for prenatal care and birth services) led to lower infant and child mortality.

Financing issues are more difficult to assess. In Honduras all health facilities had some funding from copayments, but the amounts were insignificant. In Nicaragua most facilities lacked maintenance funds (of the 40 health posts in the sample, only 4 non-social fund and 2 social fund facilities reported having a maintenance fund), but they may have drawn on general funds for maintenance needs. Social fund facilities were more likely than comparators to receive contributions of funds and materials for maintenance from communities. This may explain the finding that social fund facilities were much less likely to consider the ministry of health solely responsible for maintenance.

In Nicaragua the social fund recently (after the evaluation was concluded) introduced a preventive maintenance fund that provides cofinancing from the central government to community maintenance committees for social fund health posts and schools. By the end of 2001, 60 percent of social fund facilities in health and education (including 143 health posts) had accessed the fund.

Community involvement is higher in social fund-supported health centers. In Honduras these facilities have, on average, more than twice as many

Table 5.10 Indicators of Sustainability of Health Facilities
(percent, except where otherwise specified)

Country and indicator	Social fund facilities	Comparator facilities
Honduras		
Facilities with significant monthly incomes from copayments[a]	23	18
Volunteers (average number)	19	8
Volunteers who worked in previous month	66	64
Facilities that receive technical support from an NGO or similar group	63	45
Nicaragua		
Facilities with maintenance fund	13	17
Facilities that consider Ministry of Health solely responsible for maintenance funds	39	74
Facilities that charge a voluntary user fee	39	75
Facilities with poor infrastructure	30	75
Zambia		
Facilities receiving support from community	56	50
Facilities receiving support from NGO	50	14
Facilities receiving support from churches	63	36
Facilities receiving support from local benefactor	31	14

[a] Monthly incomes of more than 500 lempira.
Source: For data sources and years, see chapter 2, table 2.3.

Table 5.11 Maintenance of Health Facilities, Nicaragua
(percentage of facilities receiving maintenance)

Type of maintenance	Social fund facilities	Comparator facilities
Metal and ironwork repairs	25	0
Preventive maintenance		
On electrical systems	43	20
On sanitary systems	72	54

Source: For data sources, see chapter 2, table 2.3.

community volunteers as do comparators, and the qualitative study linked this involvement to higher utilization. The social fund facilities also receive more technical support from NGOs and similar groups. A larger share of community members participated in the social fund health projects (53 percent) than in comparator projects (25 percent). Participation was higher in all categories, including provision of labor, money, and materials.

In Zambia more social fund facilities (88 percent) have health advisory committees than do comparators (68 percent). The social fund advisory committees were more likely to meet frequently; 69 percent met monthly (for comparators, the figure was 57 percent). Social fund facilities also seem to receive more support from sources outside the government than do comparators—not only from NGOs but also from the community, church groups, and local benefactors.

Implications

Social fund investments in health facilities can lead to reductions in infant and child mortality. The Bolivia case study showed a very robust finding of reductions in mortality rates linked to usage of social fund facilities. The social fund was able to improve facility infrastructure (including sanitation), increase utilization for prenatal visits, and improve the availability of medical supplies in ways that other health facilities were unable to do. This result may have been aided by the more complete intervention in Bolivia, which included provision of a motorbike so health personnel could visit people outside the clinic, radios for contact with other facilities and medical experts, and alternative energy sources in off-grid areas for storing vaccines and other medications needing refrigeration. This package allowed for a level of "connectedness" (within communities and with other health facilities) that may have improved the outcomes of the social fund facilities over their comparators.

Despite years of reform efforts, the ability of health ministries to supply essential drugs to health clinics of all types still suffers from systemic weaknesses. This shortcoming raises several issues for the future design of social funds. First, social fund policy needs to be coordinated at the national policy level with sectoral health policies, particularly with respect to overall recurrent costs and supplies, especially medicines. Second, where weaknesses are noted, social funds should consider several actions: striking an appropriate balance in interventions between infrastructure and inputs; forming even stronger links and agreements with ministries to ensure adequate medical supplies; acting as an advocacy group to raise problematic issues relating to management, acquisition, and distribution of medical supplies; and piloting new arrangements for procurement or distribution. Governments should be encouraged to reexamine their drug policies.

Good levels of coordination with local and central governments have enabled social fund-financed facilities to obtain or keep staff, and such coordination should remain important in the future design and implementation of social funds. Local and central governments will need to continue to ensure the availability of adequate numbers of qualified staff.

In an imperfect sectoral environment, social funds may find it worthwhile to experiment by focusing on critical services that can have an important effect on outcomes. Strengthening the provision of prenatal and postnatal care and of services for children may lead to yet greater improvements in health outcomes.

To complement the provision of infrastructure, social funds should consider a broader package of demand-side interventions and outreach in the health sector. Such interventions, directed at households, may help increase utilization even more. Community involvement in social fund facilities can support increased utilization, as the qualitative study in Honduras found.

A sense of ownership is important for maintenance and sustainability. Social funds should endeavor to ensure community involvement and ownership and to plan for the participation of communities and local governments in the operation and maintenance of facilities. Experimentation with new ways of improving maintenance and sustainability, involving both communities and local governments as in Nicaragua and now in Honduras, can contribute to sustained maintenance.

6

Water and Sanitation

THIS CHAPTER EXAMINES THE IMPACT of social fund investments in water and sanitation. Empirical findings regarding the quality and utilization of water, sewerage, and latrine facilities and the resulting changes in health outcomes at the household level are first discussed. In all the cases surveyed, water investments by social funds led to net increases in household access to piped water, which translated into less distance to water sources and less time spent collecting water. The outcomes in individual case study countries included significant reductions in child and infant mortality, less frequent sickness and loss of working time, and less stunting of children's growth. Despite the gains and the generally acceptable quality of the water systems, there are some concerns about the costs of and responsibilities for construction and continuing maintenance and therefore about sustainability. The sewerage systems examined were operating well, with adequate maintenance, but they suffered from low connection rates. Perhaps for this reason, health impacts were not detected. Latrine investments financed by social funds were linked with reductions in diarrhea in some countries but not others.

Research Focus

This chapter describes results from the case study countries in which the impact evaluation included water and sanitation investments: Armenia, Bolivia, Honduras, Nicaragua, and Peru. In Zambia stand-alone water projects were not included in the evaluation, as they form a very small part of the social fund's overall portfolio. Most water and sanitation investments in Zambia are linked to school projects, which often include development of water supply (typically through boreholes) and latrine construction.

The following questions formed the core of this study's assessment of the effectiveness of social fund interventions in the water and sanitation sector:

- Are the infrastructure investments in water, sewerage, and latrines leading to improvements in the quality and availability of services?
- Have household access and utilization improved as a result of the social fund intervention?
- What is the final impact on social welfare of social fund water and sanitation investments, as measured by time and distance to water sources and by health impacts?
- Are these water, sewerage, and latrine investments sustainable?

The following aspects of the impact of social fund water and sanitation projects were examined:

- Quality and expansion of basic water and sanitation infrastructure
- Impact on utilization rates of households
- Impact on accessibility of the water supply, including time and distance to the nearest water source
- Health outcomes of water and sanitation investments, including incidence of diarrhea and infant and child mortality rates
- Sustainability of service delivery.

The weight of the social fund in national sectoral investment was less in the water and sanitation sectors than in health and education. In Nicaragua between 1991 and 1998, the social fund accounted for 7 percent of water and sanitation investments carried out by central agencies.[1] In Honduras (1993–97) the social fund accounted for 2 percent of all new rural water connections, 1 percent of new urban water connections, and 5 percent of all new sewerage connections. Between 1991 and 1997, an estimated 12 percent of the rural population benefited from water investments by the Bolivian social fund, and 2 percent of rural households benefited from sanitation projects. The social fund was the only central agency investing in water and sanitation systems in communities with fewer than 5,000 inhabitants.

---

[1] Water and sanitation made up a relatively small share of the overall social fund portfolio for 1991–98; water projects accounted for 4 percent of the portfolio, and sanitation projects, for 5 percent.

Water Systems

This section discusses the impact of social fund–financed water systems in Armenia, Bolivia, Honduras, Nicaragua, and Peru, drawing on data from a random sample of water projects in the social fund portfolio in each country. The sample includes both new investments and extensions or repairs of existing systems and represents a range of facilities, from simple wells to urban networks.

Quality and Utilization

The social fund–financed urban water network systems in the case study countries were approaching full utilization. Half of the 10 systems sampled in Nicaragua were functioning at full capacity, and connection rates across all sampled systems averaged 90 percent. In Honduras all the water projects were operating, and connection rates averaged 92 percent in social fund communities. In both Honduras and Nicaragua the social fund investments and the corresponding samples consisted mainly of network systems built or upgraded in urban or periurban areas. In Bolivia and Peru, where investments were concentrated in rural areas, data on household connection rates either were not gathered or were not reliable because of the large share of public standpipe systems in the sample.

The availability of water improved as a result of social fund investments. Nevertheless, water often was not available 24 hours a day, 365 days a year. In Armenia households in social fund areas were more likely to report improvements in the previous 12 months than were those in comparator groups. In Bolivia overall availability increased in the rural areas studied—from 79 to 89 percent of the year in five provinces in the Chaco region, and from 87 to 91 percent in the other rural provinces sampled. The changes, when compared with baseline data, point to improvements in water supply that are directly attributable to social fund investments. The results for hours of service per day were mixed: availability declined from 22 to 19 hours a day in the Chaco region but rose from 19 to 21 hours a day in the other rural areas sampled. In Honduras the availability of water improved, as shown in the table (Walker and others 1999), but half the social fund water systems reported low water production, compared with only 21 percent of non-social fund systems.

Availability of water, Honduras, 1999

Type of project	Days per month	Hours per day
Social fund	25	13
Comparator group	18	11

In Nicaragua half the sampled systems supplied water regularly and half supplied water only three days a week, on average. In Peru rural water users reported relatively consistent availability throughout the year from social fund systems. (See the table, from Instituto Apoyo 2000c.) Performance differed across regions, probably reflecting the relative abundance or scarcity of water locally.

Region	Percentage of households reporting permanent availability of water, Peru, 2000
Southern Andes	69
Northern Andes	76
Central Andes	67
Amazon	80

Social fund investments also led to improvements in water quality in the two countries where quality assessments were made. In Bolivia, where the World Health Organization provided laboratory tests of quality, improvements were detected only when projects began to include community training. In these projects the social fund intervention reduced the share of water sources with significant levels of fecal contamination from 55 percent to only 13 percent. This finding underscores the importance of training beneficiaries in adequate maintenance, especially for rural, community-run projects that generally lack access to technical staff and other resources. In Peru beneficiary households reported improvements in water quality, as evidenced by smell, taste, and color. Regression analysis confirmed that a social fund intervention had a significant positive effect (an 88 percent increase) on an index of water quality as perceived by households.

Physical and Operational Sustainability

Almost all the social fund water systems remained operational several years after completion, but some faced challenges to sustainability relating to such factors as design and construction quality, staffing, administrative capacity, preventive maintenance, cost recovery, and training. Nevertheless, in a global study of rural water systems that analyzed 10 programs, including the social funds in Bolivia and Honduras, the social fund systems had higher than average sustainability ratings (box 6.1).

QUALITY OF DESIGN AND OPERATIONS. Despite some reported quality problems, most of the social fund water systems appeared to be relatively well constructed and operating adequately. In Honduras all systems surveyed were operating. Although initial construction and equipment were adequate in almost all cases, comparator water systems tended to be better built (table 6.1).

Box 6.1 Comparing the Sustainability of Water Systems across Countries

A global study of rural water systems conducted by the United Nations Development Programme (UNDP)—World Bank Rural Water Program analyzed 10 programs, among them those of the social funds in Bolivia and Honduras. The study included measures of system sustainability, which were found to be comparable across countries. Overall, the social funds had higher than average sustainability ratings.

Sustainability Index for Water Systems

Criterion	Global average	Bolivian social fund	Honduran social fund
Financial management	3.02	4.91	5.35
Operations and maintenance	5.55	5.95	4.44
Consumer satisfaction	6.18	5.58	5.52
Physical condition	5.90	7.05	5.62
Willingness to pay	6.21	6.37	7.02
Overall sustainability	5.71	6.14	5.74
Sustainability ranking among 10 projects (1 = most sustainable)		4	5

Source: Katz and Sara (1998).

Beneficiary perceptions of social fund water systems were less positive than the technical evaluations, with 23 percent of households describing the quality of the works as poor. System operators were more likely to report low production and lack of equipment in social fund systems than in comparator systems, but social fund systems were less likely to suffer from low pressure.

In Nicaragua, of the 10 social fund water projects reviewed, 5 supplied water reliably. In general, these projects had completed construction much faster than the less reliable systems, were located in wealthier municipalities, and used subterranean water sources and electric pumps. The five less reliable systems evaluated did not supply water reliably, were located in poorer areas, had experienced construction delays, and were dependent on surface water sources and gravity-based technology.

In Peru community members considered most of the systems to be operating well. At the time of the survey, 93 percent of the systems installed in the previous four years were operating, but the share dropped to 85 percent for the oldest systems, completed in 1996. This may point to problems with long-term sustainability, although the improved performance of the more

Table 6.1 Quality of Water Systems, Honduras, 1999

Rating	Original construction	Works maintenance	Equipment and supplies	Equipment maintenance
Technical evaluation (percentage of systems rated)				
Social fund systems				
Good	70	69	61	53
Adequate	23	28	35	46
Poor	6	3	3	2
Comparator systems				
Good	91	50	60	46
Adequate	9	50	40	51
Poor	0	0	0	3

Beneficiary perceptions of social fund systems	Percentage of households giving rating
Good	46
Adequate	11
Poor	23
Don't know/no response	20

Source: Walker and others (1999).

recent projects may reflect the effect of the mandatory training programs that the social fund instituted after 1997 for community-based water users' associations. A study by Instituto Apoyo (2000c) of a sample of 380 water projects found that only 3 percent of systems were not functioning, but it noted the same trend toward an increase in problems over time.

STAFFING. In Honduras staffing was relatively low for both social fund and non-social fund systems. Social fund systems were more likely to receive volunteer support, as shown in the table (Walker and others 1999).

	Staff per 1,000 connections	
Type of staff	Social fund	Comparator
Paid	2.35	2.33
Volunteer	1.07	0.78
Total	3.42	3.11

In Nicaragua all of the systems reviewed except the one in the capital, Managua, employed fewer than six people. In Peru almost all of the systems studied (all of which were rural) were managed by community volunteers. Only 15 percent of system operators reported receiving payment for their work. Nearly all the volunteers (96 percent) reported having participated in the execution of the project, and two-thirds said they had received training in water system operations as part of the project.

ADMINISTRATIVE CAPACITY. Water system operations reflect a range of administrative arrangements, with community-managed systems and those in poorer areas facing greater challenges to sustainability. System management was led by the water ministry or a community water board in Honduras, by local government or the water and sanitation agency in Nicaragua, and by community water committees in Peru. In both Honduras and Nicaragua urban systems operated by the water ministry had better access to technical assistance and to critical supplies such as chlorine. Systems run by the national water agency were more sustainable and tended to be located in better-off areas.

MAINTENANCE. In Nicaragua the high-supply water systems kept better maintenance records, experienced less deterioration, and carried out more necessary maintenance activities than did low-supply systems. Most of the Nicaraguan systems used chlorination; the Bolivian social fund systems did not use chlorine until after community training had been conducted. In Honduras equipment maintenance activities were reported to be good in 53 percent of social fund water systems, compared with 46 percent of the comparator group systems (see table 6.1, above). In Peru 90 percent of system operators reported performing general cleaning, 68 percent reported making general repairs, and 15 percent reported that another institution was also involved in maintenance of the system.

COST RECOVERY. Cost recovery in social fund–financed water systems, even when higher than in comparator groups, was generally inadequate. In Honduras revenues per connection for social fund systems were almost twice those for comparator group systems but still did not fully cover operational costs in 83 percent of the systems. In Nicaragua half the sampled water systems reported that revenues were inadequate to meet costs. In communities with high water supply, 33 percent of users were behind in their water payments ($4.40 per month per user), while in communities with low supply, where poverty levels were higher, 41 percent were behind in their payments ($1.45 per month per user).

In Peru about half the community members interviewed reported paying fees for water, although this rate was affected by the inclusion of standpipe systems in the sample. (About 50 percent of the sample projects installed public standpipes rather than household connections.) The larger projects, which were probably household connection systems, tended to have higher payment rates. A larger share of the older projects collected fees from community members; 48 percent of the projects completed in 1996 reported payments, compared with only 18 percent of projects completed in 1999. As households connect to water sources, the likelihood of their paying fees increases. Rural households reported paying an average $0.52 a month. Fees were at least three times as high in the Amazon region, where communities tend to have pump-based systems that are more expensive than the gravity-fed systems prevalent in the Andes. In communities that had local water users' committees, two-thirds of households reported paying for service, while in communities without a water users' committee, only a third reported paying.

COMMUNITY PARTICIPATION AND TRAINING. Community participation and training varied among social fund–financed water systems. In Armenia only 6 percent of the households in communities that had completed a social fund water project reported belonging to a water association, but membership was even lower (3 percent) in matched comparison communities. In Nicaragua system operation and maintenance were largely the responsibility of central and municipal agencies; only one of the 10 sample projects involved users in operation and maintenance. In Honduras, by contrast, half the social fund projects reported a functioning local water committee.

Case studies suggest that community participation and training tend to have positive effects on the sustainability of community-managed systems. In Honduras training had the best results where it left behind an organizational legacy such as a water board. Such organizations became critical to the sustainability of projects, channeling the participation of communities. The qualitative investigation found that some communities were satisfied with the training received, but others, especially those in charge of the maintenance and administration of rural water projects, felt they needed more.

Peruvian projects in which a greater share of community members had been trained tended to break down less often. Where the operator had received no training, problems were slightly more likely to meet with a slow response or none at all. In communities that had received extensive training, 77 percent of households covered the water cisterns and 50 percent treated water before consumption, while in communities that had not received training, the shares were 61 and 43 percent, respectively. The existence of a formal water association or a trained system operator affected the payment of fees only slightly, but in communities that had a formal water association and fee payments, beneficiaries perceived the system as functioning better.

In Peru female-headed households were less likely than male-headed households to participate in identifying and executing a project, but, as the table shows, they were more likely to receive training in system maintenance and water use in households (Instituto Apoyo 2000c).

Percentage of households participating in social
fund water projects, by gender of household head

Form of participation	Male	Female
Selection of the project	78	71
Execution of the project	88	73
Maintenance	59	47
Training	28	37

Women from female-headed households were more likely to participate than were women from male-headed households. Participation in maintenance by female-headed households was correlated with their participation in the local project committee and in training activities. The longer female-headed households had been in the community, the more likely they were to participate in training. They were also more likely to participate if they had taken part in selecting the project and in forming the local project committee.

Household-Level Impacts

Social fund investments in water improved households' access to piped water in each of the cases evaluated. In most of the countries studied, the investments also led to improvements in health.

ACCESS. According to household data for Armenia, 93 percent of households in social fund communities had access to running water, compared with 87 percent in matched communities and 72 percent in pipeline communities. In Bolivia the impact evaluation found that in rural areas where the social fund financed water systems, the share of households with direct access to piped water rose—from 49 to 67 percent in the Chaco region, and from 44 to 54 percent in the other rural sample.[2]

In Honduras 92 percent of social fund households reported having access to piped water, compared with 87 percent in the pipeline comparator group. The high levels of household access in both groups reflect the predominance of urban systems and of projects for improving existing systems rather than making new household connections. In Nicaragua social fund investments increased the share of households with access to piped water

[2] The comparatively low rates of direct household access to piped water reflect in part the prevalence of public standpipe systems. Indeed, the results for household-level impact suggest that the water investments have been quite successful in increasing access to water and improving health outcomes.

Table 6.2 Impact of Social Fund Water Investments on Under-Five Mortality, Bolivia, 1993–97
(number of children in sample, unless otherwise indicated)

Indicator	1993	1997
Total number of children in sample	1,714	1,344
Surviving children under five	1,547	1,247
Percentage of total	90.26	94.27
Deaths of children under five	167	77
Percentage of total	9.74	5.73
Pearson design-based F(1,28)	14.715	
p-value	0.0007	

Source: Newman and others (2002).

by about half, from 57 percent in 1993 to 85 percent in 1998. In the comparator group the share reporting access to piped water increased only from 52 to 58 percent.

In all cases the increase in coverage was accompanied by a decline in the distance to the water source and in the time spent collecting water. In Nicaragua the distance to the nearest water source decreased by 600 meters; in Bolivia it decreased by 154 meters in the Chaco region and by 55 meters in the other rural areas. In Honduras the time households spent collecting water each month fell by 42 minutes. In Peru families gaining a household connection saved 34 minutes a day, while those gaining access to a public standpipe saved 30 minutes.

HEALTH OUTCOMES. Consistent with international experience, social fund water investments led to improved health outcomes in Armenia, Bolivia, Peru, and Nicaragua.[3] In Honduras there was no measurable impact on the health indicator used (the incidence of diarrhea), perhaps reflecting the focus on rehabilitating existing systems.

In Bolivia social fund water investments reduced under-five mortality by 41 percent (see table 6.2).[4] No significant impact was found on the incidence

---

[3] In a review of several studies of the health impact of improvements to water supply and sanitation facilities, Esrey and others (1990) suggest that such improvements can be expected to reduce child mortality by about 55–60 percent. They point out that to maximize the health impacts of water projects, the water supply should be as close to the home as possible in order to increase the quantity of water available for hygiene. They also note that safe disposal of excreta and proper use of water for personal and domestic hygiene appear to be more important for achieving broad health impacts than the quality of drinking water.

[4] To calculate the reduction in the mortality rate, the data in table 6.2 were converted to under-five mortality rates by estimating a Cox proportional hazard model. The reduction is from 105 to 61 deaths per 1,000, or 41 percent.

of diarrhea, but the data point to possible improvements in the duration of diarrhea in other rural areas. In Peru social fund water interventions reduced under-five mortality and the incidence of diarrhea in children under age 10. The under-five mortality rate was 33 per 1,000 in social fund households benefiting from a water project, compared with 60 per 1,000 in control group communities. When other household and environmental factors were controlled, social fund interventions reduced the incidence of diarrhea by 3 percentage points in children under 10 and the incidence of acute diarrhea, or dysentery, by 1.7 percentage points in children age 2–8. These results can be explained in part by the training given to households in water use and hygiene, which stressed the need to boil or treat water and to cover water storage areas.

In Nicaragua children's health outcomes improved as a result of social fund water investments, with the incidence of stunting (low height-for-age) falling from 25 to 14 percent (table 6.3). In Armenia social fund water investments resulted in less frequent illness. In areas benefiting from a social fund water investment, 13 percent of households reported illness, compared with 17 percent in the pipeline comparison group and 19 percent of those selected through propensity score matching. Among respondents in social fund communities, 15 percent reported inactivity due to illness, versus 25 percent in the pipeline comparison group.

Sewerage Systems

The study evaluated sewerage systems in Honduras and Peru, where social fund systems were compared with pipeline comparison groups, and in Nicaragua, where they were compared with sector norms. In Bolivia researchers collected data on the impact of social fund water investments on access to sanitation services but did not survey sewerage facilities.

Supply and Utilization

In predominantly urban areas in Honduras and Nicaragua, connection rates were low overall, with 44 percent of households connected in Honduras and 61 percent in Nicaragua. The rates varied widely among systems. Nicaragua's capital, Managua, had a much higher connection rate (77 percent) than the average in other urban areas (51 percent). In Honduras one of the eight sampled projects had not yet begun operation (pending payment of a sufficient number of connection fees), and three of the other seven systems had particularly low connection rates. In neither country were connection costs or financing included in the social fund investment.

The high costs of connecting to the sewerage system and of acquiring and installing a toilet were cited as the main reasons for the low connection rates.

Table 6.3 Impact of Social Fund Water Investments on Health Outcomes and Household Access to Water, Nicaragua

Indicator	Social fund beneficiaries		Propensity score matched beneficiaries		p-value for equal means
	Number of observations	Mean	Number of observations	Mean	
Incidence of diarrhea in children under age six in previous month (percent)	79	18.8	157	21.1	0.676
Incidence of wasting (weight-for-height; percent)[a]	102	3.4	114	7.1	0.233
Incidence of stunting (height-for-age; percent)[a]	102	13.6	114	24.9*	0.034
Incidence of underweight (weight-for-age; percent)[a]	102	15.6	114	21.1	0.298
Distance to water source, 1997 (kilometers)	95	0.009	189	0.066*	0.004
Change in distance to water source, 1993–97 (kilometers)	95	−0.130	189	−0.050	0.118
Households with piped water, 1998 (percent)	95	84.6	189	58.0*	0.000
Change in households with piped water, 1993–98 (percentage points)	95	27.3	189	5.9*	0.000

* Difference is significant at the 10 percent level.
[a] Moderate malnutrition with z-scores less than –2 for children under age six.
Source: Pradhan and Rawlings (2002).

In Managua household connections cost $30, on average, while in Honduras buying and installing a toilet cost $150, more than a fifth of per capita GDP. Focus group discussions suggest that other potential factors include:

- The historical lack of access to sewerage systems. Households may have devised their own solutions for sewage disposal (such as a septic tank) or may simply not see the need for proper sewage disposal.
- Poor promotion of the projects, leaving potential users unconvinced of the benefits.
- Disincentives for people renting houses to undertake capital improvements.

Experience suggests that connectivity increases over time as households that did not initially connect to the system later decide to do so.

Physical and Operational Sustainability

In Honduras and Nicaragua most of the social fund sewerage projects extended existing metropolitan systems, so that the projects' sustainability is linked with that of the overall systems. These new systems are typically extensions of collectors to previously unserved neighborhoods and are usually under the direct management of major water and sanitation agencies. In Nicaragua the national water and sanitation agency operates all the systems and provides most of the technical assistance. In Honduras the water and sanitation ministry operates four of the eight sewerage projects analyzed; the municipal water agency of the city of San Pedro Sula oversees two; and community water boards operate the other two. The systems operated by community water boards are simple gravity-based collection systems, without pumps, treatment plants, or other features that would complicate operation and maintenance.

QUALITY OF DESIGN AND CONSTRUCTION. Systems in Honduras and Nicaragua generally operate well, while beneficiaries reported problems in Peru. In general, large urban systems seem to face fewer operational problems. In Honduras an evaluation of technical criteria found that almost all sewerage systems, whether financed by the social fund or by comparators, were of good quality (table 6.4). Beneficiary perceptions of quality were worse, perhaps reflecting the low connection rates. When asked about problems with the systems, 88 percent of beneficiaries responded that there had been none, while 13 percent cited problems with seasonal flooding. In Nicaragua the systems' operations were characterized as good. None of the five systems in Managua reported problems in operations and maintenance, but some projects in other urban areas reported scattered problems (lack of equipment and personnel).

Table 6.4 Quality of Sewerage Systems, Honduras, 1999

	Original construction		Maintenance	
Rating	Social fund systems	Comparator systems	Social fund systems	Comparator systems
Technical evaluation (percentage of systems rated)				
Good	96	100	91	0
Adequate	4	0	5	100
Poor	0	0	5	0
Beneficiary perceptions of social fund systems	Percentage of households giving rating			
Good	61			
Adequate	15			
Poor	0			
Don't know/no response	24			

Source: Walker and others (1999).

MAINTENANCE. Maintenance of sewerage systems was generally very good. Maintenance activities were carried out regularly in all the systems in Nicaragua, although less often in Managua than elsewhere. In Honduras maintenance was evaluated as good in 91 percent of the sample of social fund projects and adequate in all of the non-social fund systems (table 6.4).

Community management of sewerage systems appeared to be less successful, although comparable measures were not available. In Peru no technical evaluations of the sewerage systems were carried out. Instead, the household survey asked beneficiaries for their perceptions of performance. A quarter of the households reported that the system in their community was not working, which could mean that the system was not yet finished, that the household was not yet connected, or that the system had ceased to function. Since the incidence of systems reported as not working was much higher in projects completed in recent years, the first two explanations are the more likely. For the projects completed in earlier years, about 10 percent of households reported some problems with the system, and 4 percent reported major problems (figure 6.1).

COMMUNITY PARTICIPATION. Community participation in social fund sewerage projects was strong in Honduras in the initial stages of the projects but weak in Nicaragua, particularly in the later stages. In Honduras more communities with social fund projects than with non-social fund projects were consulted about the projects (85 and 36 percent, respectively), and more social fund communities contributed labor, money, and materials (64 percent,

Figure 6.1 Household Perceptions of FONCODES Sewerage Systems in Peru

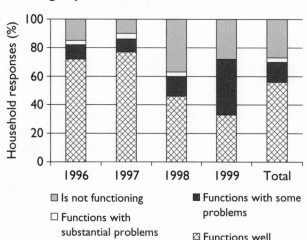

compared with 38 percent). In Nicaragua the communities receiving the five sewerage projects in Managua made the initial request for the projects, but no other community participation was noted in Managua or elsewhere in the country. The higher participation in Honduras did not seem to affect household connection rates.

Household-Level Impacts

Social fund investments improved households' access to sewerage but had little measurable impact on health.

ACCESS. Social fund investments increased the share of households with sewerage connections from 6 to 40 percent in communities with such investments in Honduras and from 43 to 64 percent in Nicaragua. In Nicaragua the increase in access was mirrored by an increase in households with a toilet: between 1993 and 1998 the number of households that reported using a flush toilet rose by 34 percent in communities receiving a social fund investment but by only 3 percent in the comparator group. In Bolivia water investments led to an increase in accompanying sanitation services, from 58 to 61 percent of households in the Chaco region, and from 27 to 71 percent in the other rural areas in the sample.

HEALTH OUTCOMES. The improved access to sewerage systems did not translate into improved health status for households. Given the low household connection rates, this result is consistent with those from other international studies (see box 6.2).

Box 6.2 International Evidence on the Health Effects of Sewerage Investments

Research by Hogrewe, Joyce, and Perez (1993) on the health effects of periurban sewerage investments found that individual household sanitation improvements did not have a significant health impact unless the surrounding households also improved their sanitation.

The study found less stunting in children who had access to a flush toilet when compared with those with access to latrines and to those without access to sanitary services. But sanitation coverage of 75 percent or more of a densely populated community was required to generate a health impact.

These results imply that efforts are needed to ensure communitywide access to sewerage when these investments are made. From a methodological standpoint, the study suggests that community measures of sanitation provide a better indicator of health risk than individual access to improved sanitation.

No statistically significant impact on health outcomes was found in Honduras, but it is worth noting that in almost all the cases reviewed in the qualitative study, the sewerage investments were made to replace latrines that were full. During the rainy season the latrines overflowed into the street, increasing the risk of malaria and other illnesses. Many dwellings lacked space for new latrines. In such urban settings, sewerage is the optimal solution, but health impacts may not be observed until higher connection rates are achieved and waste from full latrines is treated.

In Nicaragua social fund investments in sewerage may not have resulted in positive health impacts at the household level, but they did seem to have had such effects at the community level. Only 9 percent of social fund households reported diarrhea in children under age six, as against 22 percent in the comparison group communities. The difference, however, was significant only at the 85 percent level, a result of the limited sample size imposed by low connection rates. In communities with social fund investments in sewerage, 90 percent of respondents reported lower incidence of sickness and fewer problems with streams and puddles resulting from wastewater dumped in the street, and 80 percent reported improved street conditions and fewer insects.

In Peru the incidence of diarrhea was similar for social fund and comparison group households. But whereas no households benefiting from social fund investments in sewerage reported cases of acute diarrhea (dysentery) in children age six months to two years, 8–12 percent of control group households did. Again, however, small sample sizes may have limited the ability to measure significant changes.

Latrines

The study evaluated social fund latrine projects in Honduras, Nicaragua, and Peru. In all three, social funds built latrines on the sites of private dwellings in low-income communities. Only in Honduras were comparator latrines assessed.

Quality and Utilization

Household survey respondents in Honduras indicated that social fund—financed latrines were in better physical condition than comparator latrines, and all respondents with social fund latrines reported using them. The social fund latrines were of higher quality, were better maintained, had better finish work (doors and seats), and were cleaner (see table 6.5). Only 11 percent of households reported having had operational problems in the previous year. The qualitative study found that social fund latrines generally functioned better where beneficiaries had undergone training and where the soil was absorbent.

Utilization was also high in Peru, where 89 percent of households confirmed that the latrines were being used for the purpose intended. For the oldest projects reviewed (completed in 1996), the utilization rate was 98 percent.

**Table 6.5 Quality of Latrines, Honduras, 1999
(percentage of household survey respondents giving rating)**

Rating	Good	Adequate	Poor
Original construction			
Social fund households	95	5	0
Comparator households	45	25	30
Maintenance			
Social fund households	80	17	3
Comparator households	34	8	58
Doors and seats			
Social fund households	56	26	18
Comparator households	35	6	59
Cleanliness			
Social fund households	54	33	12
Comparator households	23	51	27

Source: Walker and others (1999).

Box 6.3 Concrete Benefits from Sanitation Projects, Honduras

The situation here was terrible because people went to the toilet in the open air. The project was of great benefit to us, because before you could see feces in the water sources ... but thank God, now it is different.

Men's focus group participant, El Naranjo, Honduras (Walker and others 1999)

Community participation in social fund latrine projects in Honduras was strong. The social fund projects consulted more households than did projects financed by other agencies (86 and 60 percent, respectively) and achieved participation by more households than other projects (75 versus 41 percent).

Household-Level Impacts

Social fund investments improved access to latrines in beneficiary communities. In Nicaragua 98 percent of households in beneficiary communities had access to latrines, compared with 77 percent in comparator communities. In Honduras beneficiary communities had full coverage, whereas for comparator communities, coverage was 35 percent.

In Honduras social fund latrine projects had a significant impact on the incidence of diarrhea in beneficiary communities, reducing it by 35 percent. In Peru social fund latrine projects had no statistically significant effect on the incidence of diarrhea among children age 0–10; it did, however, decrease the incidence of acute diarrhea in this age group by 24 percent. Box 6.3 provides a vivid insight into the everyday benefits of sanitation projects for people in the community.

Implications

Several lessons for future projects emerge from the study results. Notably, the findings highlight the centrality of training and participation for the sustainability of projects.

Water Systems

Although most of the water projects evaluated are of acceptable quality, many exhibit problems that indicate a need for increased oversight of initial construction and of the physical infrastructure. In most countries there were reports of low-grade material being used in construction, which led to system deterioration. The importance of proper maintenance, and the critical role of training when communities are responsible for maintenance, are underscored by the case of Bolivia, where water quality improved dramatically after community training was provided.

The Nicaraguan case suggests that the type of water system administration and users' ability to finance operations and maintenance are keys to project success in large network systems. In Nicaragua the more successful water systems were those managed by the national water agency, which regularly provided staff and maintenance and supplied chlorine. Those systems, however, were also costlier; they generally depended on under-

Latrine financed by the social fund in Iquitos, Peru.

ground water sources and electrical pumps, which translated into higher initial connection charges and higher monthly fees. Accordingly, they were found in more urban and less poor areas.

For community-managed systems, which tend to be in poorer, more rural locations with low technical and economic capacity, training is critical for sustainability. To be effective, training should include orientation and materials to support system administration and physical maintenance. Most social funds have adopted mandatory training for local water associations, but further monitoring and research will be needed to determine the effectiveness of this training and the sustainability of the systems.

Systems and fees should be fully discussed with community members before a water project is initiated. For both social fund and control group facilities, fee collection was insufficient—a matter of concern for long-term sustainability. In rural areas, where setting aside significant cash reserves is difficult, stronger community participation may be a way to meet repair needs.

Sewerage Systems

The targeting data reveal that sewerage projects tended to reach better-off populations. The findings point to the need to improve not only targeting outcomes but also technical design, community awareness and participation, and the administrative capacity of the organization responsible for operations and maintenance. There is some evidence that connection rates were lower in poorer areas, and administrative capacity may also be weaker. Additional training and technical assistance may be necessary to ensure that systems in poorer areas are sustainable, particularly if improved targeting of these investments becomes a priority.

The potential health benefits from sewerage investments will not be realized without higher connection rates. Possible strategies for increasing connection rates include greater social mobilization to inform consumers of the potential health benefits, and grant- or credit-based financing of house connections.

Latrines

Latrine investments should be accompanied by training in physical maintenance, as well as in use and hygiene. Cleanliness could be furthered through training in routine use and maintenance. Although no net impacts of training on diarrhea incidence were found, there was an effect on hygiene habits and appropriate usage.

Health outcomes are maximized where latrines provide households with new sanitation services rather than replacing existing latrines. Social funds should therefore consider the existing state of sanitary facilities in a community when appraising a latrine subproject.

7

Community Dynamics

THIS CHAPTER EXAMINES TWO ISSUES that affect sustainability: whether social fund investments reflect local priorities, and whether citizens have been engaged in the identification and execution of these small-scale investments. Evidence from household surveys and qualitative assessments shows that social funds do finance subprojects which represent community priorities. Citizens have been actively involved in the identification of subproject proposals, but less so in the technical design stage. Participation during execution and in subsequent operations and maintenance varies among social funds. The findings from the study indicate that community members are more actively involved in social fund–financed facilities than in comparators. Participation is positively correlated with indicators of project success and impact.

Research Focus

Community consultation, participation, and organization are critical in ensuring that investment projects are relevant, effective, and sustainable. Experience suggests that investments which reflect local priorities and engage the citizenry are more likely to be used and maintained by the local population.[1] Those that do not match local priorities are likely to join the ranks of failed development projects—underutilized health clinics, poorly accessible schools, and latrines that end up being used for grain storage or

---

[1] For a summary of the effects of participation on project outcomes, see World Bank (1996c).

are simply ignored. Moreover, proponents of participatory processes claim that participation is a good in itself and that participatory processes may strengthen a community's capacity to undertake development projects.

This chapter explores the evidence from the six case study countries regarding local investment preferences and participation. Although examining these issues was not the main purpose of the impact evaluation, both the household surveys and the complementary qualitative assessments allowed insights into these cross-cutting aspects of social fund interventions. The basic research questions posed were:

- To what extent do the investments financed by social funds match the priorities expressed by communities?
- To what degree do citizens participate in the identification, the execution, and the subsequent operation and maintenance of social fund investments?
- Is there any evidence linking participation with successful outcomes?

The analysis of community preferences and participation is based on structured household interviews and focus group discussions with community members.[2] It draws on responses from the household questionnaires used in the overall impact evaluation work and on complementary qualitative assessments. The assessments were conducted either in conjunction with the broader impact evaluation work (through focus group interviews in a selection of the communities included in the impact evaluation, as in Honduras and Nicaragua) or as free-standing beneficiary assessments covering projects completed within the same time frame as the impact evaluations. In some cases the research used representative samples with a basic structured interview format. In other cases, such as the beneficiary assessments in Zambia, more in-depth participatory techniques, including participatory rural appraisal approaches, were employed.

Response to Community Priorities

This section examines the performance of social funds in responding to the priorities expressed by communities.

How Projects Are Identified

Unlike many development agencies, social funds do not predetermine the nature of the intervention to be carried out in a community. Instead, they establish a range of investment options across sectors and allow communities

---

[2] See chapter 2, box 2.2, for the qualitative data sources used in this chapter.

to determine their own investment priorities. Depending on the social fund, communities can express their priorities in one of two ways: they can form a project committee and develop a funding proposal, or a local intermediary, such as the local government, an NGO, or a parent-teacher association at a local school, can submit a proposal on behalf of the community. Both mechanisms contrast with models in which central agencies and planners determine the type and location of public investments. The decentralized selection of investment is commonly referred to as "demand driven," denoting its basis in local preferences and actions that are closely, if not directly, linked to citizen choice.

Proposals for social fund projects do not necessarily derive from a formal process of community needs assessment or participatory local planning. Some social funds adopt relatively ad hoc arrangements in which communities develop project proposals in a variety of ways. A local NGO could find out about the social fund program through the national media and submit a proposal to the social fund. A local government might request financing for an investment following presentations by social fund staff about program objectives and procedures. Grassroots organizations such as parents' associations or women's groups might hear about funding opportunities "through the grapevine" and seek information about application requirements. Local contractors might offer their design services to one of these groups to help develop the technical aspects of a proposal. Local politicians might learn of the program and try to motivate communities to apply for funding. An established religious organization might work through its network of social service providers to spread the word about program opportunities. And community leaders might assist the local population in convening a local project committee and putting forth a proposal.

All these arrangements are possible within the range of operating procedures used by the case study social funds. Most social funds conduct fairly vigorous outreach efforts that combine the mass media, briefings of regional and local authorities, and information campaigns conducted by intermediary organizations. Some funds have recently developed a more structured process for upstream identification of projects. Since 1995, the social fund in Bolivia has required that all project proposals go through the formal municipal investment planning process. In Honduras in recent years the social fund has sponsored participatory town hall meetings (*cabildos abiertos*) under the auspices of the local government to develop consensus-based lists of community priorities. In Armenia local governments, established community-based organizations, and community members together form an implementing agency to develop project proposals and oversee implementation. For the most part, however, the impact evaluations in the six case study countries cover projects identified under the more ad hoc arrangements.

The nature of the investment may influence which project is proposed for financing. A community may express a strong need for a piped water system, but it may find that the only viable technical solution is prohibitively costly. Or a community may have a strong interest in a social assistance program, such as child nutrition, but lack contacts with an NGO or other agency that could deliver the services. So, communities may gravitate toward what is feasible as well as desirable.

Program rules can distort "true" demand. By setting up limited menus of eligible investments that reflect national priorities, social funds constrain community choice. Under the rules of most social funds, for example, a community may want to invest in a hospital but can obtain financing only for primary health care. Making the investment conditional on a community contribution may also affect the choice of project. If, say, a 25 percent upfront contribution is required, investment choices may be biased toward infrastructure projects for which it is easier to generate in-kind contributions (in the form of labor and materials) rather than toward projects such as training programs that would require cash (Owen and Van Domelen 1998).

Given the diverse ways in which proposals come to social funds, whether these investments truly reflect community priorities is an important issue. Communities are complex organizations made up of groups and households with differing needs and opportunities, and local intermediaries acting on behalf of citizens bring their own preferences and distortions. Each of these intermediaries is capable of facilitating the expression of local preferences or of skewing them.

Findings

Evidence from national household surveys and qualitative assessments showed that in every country surveyed, social fund investments were consistent with the expressed priorities of the majority of community members.[3] For example, in Armenia, when community members were asked whether

---

[3] A separate World Bank review of social funds (World Bank 2002) commissioned case study fieldwork in a total of 17 communities in four countries: Jamaica, Malawi, and two of the country studied in this report, Nicaragua and Zambia. The approach relied on a recall question concerning what community members perceived as the main problem facing the community in the year the social fund was created. The problems identified were then matched with the type of investment eventually carried out. The report found that in 9 of the 17 communities the top-priority problem had been addressed, and in 4 of the other 8 communities, the second-priority problem was addressed. When asked whether they would have preferred another project instead, most of the respondents in the four countries answered in the negative. These findings are broadly consistent with those reported in this study: community investments are generally in line with community priorities, and community members are satisfied. Drawing on the data from the communities in Jamaica, Rao and Ibáñez (2001) find that although community leaders tended to dominate the process within communities, most citizens were satisfied with the result and that the communities appear to have increased their capacity for collective action.

the project selected had solved the most important problem in the community, 79 percent reported that it had. Another 17 percent thought that it had addressed an important problem but that more important ones remained. Only 3 percent said the project had dealt with a problem that was not at all important (Development Programs, Ltd. 1999).

In Honduras the household survey asked whether the project financed was the most needed one among the eligible options and whether the respondents would have preferred another type of project. About 70 percent of the households sampled regarded one of the types of investment on the social fund menu as the top priority. Water projects reflected the greatest convergence between community preference and type of investment: in communities that had undertaken a water project, 64 percent of the respondents ranked water as the top priority (table 7.1). Health and education projects generated less consensus but were still ranked as the top priority in communities that had implemented such investments. Latrine and sewerage investments did not reflect the felt needs of the community. Where the project financed was not the top priority, community dynamics and external factors were often involved in the choice (box 7.1).

In Nicaragua, when community members were asked to compare social fund investments with other investments made in the community, 72 percent of survey respondents said that the social fund projects had benefited the

Table 7.1 Community Investment Priorities and Choices, by Project Type, Honduras (percentage of households identifying type of project as a priority)

Options	Health	Education	Water	Sewerage	Latrines	Average
On social fund menu						
Health	**35**	11	3	18	6	15
Education	1	**47**	1	6	5	12
Water	4	7	**64**	10	23	22
Sewerage	9	3	3	**4**	5	5
Latrines	6	1	1	0	**7**	3
Not on social fund menu						
Electricity/public lighting	13	0	3	1	15	7
Roads and bridges	8	11	5	28	6	12
Secondary education	8	0	0	0	0	2
Preschool	3	0	0	1	14	4
Other	8	10	6	19	7	10
Don't know/no opinion	5	9	15	13	13	11
Total	100	100	100	100	100	100

Note: Numbers may not sum to totals because of rounding.
Source: Walker and others (1999).

Box 7.1 Selection of Lower-Priority Projects: Two Cases in Honduras

In the few instances in Honduras where communities' top priority had not been financed, focus group interviews explored the reasons and the community dynamics behind the actual selection. Two cases are described here.

- In the village of La Empalizada, Olancho, the community would have preferred a new drinking water system (as reported by the men's focus group) or a new health center (as reported by the women's focus group) to the new school that was actually built. The water project proposal was developed before the school proposal and had the mayor's support but was blocked by the refusal of a neighboring village to share its water source. Meanwhile, the teacher in the deteriorated school had mobilized community support for including a new school building in the municipality's request to the social fund. In the end, the school proposal won out over the health center proposal; the teacher's post already existed, whereas the health ministry would have had to be lobbied for personnel to staff the center.
- In Marale, Francisco Morazan, a large part of the community would have preferred a new drinking water system or agricultural production support projects, but a sewerage system was constructed instead. According to the former mayor, the sewerage project was chosen in order to take advantage of additional resources from a Swiss fund that was limited to this type of project.

Source: Walker and others (1999).

---

community the most; 25 percent felt that other projects had benefited the community at least as much; and 3 percent said that other investments had yielded more benefits. Sewerage projects tended to reflect community priorities less: only 57 percent of those benefiting from a sewerage project felt that it was the best local investment.

In Peru community members were asked how much of a priority the project selected was. Ninety percent of the respondents—and 92 percent of the women—said that the social fund project selected was the highest-priority investment. When asked to judge the necessity of the project, 58 percent said that the project selected was very necessary, 40 percent that it was necessary, and 1 percent that it was not necessary (Instituto Apoyo 1995).

The 1994 beneficiary assessment in Zambia found that most of the social fund projects matched the highest-ranking community needs. The assessment conducted an in-depth analysis, deploying multidisciplinary teams who spent a week in each of 12 sampled project communities, and using participatory rapid appraisal techniques, including community workshops, focus group discussions, and individual interviews. Of the new social fund projects, 83 percent corresponded to the community's first priority, as did 67 percent of the ongoing or completed projects (University of Zambia, Participatory Assessment Group, 1994). The communities identified additional needs, typically relating to social infrastructure (water, schools, and health clinics) or to productive infrastructure such as roads, mills, and farm inputs. In a quarter of the communities food was a main priority, even though it was ineligible for financing. The assessment concluded that where the project funded did not coincide with people's priority needs (28 percent of cases), the reason may be that "often schools and health centers are run by people who know where to go when they want assistance to improve their respective institutions" (University of Zambia, Participatory Assessment Group, 1994: 40).

Participation throughout the Project Cycle

International experience suggests that community members and local organizations should be actively engaged in identifying, designing, implementing, operating, and maintaining local investments, to ensure that the investments have the desired impact and to improve their sustainability. Each of the case study social funds took a slightly different approach to community participation in the various stages of the project cycle. This section examines the level of community participation and its influence on project outcomes. To the extent that the data allowed, participation in social fund–financed infrastructure and services is compared with household participation in similar non–social fund facilities.[4]

Project Identification

Although the degree of community consultation varied among countries, it was quite high in most cases, both for the social funds with structured processes for determining community priorities and for those that relied on ad hoc expressions of demand through local organizations.

In Armenia about half of the community members queried in the two beneficiary assessments stated that the community had selected the project

---

[4]Caution must be exercised in attributing causality to differences in participation levels. Communities and households that have a higher propensity to engage in collective action may also be more successful at accessing social fund resources. For those results that report differences in household behavior obtained through the propensity score matching exercises, the use of pipeline communities should control for any such unobservable selection bias. For the results based on the facility-level data, it is not possible to differentiate between potential social fund effects and underlying community characteristics.

(54 percent in 1997 and 40 percent in 1999). Only 12–17 percent of respondents said that they had been personally involved in selecting the project, but the majority (56 percent) expressed satisfaction with participation, since the community had elected the implementing agency (a community organization, elected during project identification, that consists of representatives from the community and from local government).

For Bolivia no systematic data were available on participation during project identification, but comments from focus group participants pointed to weaknesses in the identification process. According to some informants, there was a general lack of knowledge on the part of the community regarding the process for selecting the type of project to be implemented. The opinion was often expressed that the community consultation process would improve as a result of the decentralized local planning processes being put in place by the government (Coa 1995).

More Honduran households said they were consulted on social fund projects than on projects by other agencies (73 percent, as against 50 percent), with consultation highest for latrine and sewerage projects and lowest for water projects (table 7.2). Only for water projects was the social fund "less consultative" than other agencies, in part because the other agencies tended to use participatory approaches more often in water projects than in other types. In 75 percent of the communities in which focus group interviews were conducted, a community organization had taken the lead in developing the project proposal.

In Nicaragua 79 percent of community members said that they had participated in identifying needs—a share that was fairly consistent across levels of poverty, among types of projects, and between rural and urban settings.[5] In Peru, where formal community assemblies convene to select projects,

Table 7.2 Share of Beneficiary Households Consulted about Social Fund and Other Projects, Honduras (percent)

Type of project	Social fund project	Projects by other agencies
Schools	68	39
Health center	75	34
Water supply	66	73
Sewerage	85	36
Latrines	86	60
Total	73	50

Source: Walker and others (1999).

[5] Fieldwork in Nicaragua for a separate World Bank social funds study (World Bank 2002) found that 60 percent of respondents said they knew about meetings to decide about the project, but only 27 percent said they attended.

Box 7.2 On the Responsiveness of Local Governments in Armenia

Local governments are well aware of the region's social infrastructure problems, and there is no doubt they have put problems of strategic importance forward for community discussion.

—*Focus group participant, Armenia (Development Programs, Ltd. 1999)*

---

between 58 and 67 percent of community members surveyed confirmed that they had participated in such an assembly. More women than men reported participating. Almost all respondents said that the projects had been selected by majority vote, and 59 percent of those who had attended had spoken at least once during the meeting.

In tandem with community members, local governments played an important role in identifying community needs and drafting project proposals in several countries. In Armenia between 28 and 38 percent of community members reported that the local government had selected the project proposed for financing (see box 7.2). In Peru 7 percent of those surveyed said that the local government had selected the project. And in Nicaragua the local government was perceived as the most active participant during project identification: 54 percent of respondents acknowledged local government participation in identifying needs, 18 percent said that the local government had also helped establish priorities, and 21 percent said that it had selected the project proposed. Participation by local government was highest in extremely poor areas.

Evidence suggests that private sector interests had only limited involvement in determining community priorities. In Armenia community members almost never named private contractors among the local actors involved in identifying and selecting projects, perhaps because contractors enter the process later, almost always through national competitive bidding. In Zambia all projects rely on community self-help construction, so contractors are rarely involved. In Peru, the *proyectista* (design engineer) did play a role, though a marginal one: when asked who determined which project was selected, 66 percent of community members named the local population; 8 percent, the local project committee (made up of community members); 7 percent, the local municipality; and 6 percent, the *proyectista*. Asked whether it was the *proyectista* who had first suggested the project, a third said yes, a third said no, and a third did not know. So, even where the contractors may have provided an important impetus by informing the community of the program, in a majority of the cases community members did not perceive them as having determined project selection.

Design

Community participation fell off considerably in the design phase. Whereas almost 80 percent of community members in Nicaragua participated in identifying a project, only 5 percent claimed to have been involved in project design. Results were similar in Armenia, where only 4 percent of community residents stated that they had participated in formulating the project proposal. This narrowing of community input during design may reflect the transfer of technical design work to project committees, NGOs, local governments, private design firms, or other agents. The risk associated with low levels of community participation in this phase is that decisions on technology, location, future utilization, and other aspects of the project may not reflect the wishes of the broad community.

Implementation

Community participation during implementation of social fund projects was often extensive, although it varied in method and intensity among countries and in some cases between rural and urban areas. Participation typically took two forms—community groups and committees assumed project management functions, or citizens donated labor, materials, or cash. In Armenia, Peru, and Zambia communities have direct responsibilities for project management, which is carried out through the local project committee elected for this purpose. The committees organize counterpart contributions, enter into contracts with the government, receive and disburse funds for project activities, and report progress to the community and the social fund. In Peru and Zambia they also handle all the contracting of civil works and all the equipment purchases. In Bolivia, Honduras, and Nicaragua the local intermediary organizations or the social funds perform these functions.

In Armenia 16 percent of community members provided contributions, 8 percent participated in construction, and 13 percent took part in implementation meetings. About 58 percent stated that they

Community members dig water line in Huancarani, Peru.

had not participated at all, perhaps reflecting a weaker tradition of citizen participation, particularly in the urban areas where the social fund investments were focused. In Peru 83 percent of those interviewed said that the community had participated in implementing the project. About 67 percent said that they had participated directly, most commonly by providing labor (90 percent), cash (11 percent), or materials (8 percent). Half of the women surveyed reported having participated, mostly by providing labor but also by contributing cash. Participation was slightly higher in indigenous communities. In rural Zambia 64 percent of households reported participating in project execution, compared with 57 percent in the comparison group. In urban areas this finding was reversed: 23 percent of beneficiary households reported providing inputs to social fund school projects, as against 39 percent of comparator households.[6]

In Honduras 58 percent of household survey respondents participated in some way in social fund projects, compared with 30 percent for other agencies' projects (table 7.3). Among those participating, 36 percent donated labor, 17 percent money, and 8 percent materials. Communities also made indirect contributions by, for example, paying the transport costs, daily living expenses, and paperwork fees of their representatives during negotiation of a project. In Nicaragua 31 percent of community members surveyed said that they had participated in construction, and another 13 percent reported helping supervise project implementation.

Requirements for community cofinancing ranged from zero to 25 percent of total project costs. The Zambian social fund had the largest requirement, with communities financing 20–25 percent of the cost. In Armenia, communities had to contribute 10 percent. In Honduras, Nicaragua, and Peru community contributions were encouraged but not required. In these ad hoc arrangements,

Table 7.3 Beneficiary Households Participating in Project Execution, Honduras (percent)

Type of project	Social fund project	Projects by other agencies
Schools	54	29
Health center	53	25
Water supply	54	68
Sewerage	64	38
Latrines	75	41
Total	58	30

Source: Walker and others (1999).

---

6 The fieldwork conducted for the World Bank (2002) social funds study in five communities in Zambia found that 49 percent of all households and 83 percent of those that had heard of the social fund said they contributed during execution.

Box 7.3 The Importance of Ownership: Comments from Honduras and Zambia

When we arrive and give away everything, that is definitely destructive . . . the best projects are those where the community has contributed, either with money or with voluntary work: they take care of them, they give them follow-up, you can see a clear difference.

—*Virgilio M. Padilla, mayor of El Progreso, Honduras (Walker and others 1999)*

We have not suffered any vandalism or theft from the time the clinic was constructed. This is because people feel they own it.

—*Community member, Mutanda, Zambia (University of Zambia, Participatory Assessment Group, 1998)*

---

contributions were typically less than 10 percent. The qualitative assessments revealed that communities saw their contributions and participation as giving them a greater sense of ownership of the project (see box 7.3).

Operation and Maintenance

Community participation in the operation and maintenance of social infrastructure can be crucial for the sustainability of the services provided. One strategy for ensuring continued delivery of services after social fund financing ends centers on securing formal community commitments for operation and maintenance, by, for example, establishing and training local maintenance committees. Other important steps include providing personnel and operating budgets (from line ministries or local governments), ensuring the technical quality and appropriateness of the initial investment, and setting clear guidelines for responsibilities for operation and maintenance.[7]

Up to half of the community members in Armenia and Peru reported being directly involved in the operation and maintenance of projects. In Honduras, Nicaragua, and Zambia social fund projects were more active in community fund-raising and other local support:

---

[7] The fieldwork carried out for the separate World Bank social funds study in selected communities in Nicaragua and Zambia included sustainability issues. Seventy-one percent of Nicaraguan and 90 percent of Zambian households said they would be willing to pay for maintenance, and 94 and 64 percent, respectively, felt that the facilities were always or usually clean and well maintained. Only 29 percent of the households in Nicaragua and 10 percent of those in Zambia said that necessary repairs were done quickly, and 9 and 13 percent, respectively, said that it always took a long time to carry out repairs (World Bank 2002).

- In Armenia 15 percent of households reported providing financial support, and a third provided physical support. But 54 percent reported no involvement in maintenance either because they did not consider maintenance necessary or because they lacked the means. This perhaps reflects a lingering belief that the government is responsible for solving all problems.
- In Honduras 92 percent of the schools that received social fund support had a committee or board in charge of maintenance.
- In Zambia social fund–supported schools reported higher payment rates for parent-teacher association fees than did comparator schools. Social fund households spent more than comparison groups on education. Social fund health centers were more likely to have a maintenance committee (50 percent, compared with 14 percent for the comparison group).
- In Nicaragua social fund schools were more active in fund-raising. Social fund rural health posts had, on average, more than twice as many community volunteers as non–social fund posts (19 and 8, respectively). Community participation in maintenance received higher ratings than did that of the local government or the line ministry (see box 7.4).
- In Peru more than half of the respondents were aware of the community's commitment to maintaining the project. Such a commitment was more likely for education, irrigation, water supply, family planning, and electrification projects and less likely for health centers, sewerage projects, and community centers.

Does Participation Matter?

Household data from the impact evaluations indicated that community participation during the project cycle did increase utilization. In Bolivia and Honduras, if community members were more actively engaged in a project, they tended to use the services delivered by the project more than they did those of similar investments carried out with less community participation. In these cases the participatory analysis was carried out as part of the impact evaluation and therefore sought to control for selection bias and potential endogeneity problems.

In Bolivia community participation in setting up a social fund health center significantly increased a household's use of health care services, including women's prenatal care. The decrease in infant mortality was associated with both the utilization of health services by households and an increase in prenatal visits, indicating that participation contributed directly to use patterns that improved health outcomes.

Box 7.4　Participation in Maintenance in Nicaragua

The qualitative assessment in Nicaragua asked various groups—community members, the local government, and line ministry staff—how they perceived their own participation in the maintenance of social fund investments and the participation of other local agents. In almost every case each group had a higher opinion of its own participation than others did. In general, community participation received higher ratings by everyone than did participation by government entities.

Ratings of Participation in Maintenance of Social Fund Projects in Nicaragua (percentage of respondents)

Quality rated and type of respondent	Good	Average	Inadequate	None
Community participation in maintenance				
Community	55	21	6	19
Local government	33	23	7	37
Line ministry	23	13	16	48
Participation by local government in maintenance				
Community	14	8	7	71
Local government	43	37	3	17
Line ministry	19	12	4	65
Participation by Ministry of Health in maintenance				
Community	9	14	6	71
Local government	17	23	3	57
Line ministry	12	12	12	65
Participation by Ministry of Education in maintenance				
Community	14	9	2	76
Local government	13	17	3	67
Line ministry	23	12	1	64

Source: IDEAS (1998).

In Honduras consultation of beneficiaries increased the utilization rate for all types of projects—from 55 to 81 percent of households for latrines, from 78 to 99 percent for water systems, from 83 to 96 percent for health centers, from 70 to 87 percent for schools, and from 62 to 98 percent for sewerage. The effect of participation—not just consultation—was especially marked: in all cases more than 85 percent of the households that participated in executing a project used its services, and for most types of subprojects the share was close to 100 percent. Whether a household provided labor, money, or materials appeared to make little difference to utilization rates.

In a study of social fund projects carried out in Peru, community participation was associated with other aspects of project success. Multivariate regression analysis using indexes of success and participation for social fund projects found that higher levels of community participation were strongly associated with successful outcomes (see box 7.5). Other factors in project success included training in operation and maintenance (particularly important for water projects), a local project committee that is perceived as being of high quality, and the presence of other public sector institutions and community-based organizations. Project success was negatively correlated with remoteness and with the prevalence of non–Spanish speaking households, and poverty levels were not correlated with project success, either negatively or positively.

The size of the participation effect depended on community and project characteristics. Participation had a larger effect on project success in communities with lower indexes of poverty. In poorer communities participation had a smaller (though still positive) effect on project success. Participation was more effective in increasing project success when the stock of human capital in the community (as determined by the percentage of the adult population with primary schooling) was larger. The impact of participation on project success was greater in smaller communities; in larger, more populous communities, organizing and efficiently supervising community participation are much more challenging tasks. The type of project also matters. For example, participation is more effective in water and sanitation projects, which emphasize community training.

Implications

Social funds have sought to encourage consultation and participation, with varying degrees of intensity and success. The importance of these factors for the effectiveness and sustainability of investment projects suggests some lessons for future efforts:

- *Link project identification with a more formal participatory planning process.* Because of the scarcity of investment resources, particularly in poorer, more remote communities, social funds need to match investments to broad community demand, look for synergies between investments at the local level, and link these investments with the development strategies of local agents. All these needs point to the advantage of using participatory planning processes rather than more open, ad hoc arrangements for preparing and submitting project proposals.
- *Broaden community input in the project design phase.* Building consultation regarding design into the project cycle helps avoid the adoption of

Box 7.5 Participation and Determinants of Success in Social Fund Projects in Peru

The Peruvian research group Instituto Apoyo carried out multivariate regression analysis to determine what factors were associated with the success of social fund projects. It constructed indexes of success and participation using data from three ex post evaluations of completed social fund projects. The indexes of success and participation selected depended on the indicators available from each survey. The regression results are shown in the table.

Measures of success available from the surveys

- The project addresses the principal needs of the community.
- The project functions adequately.
- The project benefits the neediest in the community.
- The project benefits the entire community.
- No problems were reported during implementation.
- No delays occurred in construction.
- The project does not work/has minor problems/works well.

Measures of participation available from the surveys

- Presence of a community project committee.
- Whether the project committee was elected by a majority of the population.
- Number of people who participated in project selection.
- Number of people who participated in project implementation.

Regression Results: Determinants of Success for Social Fund Projects, Peru

	Data source[a]		
Explanatory variable	4	5	6
Participation			
General participation variable (not interacted)	0.499**	0.559*	—
Presence of project committee	—	—	0.510***
Number of people participating in selection and implementation	—	—	0.076*
Participation × education	0.028*	0.069*	1.119***
Participation × poverty	−0.515**	−0.664**	−0.553***
Participation × community size	—	—	−0.468***
Participation × water and sanitation project	1.839**	—	—

(Box continues on the following page.)

Box 7.5 (continued)

Training

Number of beneficiaries trained	0.593***	—	—
Responsible operator trained	—	—	1.377***
Existence of operations and maintenance manuals	—	—	0.756***

Management

Frequency of inspector visits	—	—	0.515***
Quality of community committee			0.712***

Community institutions and organizations

Number of public institutions present	—	0.893***	1.331*
Index of presence of community organizations	—	—	19.417***

* Significant at the 10 percent level.
** Significant at the 5 percent level.
*** Significant at the 1 percent level.
Note: The dependent variable is an index of project success (see box 7.5).
a Data sets from the fourth, fifth, and sixth ex post evaluations of the Peruvian social fund projects.
Source: Instituto Apoyo (2000a).

inappropriate technology. Technical proposals should be discussed in depth with local citizens to ensure that they incorporate local preferences on use, location, and other aspects of design.

- *Clarify expectations about participation by the community in project execution and in operation and maintenance.* Some social funds have clear rules on the type and level of counterpart contributions expected from communities, while others use more ad hoc procedures. Clear understandings about financial contributions and, more important, the role of community members in implementation and in operation and maintenance are critical to successful outcomes.
- *Increase community contributions where appropriate, given the changing purposes of social funds.* Social funds that originated as emergency mechanisms for generating employment tended to require little contribution from communities. As these funds shift to longer-term development objectives, they need to revisit their policies on community contributions. Clear and consistent cost sharing yields benefits beyond the ability to extend resources to more communities; it also leads to a greater sense of local ownership of investment projects and improves the projects' utilization and sustainability.

- *Conduct intensive organizing and training efforts in marginal communities.* Communities identified as having less potential for successful partici- pation—those with limited social and human capital—may need more concentrated organizing and training efforts. Social funds could finance such efforts as stand-alone investments in community capacity building or could build them into the identification and implementa- tion of projects.

8

Cost Analysis of Social Funds

THIS CHAPTER EXAMINES THE RELATIVE EFFICIENCY OF SOCIAL FUNDS compared with similar investment mechanisms, including NGOs, line ministries, and local governments. The review focuses on two aspects of cost-efficiency: unit costs of subprojects, and administrative expenses of the program as a whole. After discussing the methodological complications of this type of study, the chapter outlines the results of the assessment of unit costs, looking at the education, health, and water and sanitation sectors in turn. There is strong evidence that in all the countries studied, community management of resources and contracting tends to reduce unit costs, both in projects financed by social funds and in other programs. The findings show no consistent comparative cross-country advantage in efficiency for social funds, other central agencies, local governments, or NGOs; the results varied greatly by country, program, and sector of intervention.

Social funds typically had substantially lower overhead expenses than other agencies carrying out social investments—an advantage that can be attributed to their larger scale, lower fixed costs, and greater managerial capacity. Comparison of the implementation record of various agencies at the country level reveals generally efficient results from the social funds studied, with some evidence of longer execution periods when voluntary community labor is involved. Community contributions varied widely by sector and type of program, reflecting the absence of consistent national policies on cofinancing, and creating confusion and conflicting incentives for communities undertaking investments.

157

Research Focus

Many delivery mechanisms are available to countries for financing small-scale infrastructure, including social funds, line ministries, local governments, NGOs, and the private sector. The programs often differ in technical design, procurement systems, quality of materials, and approaches to community participation, and there may be variations between similar types of agencies. This chapter examines the relative efficiency of social funds versus comparator investment mechanisms in the six case study countries. For the purposes of this study, the efficiency analysis centers on comparative costs.

The review of efficiency focuses on two levels: (a) the unit costs of social fund investments at the subproject level, and (b) social funds' program efficiency, as measured by overhead and process efficiency. The following questions form the core of the assessment of the efficiency of social funds:

- How do the unit costs of social fund investments compare with investments in similar infrastructure by other agencies?
- What is the general level of overhead or administrative costs associated with carrying out a given investment, and how do the overhead costs of social funds compare with those of other agencies?
- How efficient is the implementation process in terms of duration of execution?
- To what extent do social funds and other social infrastructure programs leverage local resources in the form of community contributions?

Several approaches were used to measure the unit costs of investments, and some country case studies employed more than one methodology. One approach, used in Bolivia and Honduras, is to analyze average unit costs across the portfolio of a given program on the basis of data extracted from management information systems. Systematic data on the whole portfolio of investments were typically available only for social funds. Another approach, applied in Bolivia and Zambia, is to compare the estimated costs of the standard infrastructure designs used by different programs. This method helps control for some of the variance among types of investment in the same sector but may only apply to a small range of the total investments carried out by programs. Yet another approach, employed in Nicaragua and Peru, is to isolate a smaller universe of actual investments that appear to be similar in scope and scale and carry out a case study analysis of these investments, with site visits to observe quality and functionality issues.

Complications and Caveats

There are inherent difficulties in reaching precise conclusions about comparative unit costs across programs within the same country, much less between countries. The researchers could not fully overcome many of these problems, although they attempted either to achieve greater comparability or, where this was not possible, to explain clearly why not. The findings should therefore be treated as indicative, rather than conclusive, and as illustrating general tendencies.[1] The difficulties encountered highlight the need for better program accounting of costs.

In most cases, identifying valid comparator programs proved extremely difficult. This problem was particularly acute in Bolivia, Honduras, and Nicaragua, where the social investment funds undertake most of the community- and primary-level sector investments in basic health and education infrastructure. Even where other programs could be identified, their particular traits often reduced their applicability as comparators. For example, most social funds are national in scope and include both urban and rural areas, while most NGO and local government comparators have a regional focus. These differences directly influence unit and overhead costs.

This type of analysis suffers from a classic problem involving the noncomparability of specific investments. For example, one agency's "standard" primary school construction project may include desks, blackboards, sanitary facilities, and investments in outdoor play spaces, retaining walls, and the like, while another agency's investment may cover only basic classroom construction. Similarly, "rural water systems" embrace a variety of technologies—pump based and gravity fed, house connections and public standpipes, and so on—as well as different volumes of service, confounding unit cost comparisons. In addition, costs for the same type of investment may vary greatly by location. For example, in Nicaragua the transport costs of materials increased total costs within the same region by 5 to 80 percent, depending on location (Araujo, Hurtado, and Lema 2000).

Unit costs vary both by agency and among investments by the same agency. Even where the same program carried out similar investments, large variations in unit costs occur.[2] These variations arise from differences in, for example, location, materials used, intensity of use (number of beneficiaries),

---

[1] The caveat is particularly applicable to the results for Honduras, which should be treated as only preliminary and suggestive.

[2] The coefficient of variation (the standard deviation between unit costs among projects in the same sector compared with the average cost) of the cost per beneficiary in the Bolivia social fund ranges from 0.48 for multigrade schools to 1.96 for health projects. In Honduras cost per beneficiary for preschool construction projects ranges from a low of $353 to a high of $1,199, with similar wide variations for the other types of investment financed by the social fund.

complexity, and number of subcomponents within an investment. Given these variances, extrapolating average unit costs from a small number of actual projects reviewed, as much of the cost analysis fieldwork did, can be misleading.

There is no standard practice for classifying or valuing expenditures, either between programs within the same country or between countries. Only some of the programs studied account for the full value of community contributions, including donated materials and labor. Similarly, some programs consider supervision costs part of investment costs, while others classify them as an administrative cost or do not record them at all. Finally, some implementing agencies face national value-added taxes, while others, such as NGOs, may enjoy exemptions that artificially lower their unit costs.

Reliable information was often not available. Social funds consistently kept more accessible and more complete information than the other programs studied. Comparator programs, within both central ministries and NGOs, carried out very little systematic archiving of cost information. They often could not provide data on community contributions, number of beneficiaries, and changes in costs during construction. Several donor-financed programs also had this problem. Many programs, especially NGOs, did not report administrative and overhead cost information.

Even when researchers can address comparability and data problems, the results may be prone to misinterpretation. Lower unit costs do not necessarily translate into more efficient investments, particularly when builders use substandard designs and materials, reducing the expected lifetime of an investment. Higher unit costs may be "better" if they result in longer amortization periods for investments and better quality of services provided by the infrastructure itself. Unfortunately, the data in this study do not allow for full life-cycle cost analysis.

Comparators

The comparator programs selected varied by country and type of project. In general, the research included relatively few NGO comparators. The reasons for this include the less than national scope of most NGO programs, the smaller scale of most NGO investments (rehabilitation, rather than new infrastructure), and, in many cases, the unavailability of information on the unit costs of NGO investments. Only in Honduras and Nicaragua could local government be included. In Armenia, Peru, and Zambia local governments have few resources and rarely invest in the sectors represented. In Bolivia, although municipal investments in social infrastructure are substantial, they are typically cofinanced by the social fund and hence are not usable as comparators. Central agencies were included in Armenia, Honduras, Nicaragua, Peru, and Zambia. Table 8.1 presents a full listing of the social fund programs and comparators studied. In some instances the social fund was active in a

Table 8.1 Glossary of Social Funds and Comparator Programs Used in the Cost Analysis

Name of program	Classification	Sectors analyzed
Armenia		
Social Investment Fund (ASIF)	Social fund	Education, water
Ministry of Education	Central agency	Education
All Armenia Fund (AAF)	NGO	Education
Save the Children	NGO	Education, water
Oxfam	NGO	Water
Bolivia		
Social Investment Fund (FIS)	Social fund	Education, water[a]
Plan International– Altiplano (PIA)	NGO	Education
Honduras		
Honduran Social Investment Fund (FHIS)	Social fund	Education, health, water and sanitation
Ministry of Education	Central agency	Education
Ministry of Health	Central agency	Health
National Water and Sanitation Agency (SANAA)	Central agency	Water
Municipal Water Division of San Pedro Sula (DIMA)	Local government	Sanitation
San Pedro Sula	Local government	Education
Puerto Cortes	Local government	Education, water
Progreso	Local government	Sanitation
Villanueva	Local government	Education, sanitation
Plan International	NGO	Water
Nicaragua		
Emergency Social Investment Fund (FISE)	Social fund	Education, health, water and sanitation
Ministry of Education (Aprende)	Central agency	Education
National Water and Sanitation Corporation (Enacal)	Central agency	Water and sanitation
Protierra	Local government	Education, health, water
Program for Local Development (Prodel)	Local government	Education, water and sanitation

(Table continues on the following page.)

Table 8.1 (continued)

Name of program	Classification	Sectors analyzed
CARE	NGO	Water and sanitation
Doctors without Borders	NGO	Health, water and sanitation
Peru		
National Fund for Compensation and Social Development (FONCODES)	Social fund	Education, health, water and sanitation
National Institute of Health and Education Infrastructure (INFES)	Central agency	Education, health
CARE	NGO	Water and sanitation
Zambia		
Social Recovery Program/Micro Projects Unit (SRP/MPU)	Social fund	Education
Ministry of Education, Education Sector Support Program (ESSP); supported by FINNIDA	Central agency	Education
Ministry of Education, Basic Education Support Program (BESP); supported by Irish Aid	Central agency	Education
Ministry of Education, School Improvement Program; supported by JICA	Central agency	Education
Ministry of Education, Zambia Education Project Implementation Unit (ZEPIU); supported by AfDB and OPEC	Central agency	Education

particular sector but no valid comparator programs could be found, as was the case with health infrastructure investments in Bolivia.

Education

The education projects of the social funds in Armenia, Peru, and Zambia had consistently lower unit costs than for other investment mechanisms in those countries, whether central agencies or NGOs (table 8.2). In Bolivia, Honduras,

Table 8.2 Unit Costs in School Infrastructure Projects (index: social fund unit costs = 1.00)

Country, type of project, and implementing agency	Cost per student	Cost per square meter
Armenia		
New construction of schools		
Social fund	1.00	1.00
Central agency (Ministry of Education)	1.56	3.76
NGO (All Armenia Fund)	0.91	2.97
Bolivia		
New construction		
Social fund	—	1.00
NGO (Plan International–Altiplano)	—	0.90
Honduras		
Mix of new construction and rehabilitation		
Social fund	1.00	1.00
Central agency (Ministry of Education)	1.20	0.74
Local governments	0.46–0.76	0.36–0.71
Nicaragua		
New construction of rural schools[a]		
Social fund	1.00	1.00
Central agency (Aprende)	0.73	0.69
Local government (Protierra)	0.24	0.57
New construction of urban schools[a]		
Social fund	1.00	1.00
Central agency (Aprende)	0.66	0.64
Local government (Prodel)	0.42	0.83
New construction of classrooms[b]		
Social fund	—	1.00
Central agency (Aprende)	—	0.74
Local government (Protierra)	—	0.80
Peru		
New construction		
Social fund	1.00	1.00
Central agency (INFES)	1.41	1.65
Zambia		
New construction of 1 × 2 classroom blocks		
Social fund	—	1.00
Central agency (Ministry of Education, ZEPIU/OPSUP)	—	1.11
Central agency (Ministry of Education, ESSP)	—	1.11

(Table continues on the following page.)

Table 8.2 (continued)

Country, type of project, and implementing agency	Cost per student	Cost per square meter
Central agency (Ministry of Education, ZEPIU) (AfDB)	—	2.09
Central agency (Ministry of Education, ZEPIU) (JICA)	—	3.02
Central agency (Ministry of Education, BESP)	—	1.09

Note: For definitions of program abbreviations, see table 8.1.
[a] Data are from GB Consultores (2000).
[b] Revised data from Araujo, Hurtado, and Lema (2000).
Source: For data sources and years, see chapter 2, table 2.3.

and Nicaragua the social fund's construction projects in education cost more than comparators', although only slightly so in Bolivia. These findings are from a unit cost analysis that included both new construction and rehabilitation of primary schools. Given the large variation in rehabilitation projects, new construction provides better comparisons.

The Armenian social fund's cost per square meter of new construction was only about a quarter of the cost for the Ministry of Education and only a third that for an NGO, the All Armenia Foundation (AAF). Even though the social fund's cost per square meter was significantly lower than the AAF's, costs per beneficiary were similar because the AAF concentrates on urban areas, where enrollments are larger. Design goals also differ. Whereas the AAF pays greater attention to comfort and exterior features and emphasizes superior design quality, the social fund prizes functionality and modest designs, since it has been seeking to rebuild basic community infrastructure at the lowest cost.

Schools built by social funds in Nicaragua (left) and in Peru (right).

In Bolivia the difference between the social fund's cost per square meter of school construction and that of the NGO comparator program, Plan International–Altiplano (PIA), was quite small, but the social fund's cost was 11 percent higher. Both agencies used similar classroom designs, although the PIA's slightly larger classrooms raised its costs by about 2 percent. The PIA paid less for construction materials but tended to use them more intensively. What had the greatest effect on unit costs was the contracting approach. Other things being equal, the social fund's delegation of construction to contractors raised average costs by about 25 percent more than the PIA's self-help approach.

In Honduras the unit costs of school construction varied widely. The social fund projects cost about 20 percent more per square meter of construction than Ministry of Education projects but 20 percent less per student. The social fund unit costs were higher than those of all the municipal governments examined, but the investments were generally not comparable, since municipal governments tended to carry out minor repairs and extensions rather than construct new schools. Moreover, the local governments' reporting of costs may not have completely incorporated community contributions and the use of municipal staff.

In Nicaragua, despite the comparability problems, researchers concluded that the social fund generally tended to have higher unit costs than its counterparts. This difference initially appeared to result from the social fund's construction of more complete schools, with new latrines and play areas, exterior lighting, and water supply. But even when the cost of a basic classroom was estimated, the social fund's costs averaged about 30 percent higher than those of the community-based construction program carried out through the Ministry of Education (Aprende) or the municipal development program, Protierra. The most significant difference among the programs is in the contracting approach employed. The social fund contracts civil works through private firms, and Protierra works directly with local governments. Aprende provides funds to school-level parents' associations to manage the civil works. Moreover, the social fund had the highest preinvestment and supervision costs.[3]

In Peru the social fund's unit costs were significantly lower than those of the other major national school infrastructure program, INFES. The difference was attributable in part to the social fund's focus on rural areas, where low-cost adobe can be used as the primary building material—although higher transport costs for other materials slightly erode this cost advantage.

---

[3] To the extent possible, the analysis incorporates counterpart contributions. The higher costs of the social fund are partly attributable to its higher preinvestment and supervision costs. As in some of the other case studies, this difference may reflect an underreporting of such costs by the other agencies, since time expended by Ministry of Education and local government technical staff is not fully captured.

Another factor was that INFES used private contractors, whose profits represented 6 percent of costs, while in the social fund projects community groups managed the civil works contracts. Furthermore, INFES schools included workshops and laboratories. Although the INFES schools are in urban areas and thus serve large populations, their larger enrollments did not fully offset the higher cost per square meter. Cost per student remained about 40 percent higher than in the social fund's rural investments.

In Zambia the social fund had the lowest unit costs of any national school construction program. The Zambian case presents the best conditions for comparison because several programs employ roughly similar designs in building infrastructure. In addition to the social fund, two other community-based programs, operated through the Ministry of Education with bilateral financing, use community self-help arrangements in which community groups or parents' associations manage the construction. These three programs had similar unit costs, with the costs of Ministry of Education programs slightly higher than those of the social fund. Compared with the community-based approach, contractor-based investments cost about twice as much for classrooms and more than three times as much for latrines (table 8.3).

The higher unit costs for the contractor-based approach were attributable to several factors. Higher standards accounted for about 40 percent of the difference, broken down as follows: small design modifications, 5–10 percent; higher specifications for building materials, 10 percent; inclusion of electricity and more external works, 5–10 percent; and higher standards of workmanship on finishing work, 10 percent. The other 60 percent was attributable to contractor overhead costs and profits and may indicate uncompetitive bidding.[4] Beneficiaries considered the quality of construction in all the programs

Table 8.3 Costs of Different Approaches to Constructing School Infrastructure, Zambia (U.S. dollars)

Infrastructure	Community self-help[a] Average cost	Cost per square meter	Tendering to contractors Average cost	Cost per square meter
1 × 2 classroom block	18,500	133	45,300	317
1 × 3 classroom block	26,500	124	64,800	285
Three-bed staff house	13,400	188	32,100	394
Ventilated improved pit (VIP) latrine	1,800	—	6,000	—

— Not available.
[a] Refers to the social fund and two Ministry of Education programs: the Education Sector Support Program (ESSP) and the Zambia Education Project Implementation Unit (ZEPIU). The cost data include community counterpart contributions valued at 25 percent for the social fund.
Source: Dowdall (2000).

Table 8.4 Unit Costs in Health Center Investment Projects
(index: social fund unit costs = 1.00)

Country and implementing program	Cost per beneficiary	Cost per square meter
Honduras		
Retaining walls		
Social fund	—	1.00
Ministry of Health	—	2.05
Sanitary facilities		
Social fund	—	1.00
Ministry of Health	—	0.81
Nicaragua		
Health center		
Social fund	1.00	1.00
Local government (Protierra)	0.30–0.83	0.48–0.77
NGO (Doctors without Borders)	0.18–0.50	0.42–0.68
Peru		
Health center		
Social fund	1.00	—
Central agency (INFES)	2.95	—

— Not available.
Note: For definitions of program abbreviations, see table 8.1.
Source: For data sources and years, see chapter 2, table 2.3.

acceptable, although some projects used lower-quality materials and some of the finishing work in the community-based programs could be improved.[5]

Health

A comparative cost analysis of health center investments in Honduras, Nicaragua, and Peru revealed no clear pattern of comparative advantage among agencies. In Nicaragua the social fund had significantly higher unit costs than comparators (table 8.4). Much of the difference can be explained by the social fund's more complete investments, which included electrical installations, furniture and equipment, drainage ditches, and higher-quality materials. A local government project, implemented by Protierra, included

---

[4] Dowdall (2000) estimates that this 60 percent could be reduced to 25–30 percent (the normal margin for the eastern and southern African construction market), depending on the volume of work tendered, the state of the tender market, and whether the tender takes place nationally, regionally, or internationally.

[5] A separate "value for money" audit rated the quality of workmanship on the social fund schools as follows: very good—9 percent of the projects visited; good—45 percent; satisfactory—18 percent; and fair—27 percent; no projects were rated poor or bad (ASCO Consulting 1998).

neither water nor electric power installations in the health center. In addition, the local government and NGO programs may have underreported total project costs by discounting the required community contributions, which account for only 1 percent of their reported costs, compared with the social fund average of 10 percent. The social fund's higher costs also reflect cost escalation during construction and overestimation of the number of beneficiaries at appraisal. The costs reported are based on actual beneficiary usage.

In Honduras comparable data were limited to components of health center construction projects. The social fund unit costs for constructing retaining walls were about half those of the Ministry of Health, while its unit costs for constructing sanitary facilities were roughly 20 percent higher.

In Peru's health sector, as in its education sector, the social fund incurred substantially lower unit costs than the other central social infrastructure agency, INFES. Again, much of the reason seemed to be differences in construction materials stemming from the differences in the programs' areas of focus, with INFES using bricks in its urban projects and the social fund using primarily adobe in its rural projects. Just as for schools, the larger populations served by INFES urban health centers did not translate into lower costs per beneficiary: INFES investments in health centers cost almost three times as much per beneficiary as did those of the social fund.

Water and Sanitation

This section discusses water systems and then sewerage and latrines.

Water Supply Systems

Water investments vary greatly in technology and design (and therefore costs)—from gravity-fed systems to those using electric pumps, and from public standpipes to urban household connections. They range in complexity from small-scale rural systems to large-scale urban systems serving both residential and commercial customers. This variety makes comparing the costs of programs particularly challenging. The unit cost analysis in the water sector covered urban and rural systems in Armenia, Honduras, and Nicaragua and rural systems in Peru.

In Armenia and Peru the social fund's unit costs for water investments were similar to those of NGOs, the only comparator programs in the analysis (table 8.5). In Honduras and Nicaragua the social fund's unit costs tended to be higher than those of most other investment mechanisms.

In water projects in Armenia the social fund had slightly higher costs per linear meter than the two NGOs because it undertook more extensive works and because of differences in tax treatment. The social fund rehabilitates

Table 8.5 Unit Costs in Water Infrastructure Projects
(index: social fund unit costs = 1.00)

Country and implementing program	Cost per beneficiary	Cost per linear meter (pipe connection)	Cost per daily amount of water[a]
Armenia			
Social fund			
Urban projects	0.43	0.81	0.33
Rural projects	1.00	1.00	1.00
NGO (Save the Children)	0.83	0.69	1.00
NGO (Oxfam)	1.07	0.85	—
Honduras			
Domestic connection system			
Social fund	1.00	1.00	—
Central agency (DIMA)	0.12	3.04	—
Central agency (SANAA)	0.56	0.31	—
Central agency (SANAA) (UNICEF)	0.99	0.39	—
Local government (Puerto Cortes)	0.19	0.42	—
Local government (Villanueva)	0.47	0.87	—
NGO (Plan International)	—	0.30	—
Nicaragua			
Social fund	1.00	1.00	1.00
Central agency (Enacal) (CARE)	0.32	0.12	0.46
Local government (Protierra)	0.11	0.17	0.42
Local government (Prodel)	0.26	0.51	0.53
NGO (Doctors without Borders)	0.61	0.42	1.16
NGO (CARE)	0.39	0.03	0.23
Distribution line			
Social fund	—	1.00	—
Local government (Prodel)	—	0.57	—
Peru			
Water system			
Social fund	1.00	1.00	—
NGO (CARE)	1.05	1.69	—
Training			
Social fund	1.00	n.a.	n.a.
NGO (CARE)	4.73	n.a.	n.a.

— Not available.
n.a. Not applicable.
Note: UNICEF, United Nation's Children's Fund. For definitions of program abbreviations, see table 8.1.
[a] Water unit varies among countries.
Source: For data sources and years, see chapter 2, table 2.3.

networks as a whole, including collection systems and reservoirs, while the NGOs finance relatively inexpensive rehabilitation works, mainly for pipes. In addition, whereas the social fund pays social benefits and income taxes through its contracts with small construction firms, NGOs receive preferential tax treatment. But the social fund's systems tend to deliver a larger daily amount of water than comparators and to reach more people, making its unit costs for water supply and per beneficiary competitive with those of the NGOs.

In Honduras comparisons were complicated by the variation in the scale of investments. The social fund's investments, averaging $95,270 per project, were about three times those of most of the other programs. These large investments may reflect greater complexity, which could help explain the social fund's higher unit costs. But variations in scale, design, and complexity account for only part of the difference. The social fund's water projects experienced significant cost increases during construction, with final costs averaging about 20 percent more than the appraised costs.

In Nicaragua several factors may explain the higher unit costs for the social fund's water projects compared with those carried out by the national water authority, by local governments, and by NGOs. The social fund tended to finance bigger systems, and its projects typically included well drilling, an expense not incurred by comparators. Some comparator programs, such as the local government program Prodel, saved on costs by using lower-quality materials. Comparators also reduced costs by relying on municipal staff or community self-help for administration, eliminating contractor profits.

In Peru the social fund and CARE, an NGO, had similar unit costs for construction of water systems, but CARE invested significantly more in training. Both programs work directly with community groups rather than contract with the private sector. In a UNDP–World Bank study of the costs of constructing new rural water systems in three Andean countries, the social funds had lower unit costs than most other implementing agencies (box 8.1).

Sewerage and Latrines

In the sewerage sector the social fund's unit costs were competitive in both Honduras and Nicaragua (table 8.6). In latrine projects in Nicaragua and Peru unit costs were similar across all programs.

In Honduras the cost of the social fund's investments in sewerage—both by linear meter and by beneficiary—fell within the range of costs in other programs. The two local government programs tended to have higher construction costs per meter but were able to bring their costs per beneficiary into line with those of the social fund because they served more concentrated populations.

Box 8.1 Costs of Rural Water Systems in Three Andean Countries

A 1999 United Nations Development Programme (UNDP)–World Bank study reviewed 143 rural water projects carried out by 12 implementing agencies in Bolivia, Ecuador, and Peru. In each country the review looked at the social fund and government and nongovernmental agencies. In all three countries the social fund's cost per capita was well below the national average. In Ecuador and Peru the social fund was the lowest-cost investment channel, while in Bolivia only the United Nations Children's Fund (UNICEF) had lower unit costs among the four programs that were compared (UNDP–World Bank 1999).

Per Capita Costs of Water Investments in Rural Andean Communities (U.S. dollars)

	Bolivia	Ecuador	Peru
National average	97.70	150.70	56.70
Social fund	84.50	112.90	44.40

Table 8.6 Unit Costs in Sanitation Projects (index: social fund unit costs = 1.00)

	Sewerage		Latrines	
Country and implementing program	Cost per beneficiary	Cost per meter	Cost per beneficiary	Cost per latrine
Honduras				
Social fund	1.00	1.00[a]	—	—
Central agency (DIMA)	0.70	0.84	—	—
Local government (Progreso)	1.01	1.45	—	—
Local government (Villanueva)	0.90	1.13	—	—
Nicaragua				
Social fund	1.00	1.00	1.00	1.00
Central agency (Enacal)	5.47–6.50	5.42–6.42	—	—
Local government (Prodel)	1.00	1.00	2.27	1.02
NGO (Doctors without Borders)	—	—	0.63	0.72
Peru				
Social fund	—	—	—	1.00
NGO (CARE)	—	—	—	1.14

— Not available.
Note: For definitions of program abbreviations, see table 8.1.
[a] Appraised cost.
Source: For data sources and years, see chapter 2, table 2.3.

In Nicaragua the national sanitation agency, Enacal, undertook investments in sewerage costing six times as much as investments by the social fund and a local government program. But whereas Enacal built new systems that included water treatment plants, the social fund and the local government program focused on expanding existing networks. The latter two programs had similar unit costs for investments in both sewerage and latrines. The NGO program's investments in latrines appeared to cost about 25 percent less than the social fund's, but researchers could not determine whether the program fully accounted for community contributions.

Program Efficiency

In addition to unit costs, the study looked at three measures of efficiency at the program level: overhead expenditures, speed of execution, and leveraging of community resources.

Overhead Expenditures

The cost of an investment project consists of direct investment expenses and the administrative expenses incurred in running the program. The administrative, or overhead, expenses such as—personnel, consulting and other services, equipment, transport, rent, utilities, supplies, and communications—can be significant for overall investment efficiency.

Comparing these expenses across programs is difficult because of the different terminologies and systems used in classifying administrative costs (also called overhead or operational costs—the terms are used interchangeably here). For example, some programs include preinvestment and supervision costs in a project's investment cost, while others treat them as administrative costs of the program. Most programs that spend significant resources on community outreach and capacity-building activities consider these activities to be investments in long-term capacity, but others charge them as overhead. In addition, programs run by NGOs, local governments, and line ministries rarely provide full reporting of administrative costs. Especially likely to be omitted is the work of existing administrative and technical staff. Furthermore, no programs in which community groups manage investments impute volunteer time to overhead expenses. Although the study took these differences into account as much as possible, because of the lack of accounting norms and the incomplete reporting, the data on overhead expenses should be considered only indicative.

Social funds' overhead expenses were similar among countries, falling within a range of 7–13 percent of total program costs (table 8.7). The Peruvian social fund had the lowest overhead costs, mainly because of its

Table 8.7 Annual Overhead Expenditures as a Share of Total Program Cost, by Type of Implementing Program (percent)

Country	Social fund	Central government		Local government	
Armenia	10	—		—	
Bolivia	12	20[a]	(FDC)		
Honduras	13	22	(Ministry of Education)	31	(Puerto Cortes)
		22	(Ministry of Health)	31	(San Pedro Sula)
		8	(DIMA)	9	(Villanueva)
		15	(SANAA)	9	(Progreso)
Nicaragua	10	5	(Aprende)	48	(Prodel)
				20	(Protierra)
Peru	7	23	(INFES)	—	
		17[b]	(Pronamachs)		

— Not available.

Note: Information on nongovernmental organizations was not available. In Armenia overhead costs for other agencies were not investigated. For Zambia, where the social fund is also responsible for implementation of a national poverty monitoring component, including technical assistance and support to the national household survey, overhead costs for the social fund alone could not be estimated. For definitions of program abbreviations, see table 8.1.

[a] Fondo de Desarrollo Campesino, a rural investment fund.

[b] Assumes a 51 percent community counterpart contribution toward investment costs. In the sample of projects, however, actual community contributions averaged only 13 percent of costs. If this were true across the portfolio, Pronamachs's overhead would rise to 27 percent.

Source: For data sources and years, see chapter 2, table 2.3.

large size and its public sector salaries. In most of the countries the social fund had lower overhead expenses than other programs. In Nicaragua there were two noteworthy exceptions because of differences in accounting and program design.[6] (1) Aprende, a Ministry of Education school construction program, had overhead costs of only about 5 percent because it disburses funds for school construction directly to parents' committees. The committees perform many administrative tasks that are not charged to the program. Other administrative functions are carried out by Ministry of Education staff. (2) Sanitation agencies in Nicaragua also had lower overhead costs as a result of their focus on larger investments.

Most programs working through local governments had significantly higher overhead costs than did social funds, in some cases well over 40 percent. There are two main reasons for this. First, decentralization of program administration adds costs, particularly where investment volumes are relatively small. Second, several of the local governments analyzed had

---

[6] Information on NGOs' overhead expenses is generally not available in any of the countries where these expenses were analyzed. In Peru one NGO was able to provide overhead costs but not total program costs.

relatively high fixed costs because the availability of investment funds varies from year to year but permanent staff remain on the payroll. As a result, in years with low investment, overhead costs represent a large share of total investment costs.

Speed of Execution

The speed with which investments are executed directly affects a program's administrative costs. Within the universe of donor-financed investment projects, social funds have a reputation for fast disbursement. This speed is possible largely because the funds finance many small-scale investments using streamlined (usually, community-based) procurement arrangements. By contrast, the typical investment project focuses on larger-scale works, each of which may take a year or more to contract through international competitive bidding.

Comparison of the implementation records of different agencies within countries points to generally efficient results for the social funds, with some evidence that execution took longer where voluntary community labor was involved:

- In Armenia the social fund completed its investments in schools much faster than did the Ministry of Education and in about the same time as did the NGO programs.
- In Bolivia the social fund's school construction projects took about three to four months to implement. The contracting process, which relies on national competitive bidding, took an additional three to four months. No information was available on comparators.
- In Honduras the social fund's school construction projects took 6 months from approval to completion, while its health, water, and latrine projects took 7 months. The average waiting period between submission and approval of a project proposal, however, was 8–12 months, indicating bottlenecks at the entry point. Again, no information was available on comparators.
- In Nicaragua the elapsed time between submission and approval of a proposal for a social fund project averaged about 7.5 months, and the selection of contractors, using a lottery system, averaged about 3 months. Execution ranged from about 5 months for latrines and 6.5 months for schools to 16 months for water supply and included significant delays. The large difference in the scale of investment by social funds and comparator programs clouds comparisons of execution times.
- In Peru execution times were not analyzed, but researchers observed that the productivity of voluntary, unpaid labor is lower than that of

paid workers. Programs like the social fund that rely on community contributions of labor can suffer more delays in execution of civil works.

- In Zambia school construction projects using community-driven approaches took two to three times as long to execute as did projects using contractor-based approaches. Those financed by the social fund typically took 15–18 months, the time deemed necessary to allow the community to assume the responsibility for managing the investment. Community-based investments by other programs took longer, from two to six years.

Leveraging of Community Resources

Local contributions to investment costs can stretch the scarce resources provided by the center. They typically consist of cash or in-kind contributions from beneficiary communities (the latter usually in the form of donated labor and materials) or of cofinancing by local governments. Some social funds have relatively fixed policies regarding community contributions. For example, the Zambian social fund expects communities to contribute at least 20–25 percent of project costs, much of it before the first disbursement from the social fund. Following Bolivia's fiscal decentralization in 1994–95, which transferred the mandate and resources for providing social infrastructure to the local level, the social fund established fixed cofinancing shares for municipal governments. The social funds in Honduras, Nicaragua, and Peru encourage community contributions but do not set lower limits.

Local counterpart contributions varied greatly among the social funds, from less than 10 percent of project costs to 35 percent (table 8.8). Bolivia had the largest share of local cofinancing, at 35 percent, up from an average of about 18 percent in the three years preceding fiscal decentralization (Ortuno 1998). The 25 percent requirement in Zambia represents a substantial local effort, particularly since all the financing comes directly from community members. In Peru the level varied by type of project, with the largest contributions in projects using more unskilled labor, such as irrigation.

Differences in policies relating to the payment of unskilled labor explain some of the differences in community contributions. Labor is the main way that communities provide cofinancing. For social funds such as that in Nicaragua, requiring contributions of labor would have undercut the initial objective of generating emergency employment. In Zambia voluntary community contribution of labor plays an important part in building local ownership of investments, an explicit development objective.

In Nicaragua, Peru, and Zambia local contributions varied widely among sectors and programs, reflecting a lack of consistent national policies on cofinancing and creating the risk of confusion and of conflicting incentives for

Table 8.8 Local Contributions as a Share of Direct Costs in Social Fund Projects (percent)

Country and sector	Share of investment cost
Armenia	10
Bolivia	35
Nicaragua	
Education	4
Health	8
Water	6
Sewerage	8
Latrines	6
Peru	
Education	3
Health	1
Water	4
Irrigation	10
Zambia	25

Note: For Nicaragua and Peru, the shares are averages for samples of projects and may not be representative of the social fund portfolios.
Source: For data sources and years, see chapter 2, table 2.3.

communities undertaking investments. In Nicaragua and Peru the social funds raised little community contribution to investments (table 8.9). Other programs did better, but some had no community contributions. Local government programs in Nicaragua consistently had higher levels of cost sharing. In Peru the central agency, INFES, leveraged little for health and education investments, while for water projects the comparator NGO program raised a third of the investment costs from communities. In Zambia community-based programs in education, including the social fund, raised an average of 20 percent in local support, whereas the contractor-based programs raised none.

Implications

As the data show, in many cases social funds' reputation for efficiency rests more on speed of delivery and low program overheads than on lower unit costs of investments. Among the sample countries, social funds in Armenia, Peru, and Zambia had consistently lower unit costs, while those in Honduras and Nicaragua sometimes had higher unit costs of construction.

The study identified some measures that would help improve the efficiency of basic social investments:

Develop common guidelines on factors affecting the efficiency of investments. There appears to be little exchange of information on unit costs and

Table 8.9 Local Contributions as a Share of Direct Costs in Social Fund and Other Projects, Nicaragua and Peru (percent)

| Sector | Nicaragua | | Peru | |
	Implementing program	Share	Implementing program	Share
Education	Social fund	4	Social fund	3
	Central agency (Aprende)	4	Central agency (INFES)	0
	Local government (Prodel)	48		
	Local government (Protierra)	4		
Health	Social fund	8	Social fund	I
	Local government (Protierra)	I	Central agency (INFES)	0
	NGO (Doctors without Borders)	0		
Water	Social fund	6	Social fund	4
	Central agency (Enacal)	38	NGO (CARE)	34
	Local government (Prodel)	39		
	Local government (Protierra)	16		
	NGO (Doctors without Borders)	0		
	NGO (CARE)	20		
Sewerage	Social fund	8		
	Central agency (Enacal)	0		
	Local government (Prodel)	22		
Latrines	Social fund	6		
	Local government (Prodel)	29		
	NGO (Doctors without Borders)	26		
	NGO (CARE)	23		
	Central agency (Enacal)	13		

Note: The shares are averages for samples of projects and may not be representative of the social fund portfolios. For definitions of program abbreviations, see table 8.1.
Source: For data sources and years, see chapter 2, table 2.3.

investment approaches among agencies operating in the same sector within a country. Common guidelines covering such issues as the components to be included in a particular investment, the minimum quality of materials, and the maximum cost per beneficiary would help address the wide variation among programs that now results in different standards for service.

Group similar investments under common programs to save on administrative costs. Grouping similar investments would reduce the inefficiencies observed in cases where many programs under one agency financed the same type of investment, but under different rules. In Zambia, for example, the Ministry of Education has a number of programs for education infrastructure, financed by different donors and implemented through different project management units.

Experiment with locating more control over investments at the community level. Community management of investments offers significant potential for cost savings, often on the order of 25–50 percent.

Introduce more transparent accounting of programs' investment and overhead costs. Among the most surprising findings was the poor quality or unavailability of information on investment costs and overhead expenditures. The lack of consistent, reliable information makes it difficult for governments to choose least-cost strategies for investment projects. Standard accounting nomenclature and routine reporting to central authorities would improve the transparency of the investment process.

Establish a consistent national policy on community contributions. To make rational investment decisions, communities need to face a consistent set of explicit prices. If one program requires no counterpart contribution while another requires significant inputs, that may skew the community's choice of investment. Moreover, although not requiring a counterpart contribution may be consistent with the income objectives of emergency programs, it should be reconsidered for long-range development efforts. Counterpart contributions can help develop community ownership of projects and ensure that local investments match community priorities.

9

Conclusions

THE LESSONS FROM THIS CROSS-COUNTRY STUDY are useful for informing the future design and implementation of social funds and other community-led programs, impact evaluations, and development policy. This chapter reviews key design issues for social funds that could improve poverty targeting, heighten impacts, enhance sustainability, and improve the cost-efficiency of social funds and similar community-based programs. Lessons for future impact evaluations point to the need for robust methodologies and approaches, a blend of quantitative and qualitative analysis, and the expansion of evaluation research across a broader range of development interventions. The chapter concludes with a summary of the implications for social funds within broader national poverty reduction strategies.

General Findings

The study found that social funds have met the broad objectives they were designed to address. In general, the quality of social infrastructure and the level of service provision have improved as a result of the social fund interventions, leaving social fund facilities typically better off than comparator facilities. Access to and utilization of basic services have increased. The investments have translated into tangible improvements in welfare, although the degree and type of the impacts vary among countries and sectors. Social funds do reach the poor, and the poorest of the poor, at both the geographic and the household levels. Although household targeting has been only moderately progressive, some of the poverty-disaggregated data point to larger impacts among the poorer groups. The analysis further shows that community-level investments reflect expressed local priorities.

The study results point to areas where improvements are needed. Some sectoral investments appear particularly problematic. Sewerage investments have tended to benefit better-off populations; they have not shown significant health benefits; and they were viewed as less of a priority in the communities where the investments were financed. Operation and maintenance of rural water systems remain a sectorwide challenge, as the existing administrative service systems, whether financed through social funds or through comparators, are generally unable to raise sufficient local resources through fees to ensure the sustainability of the initial investment. National health strategies have not ensured a reliable supply of essential medicines for health clinics (although improved health impacts were detected even in centers without a full complement of supplies). Infrastructure investments in schools appear to have an enrollment impact only when urban and peri-urban investments are included, raising questions about how to develop effective strategies for remedying lagging enrollment rates in rural areas. In addition, the nonpoor constitute a substantial portion of beneficiaries, and this outcome highlights the policy challenge of how to establish realistic expectations about targeting performance, given the inherent limitations of programs that primarily provide public goods through community infrastructure and services that do not restrict access by individual households.

The social fund model that began as an experiment in Bolivia a little over a decade ago has proved to be a dynamic, replicable approach to community-led development. This study does not provide definitive evidence that social funds are the best way of achieving selected development outcomes, but it does show that they can have certain important, measurable benefits. The study results serve as a benchmark for achieving certain specific impacts, against which other social sector investments with similar objectives should be measured. They provide an established record of welfare impact that has been realized on a large scale in very different countries, through the use of an alternative development model.

Key Design Issues for Social Funds

Findings on poverty targeting, impact, sustainability, and cost-efficiency point to opportunities to strengthen social fund design and the design of community-based development efforts. Moving social funds' institutional focus from emergency programs to longer-term development requires continued adjustment of procedures and criteria. Most of the social funds in this study were introduced to address crisis situations. With the transition to longer-term development objectives, many of their basic operating procedures have been and will continue to be revised. This section presents specific recommendations for the areas studied.

Improving Poverty Targeting

Most social funds aim to reach poor communities and households. To do this, they have relied on a combination of poverty maps to allocate resources progressively among districts, proactive outreach efforts, and definitions of eligible interventions that focus on goods and services which tend to be used by the poor. This method has, however, resulted in leakage to nonpoor households and has led to considerable heterogeneity in per capita district targeting results. Some of these results may be inevitable, or at least acceptable, given the main types of investments financed by social funds—social service infrastructure serving communities as a whole. Nonetheless, it would be worth exploring how to improve social funds' targeting to the neediest districts and households. Measures that may produce more progressive results include reducing access by better-off regions; introducing intradistrict targeting procedures to identify the poorest communities within districts or municipalities; and removing from the menus allowable activities that tend to have higher rates of leakage to the nonpoor.

There may be tradeoffs between improved targeting and other objectives. An example is the potential tension between scaling up to create larger national programs and achieving narrower poverty targeting objectives, particularly geographic ones. In addition, the institutional function of social funds can affect targeting outcomes. For example, some social funds have become sectoral investment mechanisms (and hence have moved away from poverty targeting objectives in favor of national coverage), while others have played a critical role in crisis response and reconstruction—for example, reaching earthquake victims in Armenia, people in hurricane-stricken areas in Honduras and Nicaragua, and other vulnerable groups that may not be among the chronic poor.

Improving the Impact

In every country studied, small-scale investments in social infrastructure improved basic welfare. The findings point to potential strategies for increasing the impact of social fund investments. Focusing on rehabilitation of infrastructure may reduce net impacts. It should also be kept in mind that there may be a tension between maximizing impact and minimizing recurrent costs. In Honduras focusing on the rehabilitation of urban water systems kept recurrent cost obligations to a minimum and generated temporary employment, in accordance with the employment objectives of the earlier phase of the social fund, but there were no measurable health impacts from the rehabilitation. In the other countries studied, strong improvements in household health outcomes seem to be associated with investments in new systems and services, particularly in rural areas. In the health and education sectors many social funds have limited the expansion of new health centers and the construction of new classrooms and schools with the aim of easing the recurrent cost burden on line ministries. Although this strategy is founded in sustainability concerns, it may have the indirect effect of limiting some of the potential impact on household welfare. Maximizing impact may entail favoring investments that provide new services.

Investments that are limited to only some parts of service delivery may reduce the potential impacts of the investments. Community-managed water projects should include training in hygiene and administration so that citizens can best use and maintain the services delivered. Investments in school infrastructure should include furniture and utilities, particularly water and sanitation. Improving the outreach capabilities of health centers— for example, by providing radios and motorcycles—may affect utilization and outcomes.

Impacts can be increased by maximizing service coverage in a particular area. For example, although latrine and sewerage investments benefit individual households, health impacts will be maximized if a critical mass of community members has access to these services. Community proposals should be reviewed to ensure that investments have enough local coverage to bring about changes in community welfare. Social funds may wish to consider piloting loan programs or other vehicles that would allow households to take advantage of these investments.

Enhancing Sustainability

Social fund–supported facilities perform as well as or better than similar facilities in each country, although more time would be needed to assess longer-term sustainability. Provision of staff has been adequate, but supply of other inputs (such as textbooks for schools and essential medicines for clinics) by line ministries remains inconsistent. This reflects broader sectoral problems; the bulk of social sector ministry expenditures still goes for personnel, with little in the way of budgetary resources allocated to drugs, textbooks, or physical maintenance of facilities. There is scope for social funds and other actors to experiment with alternative approaches to ensuring essential inputs at the local level, and the study findings suggest that these initiatives would be useful. They could take the form of support from the private sector, local government, or communities, in addition to a continued push for necessary reforms in the central ministries.

In many cases sustainability is furthered by transferring responsibility to local actors. Social funds typically support the creation of local maintenance committees. These committees have been able to provide minimum levels of routine maintenance and repairs for simple infrastructure. They should be given formal recognition and a clear set of responsibilities, particularly for facilities owned and operated by local government or line ministries. For water services dependent on user fees, investments should be based on willingness to pay and should include adequate training in operation and maintenance. For services like water systems, where it is expected that the population will be able to self-finance operation and maintenance, consumers should be fully aware of the recurrent cost implications. Training in how to administer a community-managed system is critical.

Local governments' provision of social infrastructure may enhance sustainability. Because of their potential access to resources and their more direct knowledge of local circumstances and conditions, governments at this level may be better positioned than central agencies to ensure sustainability of services. If their increased responsibilities in this area are matched with greater access to resources, local governments can make a substantial contribution to sustainability.

Increasing Cost-Efficiency

The study looked at the efficiency of social funds in terms of cost minimization, both of investments and of administrative overhead for a given output or benefit. Such efficiency allows more resources to reach more people for a fixed budget. Cost analysis revealed a wide range in performance across programs, as well as between programs within a country. Although social funds were typically more efficient than other national programs in terms of overhead expenditures, their investment unit costs tended to be more efficient only where there was significant input and control by communities. It should be noted that while the study provided information as to which mechanism is most efficient in delivering infrastructure, determining which program was most efficient in achieving outcomes such as reduction of infant mortality was beyond the scope of the study and the availability of data on comparator programs.

Several opportunities for increasing the cost-efficiency of social infrastructure investments were identified. Transferring responsibilities for management of the contracting process and control over financial resources to the local level may reduce unit costs. If decentralization is coupled with sufficient supervision and technical assistance, local groups may be able to lower unit costs. Requiring community counterpart contributions may also promote cost-effective investments. In cases where social funds were found to have higher unit costs than comparators, cost escalation during execution may have played a role. Some social funds, particularly those that work directly with private sector contractors, need to guarantee sufficient control over cost escalation during construction. In addition, life-cycle costing of systems and buildings should be considered. Higher-unit-cost investments that extend the life span of a facility and may reduce ongoing maintenance expenditures should be analyzed along with alternatives that have lower unit costs but shorter life spans. Finally, there is a need to establish national frameworks for community cost sharing and appropriate unit cost ranges. The wide variation in unit costs and in the amount expected from communities calls for the development of national policies in both areas to ensure consistency across programs and regions.

Ensuring Relevance to Community Needs and Active Engagement of Citizens

Increased citizen input and community participation in investments can improve impact and sustainability. From an operational perspective, community participation is often viewed as a "cost" because of the time and resources spent in consultations and additional training activities to enable communities to take more direct control of the identification and implementation of small-scale investments. The results of the evaluation, however, confirm many of the potential benefits of participatory processes. Reinforcing participation in social fund project cycles is justified to ensure greater relevance to community needs, lowered unit costs of investments, and greater utilization and sustainability of services. Citizen input and control should be built into all stages of the project cycle. Citizens should be fully informed about the investments that can be financed by a social fund, the rules of the game for accessing the fund, and their own potential role in the identification and implementation of these investments.

A balance may need to be struck between expanded community choice and the achievement of national development objectives. The benefits of open menus include greater choice and perhaps a better fit between community preferences and the investments selected. The drawbacks are that community preferences may not be in line with national priorities and that the programs may be more prone to elite capture if menus include public goods that tend to be used primarily by the better off. This tension can be seen in Bolivia. There, recent social fund investments in education have been integrated into the broader educational reform process, with the social fund now only financing investments in the ministry-designated hub schools that are the focus of the initial reform efforts. This conflicts with freer community choice, since some communities may give priority to school infrastructure but are not yet included in the ministry's reform plan.

Or, a national government may emphasize water investments with the aim of improving basic health, while a given community may wish to increase the reliability and convenience of the water supply, regardless of the potential health benefits. A water system that increased availability and convenience but did not improve health outcomes would be seen as unsuccessful from the national perspective but as highly successful from the local perspective. Social funds will need to consider how much weight is to be given to communities' stated priorities and how much to external social planners' indicators of success.

Key Issues for Impact Evaluation

This study is a multifaceted, multicountry analysis of the impacts of a particular type of program. The approaches applied, including experimental and quasi-experimental designs using comparison or control groups, are rarely used in evaluating development programs. The study was designed to measure not only changes resulting from the interventions but also the magnitude of these changes compared with what would have happened without the intervention. The adoption of robust methodologies creates a much stronger basis for the consideration of results and policy implications. If development practitioners are serious about responding to the growing call for performance-based evaluation, use of the type of research carried out in this study should be expanded. Ideally, equivalent information on other programs would be generated to permit informed consideration of alternative uses for scarce development resources.

The execution of robust evaluations faces significant technical challenges. The methodologies for assessing the impacts of social funds are particularly complex; the multisectoral investment menus and the demand-driven nature of social funds complicate preidentification of the type or location of the specific investments to be carried out and introduce additional challenges in addressing selection bias. This study used varying approaches, including a longitudinal evaluation in Bolivia that employed panel data using baseline measures and intervention measures collected four years later. The case studies used treatment and comparison or control groups to conduct "with and without" assessments and applied a variety of methods such as propensity scoring and other matching techniques. Qualitative methods were included to add depth to the interpretation of results and allow beneficiaries' perspectives to be reflected more directly. In all cases, international and national researchers were teamed to develop and execute the evaluations. Effective design and analysis of surveys require a high level of expertise. In most instances the lead time for designing the evaluation approach and survey instruments was substantial.

Building local capacity for conducting evaluations is critical, particularly as development assistance becomes increasingly linked to outcomes. If program evaluations are to be conducted regularly in developing countries, they must be based on local evaluation capacity and supported by policymakers who are convinced that such evaluations are worth the cost in forgone investment. Multilateral development institutions, bilateral donors, and national policymakers should continue to support capacity building to create a solid foundation for future social policy research.

In addition to improving capacity, building ownership for the process and the products of impact evaluations within developing country governments is crucial if the evaluations are to have an impact on policy. Because social funds were actively engaged in the design and were briefed on the findings, some of the country findings have already been translated into concrete changes in social fund procedures (see box 9.1).

Impact evaluations should be applied strategically to projects that can generate knowledge about development effectiveness. Because the lessons generated by impact evaluations are public goods valued by stakeholders beyond those working on the given project, external resources to help

---

Box 9.1 The Contribution of Impact Evaluation to Program Design: Honduras and Nicaragua

Impact evaluations should inform program redesign and adjustment, as happened in the following examples from Honduras and Nicaragua:

- In Honduras the impact evaluation results have led to a redesign of the criteria for supporting water systems, including training components; the development of baseline data on incoming projects to facilitate future measurement of impacts; a strengthening of subproject supervision; and efforts to ensure more systematic consultation with beneficiary communities, among other changes.

    —Information from World Bank task manager, 2001

- The Nicaragua social fund impact evaluation is leading to changes in social fund policies. The social fund has suspended the financing of new sewerage projects for two years and will begin financing more integrated infrastructure projects that will include components complementary to the basic physical works (e.g., access roads, and living quarters for teachers in rural areas). The social fund is also revising and strengthening its own project appraisal capacities and monitoring and evaluation systems.

    —World Bank (2001c)

finance the cost of evaluations are justified. In the present study, the bulk of data collection and much of the analysis were supported through project financing from multilateral loans. These evaluations were financed at the sacrifice of additional community-level investments, yet many of the lessons are transferable to other countries and programs. Since the broader development community benefits from the information generated, development agencies should make greater use of their discretionary resources to support such efforts.

Evaluations should be carried out across similar public sector programs. Far too often, only one type of intervention, such as social funds, conditional cash transfers, or active labor market programs, is subjected to thorough evaluation and analysis, resulting in an incomplete picture of the relative strengths and weaknesses of different investment mechanisms. Rigorous review would give the government a clearer picture of which approaches are most promising and cost-effective. In many cases an analysis could cover several programs in the same sector, allowing for shared costs and common methodologies.

Implications for the Role of Social Funds within Poverty Reduction Strategies

There has been a tendency to expand social funds' mandates. Each of the social funds in the case study countries began in response to economic crisis or transition. All were considered temporary at their inception. All have endured and adapted. Because of the funds' performance, governments have extended their mandates to longer-term poverty alleviation. The new tasks include supporting improved local governance through closer relationships with local governments and community groups. As mandates have expanded, so have expectations for the effects of the interventions. Short-term objectives such as providing temporary employment and shoring up dilapidated or deficient local infrastructure have given way to increased attention to ensuring sustainable service delivery and, more recently, strengthening local-level institutions and organizations.

Social funds are clearly a complement to, not a substitute for, effective sectoral policies; nor should they try to fulfill all the investment financing needs of all poor communities. Much of the impact and sustainability of social fund investments relies on effective strategies of service delivery under the mandate of other institutions, particularly line ministries and local governments. Social funds cannot substitute for good sectoral policies aimed at ensuring that, nationwide, schools and health centers are staffed with well-trained personnel and receive essential inputs in good time. Ideally, these community-level investments will further the achievement of sectoral goals and provide sufficient integration and synergy to ensure larger impacts. Social funds must work in tandem with local governments, NGOs, communities, and other development agents to leverage resources and carry out investments that serve the broader national objective of poverty alleviation.

Although investments financed by social funds appear to be sustainable, at least in the medium term, the sustainability of the social funds themselves is an outstanding question. The social funds in this study all rely on international donor support, which in many cases has been crucial in getting the programs up and running and in building modern management systems. There are social funds that are fully domestically financed, such as Chile's Social Investment and Solidarity Fund and similar community grant programs in industrial countries. Over time, it may be possible to envision a transition to more domestic financing of social funds. Many of the poorest countries, however, still rely on donor financing for the bulk of investments. Donor financing will continue to play a critical role in supporting social fund programs in the near future.

In the decade since their inception, social funds have proved to be flexible, adaptable, and proactive complements to top-down development approaches and have reached millions of poor people. By financing infrastructure investments preferred by local groups, social funds have expanded access to basic social services in poor communities and have generated important welfare benefits. The challenge now is to find the best balance between community-led initiatives and national policies in the implementation of poverty reduction programs.

Appendix

Methodology for Education, Health, and Water and Sanitation Impact Evaluations

This appendix reviews the evaluation methodologies applied in carrying out the impact evaluations of education, health, and water and sanitation projects financed by social funds. (See chapter 2 for descriptions of the methodologies and table 2.1 for a synopsis of the evaluation designs applied in each country. For a listing of the country case study reports and of *World Bank Economic Review* articles based on the studies, see box 1.)

In each country the impact evaluation used different methodologies to construct the counterfactual scenario, and common indicators of impact were not available across all countries studied. For example, specific indicators of impact on health outcomes vary across countries, although all countries use at least one main indicator of health changes. Similarly, some country cases included independent judgments as to quality of construction, while others did not.

Education

Approach

Different impact evaluation methodologies, and different combinations of methodologies, were applied in each case study country to generate the counterfactual on household impacts of social fund–financed education projects. The methodologies for assessing the effects of social fund education projects encompassed the following:

- *Experimental design.* In Bolivia's Chaco region, researchers created equivalent control and treatment groups by employing an experimental design based on the random allocation among equally eligible communities of the offer to participate in a social fund–financed education project. This evaluation methodology is widely recognized as robust, since it allows both observable and unobservable characteristics to be addressed. Bolivia is also the only country in which both baseline and follow-up data from schools and households were available—a design feature that makes possible full before-and-after measures, as well as verification of the correctness of the match between treatment and comparison groups prior to the social fund intervention.
- *Matched comparison using "pipeline" projects.* The Honduras, Peru 2 (Instituto Apoyo), and Zambia education evaluations constructed comparison groups from the pipeline of social fund projects and of communities that had not yet received a social fund investment but were due to receive an education investment in the near future. This relatively new approach allows unobservable characteristics to be addressed, notably those surrounding the selection processes of both the communities and the social funds.
- *Matched comparison using propensity scores.* The Armenia, Bolivia, Nicaragua, and Zambia evaluations used statistical propensity score matching techniques to identify similar non–social fund beneficiaries and evaluate impact.

Other techniques included the construction of a comparison group based on facility characteristics and geographic proximity in Nicaragua and Zambia and the use of instrumental variables in an econometric analysis of national household survey data in the Paxson and Schady (2002) education study in Peru.

Data Sources and Sample Sizes

The data used to analyze the impact and sustainability of education projects stem from three sources: household surveys of social fund and non–social fund beneficiaries; school facilities surveys covering social fund and non–social fund schools; and complementary beneficiary assessments.

The sampling frames for the household surveys were designed to generate representative samples of social fund beneficiaries and comparison groups at the household level. Sample sizes for household surveys in all cases are statistically representative of the universe of beneficiaries of social fund education projects. The education impact evaluation is based on a cross-country sample of more than 7,000 households selected specifically for the education analysis from household surveys conducted for the social

Table A.1 Education Evaluation: Household and Facilities Sample Sizes by Country

Country case study	Household survey sample size			School facilities survey sample size	
	Social fund treatment group	Comparison group[a]	National survey[b]	Social fund	Comparison group
Armenia	375	375	3,600	30[c]	30[c]
Bolivia[d]	940	1,020	n.a.	66	72
Honduras	320	320	n.a.	12	12
Nicaragua	240	240	4,040	24	24
Peru 1 (Paxson and Schady 2002)[e]	n.a.	n.a.	18,000 3,500 3,500	n.a.	n.a.
Peru 2 (Instituto Apoyo 2000b)	760	770		70	71
Zambia	1,020	1,020	13,500	43	25
Total	3,655	3,745	46,140	245	234

n.a. Not applicable.

[a] These comparison groups were surveyed specifically for the social fund evaluation. Other comparison groups were generated from national surveys.

[b] Total sample sizes for the national surveys are reported without the disaggregation used for the education analysis.

[c] The Armenia school survey data were not usable because of data problems.

[d] The reported sample sizes are from the follow-up surveys in Chaco and other rural areas. Households from the baseline survey that could not be located in the follow-up survey (65 percent) were replaced. The sample composition changed slightly for the school survey because a few schools could not be reinterviewed owing to the absence of key informants, or because project implementation did not directly follow project promotion.

[e] The Paxson and Schady evaluation collected no primary data. Instead, it used social fund administrative data analyzed jointly with household survey data from the 1996 Peruvian National Statistical Institute (INEI) household survey (18,000 households), the 1994 Peru Living Standards Measurement Survey (3,500 households), and the 1997 Peru Living Standards Measurement Survey (3,500 households).

fund evaluation and on analysis of national-level survey data of more than 46,000 households (see table A.1).

The evaluation sampled more than 400 social fund and non–social fund schools in the case study countries to assess the quality and sustainability of social fund education investments. On a country-to-country basis, however, the sample sizes are not large enough to generate representative samples of social fund or comparator schools. The data from the facilities surveys are not always generalizable to the whole population of schools, and the results from them should generally be treated as case studies within each country.

Country cases vary as to the urban, rural, or national focus of the data used for the evaluation. The data used for the Bolivia study and the Instituto Apoyo study in Peru were collected from rural areas, where social fund investments in these countries are concentrated. The data from all other counties are from national surveys. In Armenia 85 percent of social fund projects were carried out in the capital city, Yerevan; in the zone affected by the 1988 earthquake; and in areas affected by civil conflict. This concentration of social fund projects in distinct areas of the country made it difficult to find appropriate comparison groups.

The impacts of social fund–financed education projects on academic achievement and in indigenous communities are reported from Bolivia and Peru, respectively. In Bolivia math and language tests were applied to control and treatment group students in both Chaco and the other rural regions sampled. In Peru the Instituto Apoyo study included a representative sample of indigenous communities.

Health

Approach

Different approaches were used to develop the counterfactual on health interventions in each of the countries studied, and several of the countries used multiple approaches. The general approaches were:

- *Matched comparison using "pipeline" projects.* The Honduras and Zambia case studies generated all (Honduras) or a portion (Zambia) of their comparison groups from communities where social fund projects had been approved but not yet implemented.
- *Matched comparison using propensity scores.* The Bolivia, Nicaragua, and Zambia case studies used statistical matching techniques to develop propensity scores for creating comparison groups and evaluating impact.

In addition, the Nicaragua and Zambia analyses included the construction of a comparison group based on facility characteristics and geographic proximity. The Bolivia analysis employed life-table estimates for changes in mortality, as well as Cox proportional hazard estimates of child mortality. The Honduras evaluation included multivariate analysis.

Data Sources and Sample Sizes

The analysis of the health impact of social funds drew on three main sources of primary data: household surveys, facilities surveys, and qualitative beneficiary assessments.

The household survey sample sizes in each country are statistically representative of the beneficiaries of social fund health investments. Almost 9,000 households were specifically interviewed across the four countries studied in the impact evaluation of social fund health interventions, and an additional 17,500 households were used from national surveys (see table A.2).

Table A.2 Health Evaluation: Household and Facilities Sample Sizes by Country

	Household survey sample size			Health facilities survey sample size	
Country case study	Social fund treatment group	Comparison group[a]	National survey[b]	Social fund	Comparison group
Bolivia[c]	1,921	1,921	n.a.	90	87
Honduras	386	188	n.a.	11	12
Nicaragua	199	199	4,010	20	20
Zambia	2,150	1,900	13,500	16	14
Total	4,656	4,208	17,510	137	133

n.a. Not applicable.
[a] These comparison groups were surveyed specifically for the social fund evaluation. Other comparison groups were generated from national surveys.
[b] Total sample sizes for the national surveys are reported without the disaggregation used for the health analysis.
[c] 1998 follow-up survey data reported.

In total, 270 health facilities were surveyed to assess the quality and sustainability of social fund interventions, but in most countries the sample sizes were relatively small. As a result, the findings are not always generalizable to all the health facilities that received social fund support in the countries studied. This report thus analyzes the facilities data findings (physical aspects of clinics, supplies, staffing, and utilization as reported by the facilities) as a case study approach in a similar manner as for the education sector. Where possible, triangulation from facilities, household, and qualitative surveys is performed to give a more robust indication of impact; this was done, for example, for utilization.

Unlike education, which is a fairly common event for school-age children, significant bouts of illness occur only to a small proportion of the population at any point in time. Infant and child mortality are also relatively rare events. To capture these rarer events, much larger sample sizes are required to allow tracking of statistically significant changes in many epidemiological measures. Only one of the case studies, that for Bolivia, collected information on mortality rates and had solid baseline data for undertaking the analysis.

Water and Sanitation

Approach

The water projects sampled in the evaluation encompass a wide variety of systems. Social fund water investments included in the sample frames range from rehabilitation of existing urban distribution systems to the construction

Table A.3 Water and Sanitation Evaluation: Household and Facilities Survey Sample Sizes by Country and Subsector

Country case study	Household survey sample size			Infrastructure facilities survey sample size	
	Social fund treatment group	Comparison group[a]	National survey[b]	Social fund	Comparison group
Armenia					
Water	340	380	3,600	19	17
Bolivia[c]					
Water			—	n.a	n.a.
Baseline	1,235				
Follow-up	1,109				
Honduras					
Water	324	324	—	12	12
Sewerage	162	162		8	4
Latrines	162	162		6	5
Nicaragua					
Water	95		4,040	10	—
Sewerage	104			10	—
Latrines	234			23	—
Peru (Instituto Apoyo)[d]					
Water	1,176	1,176	—	166	166
Sewerage	224	224		21	13
Latrines	510	510		86	83
Total	5,675	2,938	7,640	361	300

— Not available.

n.a. Not applicable.

[a] These comparison groups were surveyed specifically for the social fund evaluation. Other comparison groups were generated from national surveys.

[b] Total sample sizes for the national surveys are reported without the disaggregation used for the water and sanitation analysis.

[c] No specific water facilities survey was used; households from the existing 18 projects at time of baseline were interviewed. Control group beneficiaries were statistically matched from the health sub-sample on baseline characteristics.

[d] The Peruvian impact evaluation is supplemented by data on water system performance developed through the "Sixth Ex-Post Evaluation of FONCODES" (Instituto Apoyo 2000c), which analyzed 380 water projects completed between 1997 and 1999. The evaluation surveyed 3,800 households; no control groups were created.

of new water services in rural areas. Some investments include construction of water collection systems; others focus on extending distribution systems from existing collection sources. Other differences include use of public standpipe systems versus house connections. These differences may influence the ultimate household-level impacts. For example, one would expect higher net health impacts from the provision of new services as opposed to rehabilitation of existing services. The data sets do not allow for a disaggregation among different types of water systems.

Data Sources and Sample Sizes

The impact evaluation in water and sanitation used a combination of household surveys to measure changes in access and household outcomes; facilities surveys of infrastructure to gauge quality and sustainability; and qualitative assessments to probe community perceptions and dynamics. Because of the sampling methodologies used, the most robust findings are for household impacts, while the facilities surveys should be taken as indicative. Table A.3 presents a summary of the survey design for the household and facilities surveys. Specific facility surveys were not carried out in Bolivia. In Nicaragua a lack of comparison projects limited the facilities survey sample to only social fund projects. In Armenia the water sample included both water and irrigation projects. Although it is conceptually necessary to separate water projects into their two major subcategories—irrigation and potable water—the resulting sample size for treatment and control is quite small. As a consequence, few statistically meaningful results emerge from the water facilities analysis, and so the results are not presented. In Honduras facilities surveys were carried out on all three types of investment (water, sewerage, and latrines) for both social fund and non–social fund facilities.

Bibliography

Abraham, Anita, and Jean-Philippe Platteau. Forthcoming. "Participatory Development: Where Culture Creeps In." In Vijayendra Rao and Michael Walton, eds., *Culture and Public Action: How Cultural Factors Affect Poverty Reduction in an Unequal World* (working title). Palo Alto, Calif.: Stanford University Press.

Akin, John S., David K. Guilkey, and E. Hazel Denton. 1995. "Quality of Services and Demand for Health Care in Nigeria: A Multinominal Probit Estimation." *Social Sciences and Medicine* 40 (11): 1527–37.

Alderman, Harold. 2002. "Do Local Officials Know Something We Don't? Decentralization of Targeted Transfers in Albania. *Journal of Public Economics* 83 (3): 375–404.

Alderman, Harold, and Victor Lavy. 1996. "Household Responses to Public Health Services: Cost and Quality Tradeoffs." *World Bank Research Observer* 11 (2, February): 3–22.

Alfaro, J., and F. Soto. 2000. "Analisis de costo-eficiencia de los fondos de inversión social: el caso de Perú." Background paper for the Social Funds Evaluation Study. World Bank, Human Development Network, Social Protection Unit, Washington, D.C.

Ames, Barry. 1987. *Political Survival: Politicians and Public Policy in Latin America.* Berkeley: University of California Press.

Andina Mathys, Alain, and Shirley Claure. 1999. "Estudio costos en proyectos rurales que proveen agua en la region." United Nations Development Programme–World Bank Water and Sanitation Program, Washington, D.C.

Araujo, E., C. Hurtado, and R. Lema. 2000. "Analisis complementario de costo-eficiencia del Fondo de Inversión Social de Emergencia de Nicaragua." Background paper for the Social Funds Evaluation Study. Draft. Social Investment Group, Managua.

ASCO Consulting. 1998. "Microprojects Programme: Value for Money Audit." Paper prepared for European Development Fund, Lusaka.

Aucoin, Peter. 1996. "Designing Agencies for Good Public Management: The Urgent Need for Reform." *Choices: Governance* 2 (4, April): 15–19. Montreal, Canada: Institute for Research on Public Policy.

Babajanian, B. 1999. "Armenia Social Investment Fund II Project: Cost-Effectiveness Analysis." Background paper for the Social Funds Evaluation Study. World Bank, Eastern Europe and Central Asia Department, Washington, D.C.

Baker, Judy L. 2000. *Evaluating the Impact of Development Projects on Poverty: A Handbook for Practitioners*. Directions in Development series. Washington, D.C.: World Bank.

Barrientos, J. C. 1999. "Coordinating Poverty Alleviation Programs with Regional and Local Governments." Social Protection Discussion Paper 9933. World Bank, Human Development Network, Social Protection Unit, Washington, D.C.

Barrientos, J. C., and S. Jorgensen. 1998. "A Practical Approach for Designing Community-Based Operations—with Special Reference to Implementation Arrangements." World Bank, Human Development Network, Social Protection Unit, Washington, D.C.

Batley, R. 1999. "The Role of Government in Adjusting Economies: An Overview of Findings." International Development Department, University of Birmingham, Ala.

Behrman, Jere R., Yingmei Cheng, and Petra Todd. 2000. "The Impact of the Bolivian Integrated 'PIDI' Preschool Program." University of Pennsylvania, Philadelphia. Processed. Developed for the World Bank Research Foundation Project on Evaluation of the Impact of Investments in Early Childhood Development on Nutrition and Cognitive Development.

Behrman, Jere R., Piyali Sengupta, and Petra Todd. 2000. "The Impact of PROGRE-SA on Achievement Test Scores in the First Year." International Food Policy Research Institute, Washington, D.C.

Benefo, Kofi Darkwa, and T. Paul Schultz. 1994. *Determinants of Fertility and Child Mortality in Côte d'Ivoire and Ghana*. Living Standards Measurement Study Working Paper 103. Washington, D.C.: World Bank.

Bermudez, Gustavo, ed. 1999. "Analysis institutional del FISE." Background report to the Emergency Social Investment Fund, Managua.

Brown, L. David, and David C. Korten. 1989. "Understanding Voluntary Organizations: Guidelines for Donors." Policy Research Working Paper 258. World Bank, Country Economics Department, Washington, D.C.

Carvalho, Soniya. 1994. "Social Funds: Guidelines for Design and Implementation." HRO Working Paper 34. World Bank, Human Resources Development and Operations Policy Department, Washington, D.C.

Chase, Robert S. 2000. "Supporting Communities in Transition: The Impact of the Armenian Social Investment Fund." Background paper for the Social Funds Evaluation Study. World Bank, Human Development Network, Social Protection Unit, Washington, D.C.

——. 2002. "Supporting Communities in Transition: The Impact of the Armenian Social Investment Fund." *World Bank Economic Review* 16 (2): 219–40.

Chase, Robert S., and Lynne Sherburne-Benz. 2000. "Impact Evaluation of the Zambia Social Fund." Background paper for the Social Funds Evaluation Study. World Bank, Human Development Network, Social Protection Unit, Washington, D.C.

Chaubey, J. N. 1998. "Social Fund Institutions: Concepts and Practice." Draft. World Bank, Human Development Network, Social Protection Team, Washington, D.C.

Coa, R. 1995. "Percepción de beneficios de proyectos FIS." Ministry of Human Development, Social Policy Analysis Unit, La Paz.

Cornia, Giovanni Andrea. 1999. *Social Funds in Stabilization and Adjustment Programmes.* WIDER Research for Action Paper 48. Helsinki: United Nations University/World Institute for Development Economics Research.

Dehejia, Rajeev H., and Sadek Wahba. 1998. "Propensity Score Matching Methods for Nonexperimental Causal Studies." NBER Working Paper 6829. National Bureau of Economic Research, Cambridge, Mass.

Development Programs, Ltd. 1997. "Report of Armenian Social Investment Fund Project Impact Assessment Study." Yerevan.

——. 1999. "Sociological Study: Armenia Social Investment Fund." Yerevan.

Dowdall, L. 2000. "Zambia Primary School Study: Final Report." Group 5 Consulting Engineers. Background paper for the Social Funds Evaluation Study. World Bank, Human Development Network, Social Protection Unit, Washington, D.C.

Dunleavy, P., and C. Hood. 1994. "From Old Public Administration to New Public Management." *Public Money and Management* (July–September): 9–16.

ESA Consultores. 2000. "Estudio de costo-eficiencia del Fondo Hondureño de Inversión Social." Background paper for the Social Funds Evaluation Study. World Bank, Human Development Network, Social Protection Unit, Washington, D.C.

Esrey, Steven A., James B. Potash, Leslie Roberts, and Clive Schiff. 1990. "Health Benefits from Improvements in Water Supply and Sanitation." WASH Technical Report 66. U.S. Agency for International Development, Washington, D.C.

Freeman, Howard E., and Peter Rossi. 1993. *Evaluation: A Systematic Approach.* Newberry Park, Calif.: Sage.

Frigenti, Laura, Alberto Harth, and Rumana Huque. 1998. "Local Solutions to Regional Problems: The Growth of Social Funds and Public Works and Employment Projects in Sub-Saharan Africa." World Bank, Africa Region, Washington, D.C.

Galasso, Emanuela, and Martin Ravallion. 1999. "Decentralized Targeting of an Anti-Poverty Program." World Bank, Development Economics Research Group, Washington, D.C.

———. 2000. "Distributional Outcomes of a Decentralized Welfare Program." Policy Research Working Paper 2316. World Bank, Development Research Group, Washington, D.C.

GB Consultores. 2000. "Estudio de costo-eficiencia del programa de inversión social en Nicaragua: phase 2." Background paper for the Social Funds Evaluation Study. World Bank, Human Development Network, Social Protection Unit, Washington, D.C.

Glaessner, Philip J., Kye Woo Lee, Anna Maria Sant'Anna, and Jean-Jacques de St. Antoine. 1994. *Poverty Alleviation and Social Investment Funds: The Latin American Experience.* World Bank Discussion Paper 261. Washington, D.C.

Glewwe, Paul, Margaret Grosh, Hanan Jacoby, and Marlaine Lockheed. 1995. "An Eclectic Approach to Estimating the Determinants of Achievement in Jamaican Primary Education." *World Bank Economic Review* 9 (2, May): 231–58.

Godinez, A., and J. Van Domelen. 1996. "Targeting Social Programs to the Poor." Working paper for Ecuador Poverty Report. World Bank, Latin America and Caribbean Department, Washington, D.C.

Goodman, M., S. Morely, G. Siri, and E. Zuckerman. 1997. "Social Investment Funds in Latin America: Past Performance and Future Role." Inter-American Development Bank, Social Programs and Sustainable Development Department, Evaluation Office, Washington, D.C.

Gopal, Gita, and Alexandre Marc. 1994. *World Bank–Financed Projects with Community Participation: Procurement and Disbursement Issues.* World Bank Discussion Paper 265. Washington, D.C.

Grootaert, Christiaan. 1999. "Social Capital, Household Welfare, and Poverty in Indonesia." Local-Level Institutions Working Paper 6. World Bank, Social Development Department, Washington, D.C.

Grosh, Margaret. 1994. *Administering Targeted Social Programs in Latin America: From Platitudes to Practice.* World Bank Regional and Sectoral Study. Washington, D.C.

Grosh, Margaret, and Paul Glewwe, eds. 2000. *Designing Household Survey Questionnaires for Developing Countries: Lessons from the 15 Years of the Living Standards Measurement Study.* Washington, D.C.: World Bank.

Grossman, Jean Baldwin. 1994. "Evaluating Social Policies: Principles and U.S. Experience." *World Bank Research Observer* 9 (2, July): 159–80.

Gurgur, Tugrul, and Anwar Shah. 2000. "Localization and Corruption: Panacea or Pandora's Box?" Prepared for the International Monetary Fund Conference on Fiscal Decentralization, November 20–21, Washington, D.C. World Bank, Washington, D.C.

Hanushek, Eric. 1986. "The Economics of Schooling: Production and Efficiency in Public Schools." *Journal of Economic Literature* 24 (September): 1141–77.

Harbison, Ralph W., and Eric A. Hanushek. 1992. *Educational Performance of the Poor: Lessons from Rural Northeastern Brazil.* New York: Oxford University Press.

Heckman, James J., Ichimura Hidehiko, and Petra Todd. 1998. "Matching as an Econometric Evaluation Estimator." *Review of Economic Studies* 65 (April): 261–94.

Heckman, J., R. Lalonde, and J. Smith. 1999. "The Economics of Active Labor Market Programs." In Orley Ashenfelter and David Card, eds., *Handbook of Labor Economics*, vol. 3. Amsterdam: North-Holland.

Heiser, T. 1991. "Socio-Economic Development Funds: A Guideline for Design and Implementation." Asian Development Bank, United Nations Development Programme, and World Bank, Washington, D.C.

Hentschel, Jesko, Javier Poggi, and N. Schady. 1996. "Did the Ministry of the Presidency Reach the Poor in 1995?" Report for World Bank, Latin America and the Caribbean Region, Country Operations Division 1, Washington, D.C.

Hirschman, Albert O. 1970. *Exit, Voice and Loyalty: Responses to Decline in Firms, Organizations, and States.* Cambridge, Mass.: Harvard University Press.

Hogrewe, W., S. Joyce, and E. Perez. 1993. "The Unique Challenges of Peri-Urban Sanitation." WASH Technical Report 86. U.S. Agency for International Development, Washington, D.C.

Hotchkiss, David R. 1993. "The Role of Quality in the Demand for Health Care in Cebu, Philippines." Department of Economics, University of North Carolina, Chapel Hill.

Husain, I., ed. 1997. "Portfolio Improvement Program: The Review of the Social Funds Portfolio." Report submitted to World Bank Quality Assurance Group, Washington, D.C.

IADB (Inter-American Development Bank). 1998a. "Integrating WID/Gender Issues into Social Investment Funds." Draft. July. Washington, D.C.

———. 1998b. "The Use of Social Investment Funds as an Instrument for Combating Poverty." Poverty and Inequality Advisory Unit, Washington, D.C.

IDEAS (Instituto de Desarrollo Empresarial Asociativo). 1998. *Evaluación cualitativa de beneficiarios del FISE 1993/96.* Managua.

IFPRI (International Food Policy Research Institute). 2002a. "Sistema de evaluación de la fase piloto de la red de protección social de Nicaragua: evaluación de focalización." Washington, D.C.

———. 2002b. "Sistema de evaluación de la fase piloto de la red de protección social de Nicaragua: evaluación de impacto." Washington, D.C.

Inman, Robert P., and Daniel Rubinfeld. 1997. "Rethinking Federalism." *Journal of Economic Perspectives* 11 (4, fall): 43–64.

Instituto Apoyo. 1995. "Evaluación ex-post del desempeno de FONCODES: 1994." Lima.

———. 1997. "Evaluación ex-post de los proyectos de FONCODES." Lima.

———. 1999. "Quinta evaluación ex-post de los proyectos de FONCODES." Lima.

———. 2000a. "Determinants of Project Success: Case Study of FONCODES." Lima.

————. 2000b. "Sexta evaluación ex-post del FONCODES: evaluación de impacto y sostenibilidad." Lima.

————. 2000c. "Sixth Ex-Post Evaluation of FONCODES: Study of Water Supply Projects, Lima." Lima.

Jalan, Jyotsna, and Martin Ravallion. 1998. "Transfer Benefits from Workfare: A Matching Estimate for Argentina." World Bank, Development Research Group, Washington, D.C.

Jimenez, Emmanuel, and Vincent Paqueo. 1996. "Do Local Contributions Affect the Efficiency of Public Primary Schools?" *Economics of Education Review* 15 (4): 377–86.

Jimenez, Emmanuel, and Yasuyuki Sawada. 1998. "Do Community-Managed Schools Work? An Evaluation of El Salvador's Educo Program." Impact Evaluation of Education Reforms Paper 8. World Bank, Development Research Group, Washington, D.C.

Jorgensen, Steen Lau, and Julie Van Domelen. 2000. "Helping the Poor Manage Risk Better: The Role of Social Funds." In Nora Lustig, ed., *Shielding the Poor: Social Protection in the Developing World*. Washington, D.C.: Brookings Institution.

Jorgensen, Steen, Margaret Grosh, and Mark Schacter. 1991. "Easing the Poor through Economic Crisis and Adjustment: The Story of Bolivia's Emergency Social Fund." World Bank, Regional Studies Program, Washington, D.C.

————, eds. 1992. *Bolivia's Answer to Poverty, Economic Crisis, and Adjustment: The Emergency Social Fund*. World Bank Regional and Sectoral Study. Washington, D.C.

Kammersgaard, Jesper. 1999. "Causalities between Social Capital and Social Funds." Social Protection Discussion Paper 9908. World Bank, Human Development Network, Social Protection Unit, Washington, D.C.

Katz, Travis, and Jennifer Sara. 1998. "Making Rural Water Supply Sustainable: Report on the Impact of Project Rules." United Nations Development Programme–World Bank Water and Sanitation Program, Washington, D.C.

Khadiagala, L. S. 1995. "Social Funds: Strengths, Weaknesses and Conditions for Success." World Bank, Environment and Social Policy Department, Washington, D.C.

Lanjouw, Peter, and Martin Ravallion. 1999. "Benefit Incidence, Public Spending Reforms, and the Timing of Program Capture." *World Bank Economic Review* 13 (2, May): 257–74.

Lavy, Victor, and Jean-Marc Germain. 1994. *Quality and Cost in Health Care Choice in Developing Countries*. Living Standards Measurement Study Working Paper 105. Washington, D.C.: World Bank.

Lavy, Victor, John Strauss, Duncan Thomas, and Philippe De Vreyer. 1996. "Quality of Health Care, Survival and Health Outcomes in Ghana." *Journal of Health Economics* 15 (3): 333–57.

Li, Guo, Diana Steele, and Paul Glewwe. 1999. "Distribution of Government Education Expenditures in Developing Countries." World Bank, Human Development Network, Education Unit, Washington, D.C.

Lustig, Nora. 1997. "The Safety Nets That Are Not Safety Nets: Social Investment Funds in Latin America." Draft. October 21. Inter-American Development Bank, Washington, D.C.

Marc, Alexandre, Carol Graham, Mark Schacter, and Mary Schmidt. 1995. *Social Action Programs and Social Funds: A Review of Design and Implementation in Sub-Saharan Africa.* World Bank Discussion Paper 274. Washington, D.C.

Mwabu, Germano, Martha Ainsworth, and Andrew Nyamete. 1993. "Quality of Medical Care and Choice of Medical Treatment in Kenya: An Empirical Analysis." Technical Working Paper 9. World Bank, Africa Technical Department, Human Resources and Poverty Division, Washington, D.C.

Narayan, Deepa. 1997. *Voices of the Poor: Poverty and Social Capital in Tanzania.* Environmentally and Socially Sustainable Development Studies and Monographs Series 20. Washington, D.C.: World Bank.

Narayan, Deepa, and Katrinka Ebbe. 1997. *Design of Social Funds: Participation, Demand Orientation, and Local Organizational Capacity.* World Bank Discussion Paper 375. Washington, D.C.

Newman, John, Steen Jorgensen, and Menno Pradhan. 1991a. "How Did Workers Benefit from Bolivia's Emergency Social Fund?" *World Bank Economic Review* 5 (2, May): 36–93.

———. 1991b. *Workers' Benefits from Bolivia's Emergency Social Fund.* Living Standards Measurement Study Working Paper 77. Washington, D.C.: World Bank.

Newman, John, Menno Pradhan, Laura Rawlings, Geert Ridder, Ramiro Coa, and Jose Luis Evia. 2000. "An Impact Evaluation of Education, Health, and Water Supply Investments by the Bolivian Social Investment Fund." Background paper for the Social Funds Evaluation Study. World Bank, Human Development Network, Social Protection Unit, Washington, D.C.

———. 2002. "An Impact Evaluation of Education, Health, and Water Supply Investments by the Bolivian Social Investment Fund." *World Bank Economic Review* 16 (2): 241–74.

Nordhaus, William D. 1975. "The Political Business Cycle." *Review of Economic Studies* 42: 169–90.

Ortuno, A. 1998. "Eficacia y eficiencia institucional del FIS: asesoria de evaluación de programas y fiscalia." Social Investment Fund (FIS), La Paz.

Ostrom, Elinor, Larry Schroeder, and Susan Wynne. 1993. *Institutional Incentives and Sustainable Development: Infrastructure Policies in Perspective.* Boulder, Colo.: Westview.

Owen, Daniel, and Julie Van Domelen. 1998. "Getting an Earful: A Review of Beneficiary Assessments of Social Funds." Social Protection Discussion Paper 9816. World Bank, Social Protection Unit, Washington, D.C.

Parker, Andrew, and Rodrigo Serrano. 2000. "Promoting Good Local Governance through Social Funds and Decentralization." Social Protection Discussion Paper 0022. World Bank, Human Development Network, Social Protection Unit, Washington, D.C.

Paxson, Christina, and Norbert R. Schady. 2000. "The Allocation and Impact of Social Funds: Spending on School Infrastructure in Peru." Background paper for the Social Funds Evaluation Study. World Bank, Human Development Network, Social Protection Unit, Washington, D.C.

———. 2002. "The Allocation and Impact of Social Funds: Spending on School Infrastructure in Peru." *World Bank Economic Review* 16 (2): 297–319.

Polidano, C. 1999. "The New Public Management in Developing Countries." Institute for Development Policy and Management, University of Manchester, U.K.

Pradhan, Menno, and Laura Rawlings. 2000. "The Impact and Targeting of Social Infrastructure Investments: Lessons from the Nicaraguan Social Fund." Background paper for the Social Funds Evaluation Study. World Bank, Human Development Network, Social Protection Unit, Washington, D.C.

———. 2002. "The Impact and Targeting of Social Infrastructure Investments: Lessons from the Nicaraguan Social Fund." *World Bank Economic Review* 16 (2): 275–95.

Pradhan, Menno, Laura Rawlings, and Geert Ridder. 1998. "The Bolivia Social Investment Fund: An Analysis of Baseline Data for Impact Evaluation." *World Bank Economic Review* 12 (3): 457–83.

———. 2000. "The Bolivia Social Investment Fund: An Analysis of Baseline Data for Impact Evaluation." Background paper for the Social Funds Evaluation Study. World Bank, Human Development Network, Social Protection Unit, Washington, D.C.

Prennushi, Giovanna, Gloria Rubio, and Kalanidhi Subbarao. 2000. "Monitoring and Evaluation." In World Bank, "Poverty Reduction Strategy Sourcebook," vol. 1. Washington, D.C. Available at <http://www.worldbank.org/poverty/strategies/chapters/monitoring/moneval.htm>; accessed November 18, 2002.

Prud'homme, Remy. 1995. "The Dangers of Decentralization." *World Bank Research Observer* 10 (2, August): 201–20.

Putnam, Robert D., with Robert Leonardi and Raffaella Y. Nanetti. 1993. *Making Democracy Work: Civic Traditions in Modern Italy.* Princeton, N.J.: Princeton University Press.

Rao, Vijayendra, and Ana Maria Ibáñez. 2001. "The Social Impact of Social Funds in Jamaica: A Mixed-Methods Analysis of Participation, Targeting and Collective Action in Community Driven Development." World Bank, Development Economics Research Group, Washington, D.C.

Ravallion, Martin. 2000. "Monitoring Targeting Performance When Decentralized Allocations to the Poor Are Unobserved." *World Bank Economic Review* 14 (2, May): 331–45.

Reddy, S. 1998. *Social Funds in Developing Countries: Recent Experiences and Lessons.* New York: United Nations Children's Fund (UNICEF).

Rogoff, Kenneth. 1990. "Equilibrium Political Budget Cycles." *American Economic Review* 80: 21–36.

Rosenbaum, Paul R., and Donald B. Rubin. 1983. "The Central Role of the Propensity Score in Observational Studies for Causal Effects." *Biometrika* 70 (1, April): 41–55.

Salmen, Lawrence F. 1999. "Beneficiary Assessment Manual for Social Funds." Social Protection Discussion Paper 9930. World Bank, Social Development Department, Washington, D.C.

Schady, Norbert. 1999. "Seeking Votes: The Political Economy of Expenditures by the Peruvian Social Fund (FONCODES), 1991–95." Policy Research Working Paper 2166. World Bank, Poverty Reduction and Economic Management Network, Washington, D.C.

Schmidt, M., and A. Marc. 1995. "Participation in Social Funds." Environment Department Paper, Participation Series. World Bank, Washington, D.C.

Schuknecht, Ludger. 1996. "Political Business Cycles and Fiscal Policies in Developing Countries." *Kyklos* 49 (2): 155–70.

Schultz, T. Paul. 2000. "Final Report: The Impact of PROGRESA on School Enrollments." International Food Policy Research Institute, Washington, D.C.

Stewart, F. 1995. *Adjustment and Poverty*. London: Routledge.

Stewart, F., and W. van der Geest. 1995. "Adjustment and Social Funds: Political Panacea or Effective Poverty Reduction?" Employment Paper 2. International Labour Organisation, Geneva.

Tanzi, Vito. 1996. "Fiscal Federalism and Decentralization: A Review of Some Efficiency and Macroeconomic Aspects." *Annual World Bank Conference on Development Economics, 1995,* 295–316. Washington, D.C.: World Bank.

Tendler, Judith. 2000. "Why Are Social Funds So Popular?" In Shahid Yusuf, Weiping Wu, and Simon Evenett, eds., *Local Dynamics in an Era of Globalization: 21st Century Catalysts for Development*. New York: Oxford University Press.

Tendler, Judith, and Rodrigo Serrano. 1999. "The Rise of Social Funds: What Are They a Model of?" Paper for Massachusetts Institute of Technology and United Nations Development Programme (UNDP) Decentralization Project. Draft. UNDP, New York.

Tiebout, Charles M. 1956. "A Pure Theory of Local Expenditures." *Journal of Political Economy* 64 (5): 416–24.

UNDP (United Nations Development Programme)–World Bank Joint Program in Rural Water. 1999. "Estudio de costos de los sistemas de agua." Lima. Processed.

University of Zambia, Participatory Assessment Group. 1994. "Beneficiary Assessment III, Participatory Assessment Group." Prepared for the Social Recovery Project, Lusaka.

———. 1997. "Beneficiary Assessment IV, Participatory Assessment Group." Prepared for the Social Recovery Project, Lusaka.

———. 1998. "Beneficiary Assessment V, Participatory Assessment Group." Prepared for the Social Recovery Project, Lusaka.

Urquiola, Miguel. 2000. "Analisis de costos del fondo de inversión social." Background paper for the Social Funds Evaluation Study. World Bank, Latin

America and the Caribbean Region, Human Development Department, Washington, D.C.

van de Walle, Dominique, and Dorothyjean Cratty. 2002. "Impact Evaluation of a Rural Road Rehabilitation Project." World Bank, East Asia Region, Washington, D.C.

Van Domelen, Julie 1989. "Geographical Targeting of Poverty by the Emergency Social Fund." World Bank, Resident Mission, La Paz. Processed.

Velez, Eduardo, Ernesto Schiefelbein, and Jorge Valenzuela. 1993. "Factors Affecting Achievement in Primary School: A Review of the Literature for Latin America and the Caribbean." HRO Working Paper 2. World Bank, Human Resources Development and Operations Policy Department, Washington, D.C.

Walker, Ian, Rafael del Cid, Fidel Ordoñez, and Florencia Rodriguez. 1999. "Ex-Post Evaluation of the Honduran Social Investment Fund (FHIS 2)." ESA Consultores, Tegucigalpa, for the World Bank, Latin America and the Caribbean Region, Human Development Department, Washington, D.C.

————. 2000. "Ex-Post Evaluation of the Honduran Social Investment Fund (FHIS 2)." Background paper for the Social Funds Evaluation Study. World Bank, Human Development Network, Social Protection Unit, Washington, D.C.

Wietzke, Frank Borge. 2000. "Institutional Characteristics of Social Funds." Background paper for the Social Funds Evaluation Study. World Bank, Human Development Network, Social Protection Unit, Washington, D.C.

World Bank. 1988. "Honduras—como lograr salud para todos?" Latin America and the Caribbean Regional Office, Washington, D.C.

————. 1991. "Zambia: Social Recovery Project." Staff Appraisal Report. Africa Regional Office, Washington, D.C.

————. 1993a. "Bolivia: Second Social Investment Fund Project." Staff Appraisal Report. Latin America and the Caribbean Regional Office, Washington, D.C.

————. 1993b. "Peru: Social Development and Compensation Project." Staff Appraisal Report. Latin America and the Caribbean Regional Office, Human Development Sector Management Unit, Washington, D.C.

————. 1994a. "FHIS-I Honduras." Performance Audit Report. Latin America and the Caribbean Regional Office, Human Development Sector Management Unit, Washington, D.C.

————. 1994b. "FHIS-I Honduras." Project Completion Report. Latin America and the Caribbean Regional Office, Human Development Sector Management Unit, Washington, D.C.

————. 1994c. "Honduras: Social Investment Fund Project." Staff Appraisal Report. Latin America and the Caribbean Regional Office, Human Development Sector Management Unit, Washington, D.C.

————. 1995a. "Armenia: Social Investment Fund Project." Staff Appraisal Report. Eastern Europe and Central Asia Department, Washington, D.C.

————. 1995b. "Zambia: Social Recovery Project." Staff Appraisal Report. Africa Regional Office, Washington, D.C.

————. 1996a. "Peru: Second Social Development and Compensation Project." Staff Appraisal Report. Latin America and the Caribbean Regional Office, Human Development Sector Management Unit, Washington, D.C.

————. 1996b. "SIF-I and II Bolivia." Performance Audit Report. Operations Evaluation Department, Washington, D.C.

————. 1996c. *World Bank Participation Sourcebook.* Washington, D.C.

————. 1997a. "FISE-I Nicaragua." Implementation Completion Report. Latin America and the Caribbean Department, Human Development Sector Management Unit, Washington, D.C.

————. 1997b. "Portfolio Improvement Program: Review of the Social Funds Portfolio." Poverty Reduction and Economic Management Network, Washington, D.C.

————. 1998a. "FISE-II Nicaragua." Implementation Completion Report. Latin America and the Caribbean Regional Office, Human Development Sector Management Unit, Washington, D.C.

————. 1998b. "Honduras: Fourth Social Investment Fund Project." Project Appraisal Document. Latin America and the Caribbean Regional Office, Human Development Sector Management Unit, Washington, D.C.

————. 1998c. "Nicaragua: Social Investment Fund Project." Staff Appraisal Report. Latin America and the Caribbean Regional Office, Human Development Sector Management Unit, Washington, D.C.

————. 1998d. "Nicaragua: Third Social Investment Fund Project." Project Appraisal Document. Latin America and the Caribbean Regional Office, Human Development Sector Management Unit, Washington, D.C.

————. 1999a. "FIS-I Guatemala." Implementation Completion Report. Latin America and the Caribbean Regional Office, Human Development Sector Management Unit, Washington, D.C.

————. 1999b. "Honduras: Fourth Social Investment Fund Project." Memorandum and Recommendation of the President. International Development Association, Washington, D.C.

————. 1999c. "Improving Social Assistance in Armenia." Report 19385-AM. Europe and Central Asia Regional Office, Country Department III, Human Development Unit, Washington, D.C.

————. 1999d. *Poverty and Social Developments in Peru, 1994–1997.* World Bank Country Study. Washington, D.C.

————. 1999e. "SRP-I Zambia." Implementation Completion Report. Africa Regional Office, Washington, D.C.

————. 2000a. "Nicaragua: Ex-Post Impact Evaluation of the Emergency Social Investment Fund." Background paper for the Social Funds Evaluation Study. Prepared by L. Rawlings, M. Pradhan, B. Özler, and others. Report 20400-NI. Latin America and the Caribbean Regional Office, Human Development Sector Management Unit, Washington, D.C.

————. 2000b. "Zambia: Social Recovery Project Impact Evaluation." Working paper for Social Funds 2000 Study. Human Development Network, Social Protection Unit, Washington, D.C.

————. 2001a. "Bolivia: Second Social Investment Fund Project." Implementation Completion Report. Latin America and the Caribbean Regional Office, Human Development Sector Management Unit, Washington, D.C.

————. 2001b. "Determinants of the Success of Social Fund Projects: The Case of FONCODES." Working paper for Social Funds 2000 Study. Revised draft. March. Human Development Network, Social Protection Unit, Washington, D.C.

————. 2001c. "Nicaragua Poverty Assessment." Report 20488-NI. Latin America and the the Caribbean Regional Office, Poverty Reduction and Economic Management Sector Unit, Washington, D.C.

————. 2002. "Social Funds: Assessing Effectiveness." Operations Evaluation Department, Washington, D.C.

Wurgaft, Jose. 1993. "Social Investment Funds in Latin America: Effects on Employment and Income." Working paper for international policy workshop, "Employment for Poverty Alleviation and Food Security," International Labour Organisation, Airlie House, Virginia, October 11–14.